American infantrymen advance toward the mountain stronghold of Troina as the 38-day campaign in Sicily approaches its climax. The ancient town was the scene of a major battle as the Germans funneled their forces into the northeastern corner of the island in preparation for their withdrawal to the mainland of Italy.

THE ITALIAN CAMPAIGN

WORLD WAR II · TIME-LIFE BOOKS · ALEXANDRIA, VIRGINIA

BY ROBERT WALLACE
AND THE EDITORS OF TIME-LIFE BOOKS

THE ITALIAN CAMPAIGN

The Author: ROBERT WALLACE served as an enlisted man and an officer in the U.S. Navy in World
War II and took part in the assault landings in
North Africa, Sicily and Salerno. As a staff writer at
LIFE, he wrote more than 75 articles. He has also
written a number of award-winning short stories
and television plays. His books include four volumes in the TIME-LIFE BOOKS' Library of Art series,
The World of Leonardo, The World of Rembrandt,
The World of Van Gogh and The World of Bernini,
as well as two volumes in The American Wilderness series, The Grand Canyon and Hawaii.

The Consultants: COL. JOHN R. ELTING, USA
(Ret.), is a military historian and author of The
Battle of Bunker's Hill, The Battles of Saratoga and
Military History and Atlas of the Napoleonic Wars.
He edited Military Uniforms in America: The Era
of the American Revolution, 1755-1795 and Mili-
tary Uniforms in America: Years of Growth, 1796-
1851, and was associate editor of The West Point
Atlas of American Wars.

MARTIN BLUMENSON is the author of Salerno to
Cassino, Anzio: The Gamble That Failed and
Bloody River: The Real Tragedy of the Rapido,
all on the Italian campaign. His other books include The Vilde Affair: Beginnings of the French
Resistance, and The Patton Papers, 1885-1940 and
1940-1945.

CONTENTS

SICILY: DOORSTEP TO ITALY

At Sousse, Tunisia, British troops laden with packs and weapons board landing craft waiting to take them to Sicily in July 1943.

AN AWESOME INVASION FORCE

Historically, the Allies were only the latest in a long succession of armies to set their sights on Sicily, the strategic island lying just two miles from the toe of the Italian boot. Greeks, Carthaginians, Romans, Byzantines, Saracens, Normans, Angevins and Spaniards—all had landed on the shores of this mountainous crossroads of the Mediterranean. But Operation *Husky*, as the 1943 Allied invasion of Sicily was code-named, would dwarf all of its predecessors. It was to be the most massive amphibious assault ever attempted anywhere.

In the initial 48 hours of this first Allied ground operation against Axis-held Europe, no fewer than 80,000 troops, 7,000 vehicles, 300 trucks, 600 tanks and 900 artillery pieces would be landed. It would take 3,300 seagoing craft of all kinds to ferry the invasion force to Sicily. The airborne operation that was to precede the landings by almost three hours was also a "first" for the Allies—the first large-scale Allied paratroop action of the War—and it would involve 4,600 men carried on 222 planes and 144 gliders.

For months before the invasion, logistics experts wrestled with the monumental problems of equipping and assembling the landing force. In addition to weapons and ammunition, each U.S. soldier was to be supplied with rations for four days ashore, while transports were to be loaded with seven days' additional food. Such equipment as gasoline stoves—one per squad—had to be acquired and parceled out. Quartermaster Corps planners calculated that each day of the operation, every 200 troops would need an average of one new plastic razor, 30 blades, 16 tubes of shaving cream, three toothbrushes, seven cans of tooth powder, 28 bars of soap, 200 packs of cigarettes, 400 books of matches, 25 pounds of hard candy and 400 sticks of gum.

The invasion was planned down to the last detail. As troop transports awaited the signal to depart from staging areas in England, the United States, North Africa and the Middle East, men on board were handed copies of the "Soldier's Guide to Italy"—for many the first inkling they had of their destination.

Overlooking the port at Tripoli, Libya, a signalman wigwags a command for part of the invasion fleet to shove off for Sicily on July 3, 1943.

Crammed with cargo ranging from canned food to motorcycles, supply craft for Operation Husky float side by side at Tripoli. Once ashore on Sicily, the U.S. contingent alone would need 3,000 tons of supplies a day.

American forces, equipped for combat, march in single file to board landing craft massed at the harbor of Bizerte in Tunisia.

British paratroopers struggle into their harnesses on a runway in North Africa. The British used 144 gliders in their airborne assault.

Packed cheek by jowl on a World War I landing craft, Allied troops are ferried to larger transports in the harbor at Sousse.

Ashore on Sicily, British troops heave against a stalled, driverless jeep as comrades form a chain to unload a supply craft.

1

"There is no way of conveying the enormous size of that fleet. On the horizon it resembled a distant city. It covered half the skyline, and the dull-colored camouflaged ships stood indistinctly against the curve of the dark water, like a solid formation of uncountable structures blending together. Even to be part of it was frightening. I hope no American ever has to see its counterpart sailing against us."

So wrote war correspondent Ernie Pyle, telling of the great flotilla that in July of 1943 embarked upon what still remains the biggest amphibious operation in history, the invasion of Sicily. It was code-named Operation *Husky,* and it involved 3,300 ships. Seven Allied divisions were in the assault wave—two more than would make the initial landings in Normandy, almost a year in the future.

It was, among other things, World War II's first Allied landing on Axis home soil—defended in this case by Italian troops and their German partners. That landing and the ensuing ground battle for the island of Sicily were to establish all the principal themes of the struggle for Italy—one of the longest, bitterest and most controversial campaigns of the War. The Italian campaign was marked by blunders, omissions and discord on the Allied side that occasionally approached the scandalous; it was also distinguished by a German defense of notable economy, skill and tenacity, led by Field Marshal Albert Kesselring, one of the most intelligent and effective generals in any of the armies engaged in the War.

The decisions that set the Sicilian operation in motion had been taken in January of the same year in the Moroccan city of Casablanca, while Allied forces were still fighting the stubbornly yielding Germans and Italians in Tunisia. At Casablanca, President Franklin D. Roosevelt and Prime Minister Winston S. Churchill had met with the British and American Combined Chiefs of Staff to review the Allied strategic position and to consider the steps that should be taken when the conquest of North Africa was completed, an event that appeared likely to take place within the next six months.

It was immediately clear that Americans and Britons were in deep disagreement. The American strategists, led by the U.S. Army Chief of Staff, General George C. Marshall, held that Germany was the prime enemy and that the quickest

THE FIRST BITE OF EUROPE

way to end the War was to assemble a massive force in England and send it booming across the Channel, through France and into the Third Reich. The Mediterranean was in Marshall's phrase "a suction pump" that would draw men and matériel from the main effort.

The British, after hundreds of years of experience in fighting wars on the European continent, favored an indirect, pragmatic approach. They had memories of the dreadful bloodletting at Ypres, Passchendaele and the Somme, in World War I, where the best of a generation of Englishmen had been cut down, and they were anxious to avoid a repetition. In Churchill's view it seemed wiser to nibble at the periphery of Hitler's empire, constantly harrying it by blockade, bombing and subversion until the opportunity arose to deliver a deadly stroke.

Although he made no such formal statement at Casablanca, Churchill felt that a campaign in the Mediterranean might soon knock Italy out of the War. Allied forces, after taking the glittering prize of Rome, might then drive up through the Italian peninsula, break into the "soft underbelly" of the Axis, and create all manner of havoc and opportunity. Perhaps neutral Turkey, watching this, might enter the War on the Allied side.

General Marshall was dismayed at the idea of any venture that might distract the Allies from what he regarded as "the main plot," a cross-Channel invasion of the Continent. Indeed, Marshall was prepared to say (until Roosevelt gently restrained him) that if the British insisted on their Mediterranean suction pump, the Americans would turn their main attention to fighting the Japanese in the Pacific and permit the war in Europe to drift.

In the end, Americans and Britons reached a compromise. It was clear that they had not yet built up enough strength to launch a cross-Channel invasion in 1943. Therefore, to maintain their momentum and to give employment to their battle-trained troops in Africa, they would attack and occupy Sicily—but not necessarily as a prelude to further campaigns on the Italian mainland. Three strategic advantages were seen arising from this operation: the Allied line of seaborne supply, which stretched from Gibraltar past Sicily to Suez and the Far East, would be made more secure; a little German attention would be diverted from the Russian front, in response to demands from Stalin; and the pressure on Italy might force it to withdraw from the War.

Further agreement was reached on the command of operations against Sicily. Although Britain and the Commonwealth nations overshadowed the United States in ground and naval power in the Mediterranean, the American Lieut. General Dwight D. Eisenhower was named Supreme Commander. His principal subordinates were all British: General Sir Harold R. L. G. Alexander, Air Chief Marshall Sir Arthur W. Tedder and Admiral of the Fleet Sir Andrew B. Cunningham. The time fixed for the invasion was to be "the period of the favorable July moon." This seemingly astrological note merely referred to military need. Airborne troops like to operate by moonlight while sailors, approaching a hostile shore, prefer the cover of darkness. On the 10th of July, the moon would be favorable to both, rising early and setting at about midnight.

The tactical plan for the invasion of Sicily (map, page 25) called for the British Eighth Army, under General Sir Bernard L. Montgomery, to land on the southeast corner of the island. That would be the British 5th, 50th and 51st infantry divisions, the 1st Canadian Infantry Division and two Royal Marine Commando units. The American Seventh Army, under General George S. Patton Jr., would land on Montgomery's left, throwing in the U.S. 1st, 3rd and 45th infantry divisions and, soon after, the U.S. 2nd Armored Division. While the Americans were protecting his left flank and rear, Montgomery was to drive up the east coast through Augusta and Catania to the Strait of Messina, and—if all went well— cut off the Germans and Italians.

The plan, devised at Montgomery's insistence, ruffled the feelings of top American ground commanders. They were relegated to a secondary role in the campaign while the headlines and credit were to go to Montgomery. Many of them disliked the British general intensely. They considered him a vain man and agreed with Lieut. General Omar N. Bradley, commander of the U.S. II Corps in Tunisia and Sicily, who deplored what he called Montgomery's "rigid self-assurance."

For his part, Montgomery had doubts about the fighting ability of Americans, who had suffered some embarrassing defeats in their first encounters with the Germans in North Africa. His own Eighth Army was a tested, veteran force and he believed it was entitled to a dominant role in the coming campaign. Inevitably, the bad feeling between the American and British commanders would loom larger as the campaign progressed. As the British General Sir William G. F. Jackson observed, "the seeds of discord between the Seventh and Eighth Army headquarters had been sown and were to germinate very quickly."

In the planning phase, a key question was whether the Italians in Sicily would fight, and how hard. On paper, they had at least a fair capability. There were more than five coastal divisions to defend the Sicilian shore. Stationed inland were four mobile divisions, backed up by tanks, which could be thrown into the battle when and where required. In all, the Italians had about 200,000 troops available. These were stiffened by the presence of more than 30,000 German ground troops, organized into two divisions—the Hermann Göring, an armored unit officially part of the Luftwaffe, and the 15th Panzer Grenadier, a mechanized infantry formation. Both could be tough. An Allied intelligence report referred to the Germans as "strictly hot mustard," and it was expected that they would fight bravely and well, though in fact many of their junior officers and enlisted men were inexperienced.

All of the Axis troops, German as well as Italian, were under the operational control of General Alfredo Guzzoni, a competent soldier who was commander of the Italian Sixth Army. However, the Germans maintained their own communications and chain of command and were prepared to act independently. They administered and supplied their Sicilian-based divisions from Lieut. General Hans-Valentin Hube's XIV Panzer Corps headquarters on the mainland, and their overall commander was Kesselring, headquartered near Rome. Most top Allied authorities agreed with Colonel Benjamin A. Dickson, chief of intelligence in the American II Corps, who ventured the opinion that "when the going gets tough, the Boche will pull the plug on the Eyeties and wash them down the drain."

In evaluating the forces that the enemy might be able to bring to bear in the Sicilian operation, Allied planners had to take into account two other crucial factors: the air and naval strength of the Axis. The Luftwaffe, which had recently been strengthened by transfers from Germany and from the Russian front, now had more than 800 planes on Sicily, Sardinia and the Italian mainland that could be thrown against the vulnerable troop transports and supply ships off the Sicilian beaches.

The Allies had been doing their best to whittle down the Luftwaffe before the invasion, and in several air battles over the Mediterranean they had had considerable success. It was enough, when combined with the results of constant bombing of airfields in Italy and Sicily, to establish clear air superiority over the beaches. It was also enough to prompt Reich Marshal Hermann Göring to send his pilots a vicious rebuke: "Compared with the fighter pilots in France, Norway and Russia, I can only regard you with contempt. I want an immediate improvement . . . and if this is not forthcoming, flying personnel from the commander down must expect to be reduced to the ranks and transferred to the Eastern front to serve on the ground." If the Allies had known that the Germans were receiving that sort of encouragement from their commander at home, they might have been even more apprehensive about what the Luftwaffe, with its back to the wall, might do.

The Italian fleet, too, had the potential to deliver a desperate, last-ditch blow at the invasion ships. During the past three years of the sea war the British had harried the Italians so successfully that their surface navy now spent most of its time in port; the Allies had unquestioned naval superiority in the Mediterranean. But Mussolini still had 10 destroyers, six cruisers and four battleships—two of them modern vessels mounting 15-inch guns and capable of 30 knots—that might come boiling out of ports in the Adriatic and the Gulf of Genoa. The Italians lacked modern radar and were short of oil, but they were unpredictable. In line with Mussolini's favorite dictum—"Better one day as a lion than fifty years as a sheep"—might they now come out to fight?

The ground invasion of Sicily was preceded by landings of British and American airborne troops, aimed at blocking Axis counterattacks against the beaches and barring Axis reinforcements by seizing key bridges. The plan had been to drop the airborne troops around midnight, three hours before the first assault waves hit the beaches. The main objective of the Americans was an important piece of high ground near Gela called Piano Lupo; the British were to take a vital bridge, the Ponte Grande, south of Syracuse.

The British went in gliders, while the Americans used

The rugged terrain of Sicily and the Italian peninsula produced some of World War II's most brutal fighting. The Germans took full advantage of the terrain by establishing heavily fortified defensive lines at critical locations—especially the Winter Line at Cassino and the Gothic Line in northern Italy—besides blowing up communications and anything else that could be of use to the Allies. So effective were the demolitions that General Dwight D. Eisenhower said, "With railroads wrecked, bridges destroyed, and many sections of roads blown out, the advance was difficult enough even without opposition from the enemy."

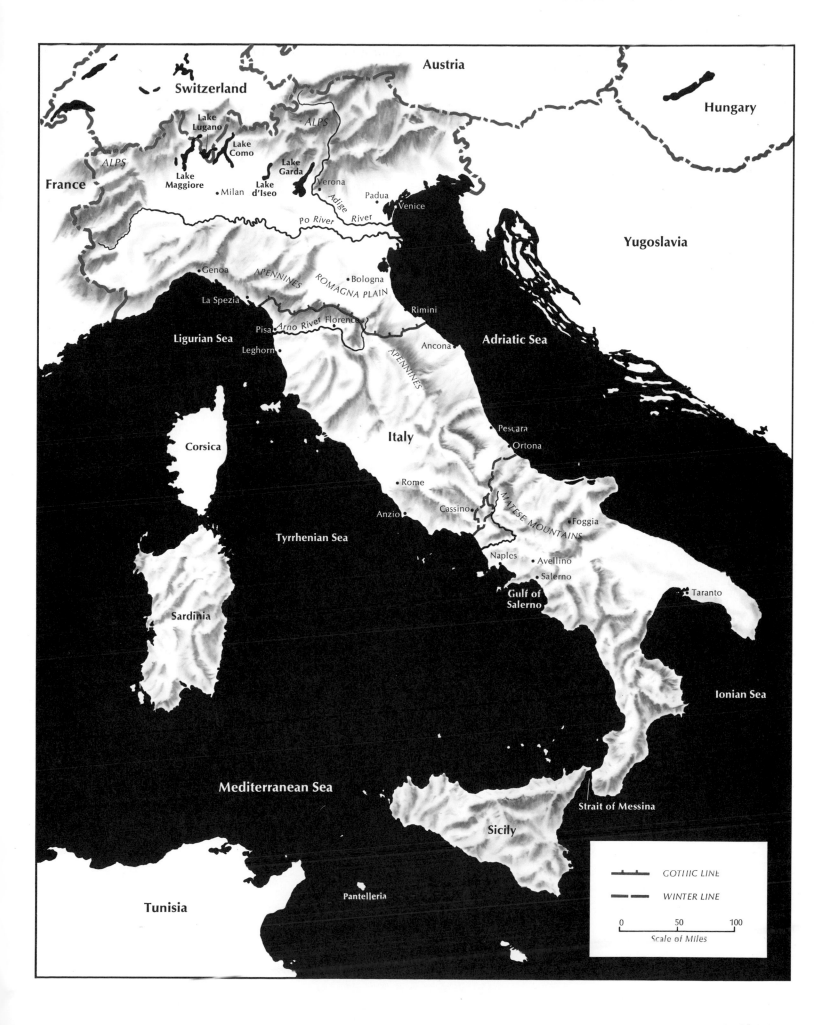

Switzerland

Austria

Hungary

ALPS

Lake
Lugano

Lake
Como

Lake
Maggiore

Lake
Garda

Lake
d'Iseo

France

ALPS

Milan

Verona

Adige River

Padua

Venice

Yugoslavia

Po River

Genoa

APENNINES

ROMAGNA PLAIN

Bologna

La Spezia

Rimini

Pisa

Arno River Florence

Ligurian Sea

Leghorn

Ancona

Adriatic Sea

APENNINES

Corsica

Italy

Pescara

Ortona

Rome

Cassino

MATESE MOUNTAINS

Foggia

Anzio

Tyrrhenian Sea

Naples

Avellino

Salerno

Sardinia

Gulf of
Salerno

Taranto

Ionian Sea

Mediterranean Sea

Strait of Messina

Sicily

Tunisia

Pantelleria

GOTHIC LINE

WINTER LINE

0   50   100
Scale of Miles

21

parachutes. The pilots and navigators of most of the transport planes in both operations were American. These aircrews had not been adequately trained. They were acquainted with the Sicilian landscape only through aerial reconnaissance photographs taken by day, and had little idea of its appearance by night. Moreover, to avoid being shot at by the invasion fleet, they were obliged to fly a devious, dog-legged course.

The planes ran into high winds shortly after taking off from bases in North Africa. Their V formations broke up before reaching Sicily. Landmarks became impossible to find in the dark and the planes approached the drop zones blindly from every direction. Italian and German antiaircraft batteries fired at them. "We couldn't hear the bursts over the roar of the engines," said one aircrew member, "but were rocked again and again by explosions, and the gun flashes were visible below." The 3,400 American paratroopers who jumped were scattered all over southeastern Sicily. Most of them were nowhere near their targets; the American commander, Colonel James M. Gavin, was not even sure that he was in Sicily when he touched ground.

The British glider troops fared far worse. Of 144 gliders that took off from bases in North Africa, nearly 70 were released prematurely and fell into the sea; the remainder were dispersed for many miles across the landscape and only a dozen landed where planned. Only 87 of the troops reached the area of their target, the Ponte Grande, and there all but 19 were killed or wounded. But the survivors were able to hold the bridge until other British soldiers, coming in from the beaches, relieved them.

The chaotic scattering of the airborne troops was confusing to the Allied commanders as they tried to assemble a picture of what was happening. But it was even more confusing to the Germans and Italians, who got so many reports of landings at so many points that some assumed the Americans and British had dropped between 20,000 and 30,000 men on them. (The actual total was 4,600.)

In the meantime, things were going much better for the ground forces landing on the island's southern and eastern shores. In the American sector, troops of the U.S. Seventh Army landed at Licata, Gela and Scoglitti. At Gela, U.S. Rangers came under heavy fire 500 yards offshore. They lost a whole platoon to enemy rifle and machine-gun fire, but by dawn they had pushed into the town. Near Licata, U.S. troops walked unopposed into a hastily abandoned Italian command post whose defenders had vanished without firing a shot. Among the first to enter it was an American correspondent, Michael Chinigo, of International News Service. The telephone rang. Chinigo, who spoke Italian well, picked it up and said, "Chi c'è?" (Who's there?) A high-ranking Italian officer was on the line, wanting to know whether it was true that Americans were landing in the neighborhood. "Of course not," said Chinigo. "Fine," said the officer, and hung up.

Off to the east, the four heavily reinforced divisions of the British Eighth Army had successfully landed in the area surrounding the Pachino peninsula near Syracuse. That evening, the British 5th Division offered an augury of effortless success in Sicily—a sign as false as it was unexpected—by marching virtually unopposed into the port of Syracuse, a major Allied objective.

The first serious trouble for the ground troops came on the American front, in the Gela section, as D-day wore on. Prior to the invasion the Axis commander, General Guzzoni, had designated one of his mobile Italian divisions, the Livorno, and two mobile groups equipped with obsolescent tanks, to counterattack at Gela alongside the bulk of the Hermann Göring Division. The commander of the German division, Major General Paul Conrath, was alerted to the landings initially by his own reconnaissance patrols and by the Rome headquarters of Field Marshal Kesselring; Conrath decided to counterattack on his own immediately. But because his telephone communications with Guzzoni's headquarters were disrupted by Allied bombing, Conrath had never received orders from Guzzoni to coordinate with the Italians.

With a mixed force of tanks and infantry, Conrath jumped off from his positions near Caltagirone, some 20 miles from Gela, at about four in the morning on July 10. Allied bombers and ambushes by the airborne troops slowed him down; at times, things got so hot that Conrath had to move among the greener of his men to prevent panic. But the Hermann Göring Division kept going toward Gela.

Farther west, troops of the Livorno Division and tanks of the mobile groups had better luck—at any rate for a while.

Nine or 10 tanks managed to make it into Gela, albeit unsupported by infantry. There they clanked up and down the streets, while Rangers and engineers played a deadly cat-and-mouse game with them, nipping in and out of houses to fire rocket launchers and throw grenades.

In the beginning the American troops got the worst of it. But a formidable young Ranger lieutenant colonel named William O. Darby finally lost his patience after firing 300 rounds of .30-caliber ammunition at one Italian tank and watching the bullets bounce harmlessly off it. Darby leaped into his jeep, dashed down to the shore and commandeered a 37mm gun and crew that had just come ashore. He then hoisted the gun into the jeep, raced back into the center of town, went into action with the makeshift tank destroyer and started shooting. Every shell fired by the demounted gun, he later reported, recoiled on the gun captain and bowled him over. Nonetheless Darby—who was awarded the Distinguished Service Cross for his act—succeeded in disabling one enemy tank and so harassed the others that they soon withdrew from the town.

As the tanks pulled back, about 600 Italian infantrymen of the Livorno Division, marching in a brave but suicidal approximation of parade-ground formation, approached Gela. American small-arms and mortar fire scythed them down, and not a single soldier reached the town.

The Hermann Göring Division, also moving toward Gela, began meanwhile to run into heavy resistance. Most of it came from naval gunfire, 5- and 6-inch shells that pounded into them from the sea, but that was not the only problem. Heavy Tiger tanks accompanying infantry units attacking through the olive groves east of Gela got hung up in the dense growths of tough trees. These were among the first Tigers manufactured and some of them had defective steering mechanisms. Nevertheless, Conrath kept up the pressure. At one point during the afternoon, his men shattered an American battalion and captured most of the survivors, including the commanding officer. This victory temporarily left the 1st Division's beaches vulnerable, but American reserves thrown into the battle held on—until suddenly, and completely uncharacteristically, the German soldiers panicked, broke and ran. Night fell on an American beachhead that was still intact.

But Kesselring, none too happy with either the Italians' or Conrath's performance, ordered the Hermann Göring Division back to the attack the next day. This time Conrath linked up with his allies. Italian guns captured by the Rangers helped stop successive coordinated Axis assaults, but again, naval gunfire was an even greater deterrent. Army Captain James B. Lyle, spotting a column of Italian troops heading for his position near Gela, called on the light cruiser U.S.S. *Savannah* for help. The *Savannah*, which had a main battery of fifteen 6-inch guns, immediately cut loose with a deadly barrage of 500 rounds that halted the attack. When Lyle and his men went out to mop up, they captured

AN ISLAND SURRENDERS TO AIR ATTACK

The Allied capture of Italy's island fortress of Pantelleria was an operation unique in history—the conquest of an enemy stronghold almost entirely by air power.

Strategically located between Africa and Sicily, the island had to be taken before the invasion of Sicily could get under way. Fortified in the 1920s and 1930s, Pantelleria had coastal batteries, an airport, and underground hangars capable of handling 80 planes. Steep cliffs and treacherous currents discouraged amphibious assaults.

Allied planes began five weeks of bombing in May 1943, with occasional support from the Royal Navy. On June 10, bombers were so thick that some had to circle while waiting for a chance to drop their bombs.

Next day the British landed, unopposed by 11,000 stunned Italian troops. The sole British casualty was a soldier bitten by a local jackass. (The soldier survived.)

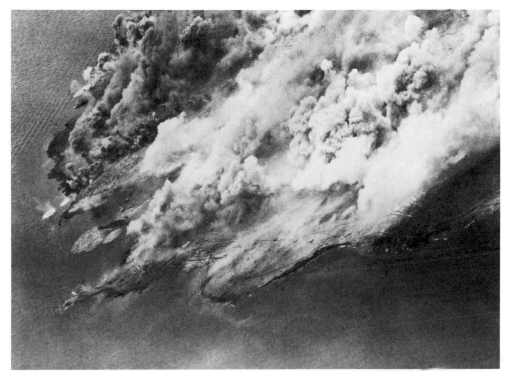

Billowing smoke covers bomb-blasted Pantelleria. Over 10 days, 4,844 tons of bombs hit the island.

almost 400 Italians, dazed and staggering, who could hardly comprehend what had hit them. The gunfire had been so devastating, Lyle reported, that "there were human bodies hanging from the trees."

Still, the fight was far from finished. The renewed assault of the Hermann Göring Division came dangerously close to throwing the Americans off the beach, and for a while the Germans thought they had accomplished it. Sixty German tanks attacked, and some of them drove to within 2,000 yards of the shore and turned their guns on the Americans there. All unloading operations ceased, as everyone grabbed a weapon and turned to fire on the attackers. Somebody on the German side got excited and reported that the Americans were reembarking. In reality, American troops were still coming ashore; among them was a field-artillery battalion that set up its guns along the dunes and opened fire on the German armor.

Slowly the tanks began to back away, and as the range opened up, naval guns—silent during the crisis because the combat had been at such close quarters that the sailors feared hitting American soldiers—completed the rout. Two thirds of the tanks were knocked out. "As salvo after salvo of naval gunfire split their armored hulls," wrote General Bradley, "the German panzer commanders wisely concluded that a 26-ton Mark IV is no match for a cruiser. The enemy turned and ran for the hills where the Navy could not pursue him."

All the same, the Navy did its best to reach the enemy at the longest possible range. Attached to the American fleet off Gela was a curious-looking British vessel called H.M.S. Abercrombie. The Abercrombie was a latter-day Monitor, a throwback to the 19th Century, and the ship's appearance at first aroused mild amusement among Navy men who saw her. Sitting low in the water, slow and stubborn, the Abercrombie was merely a floating platform for a great turret in which two 15-inch guns were mounted. Perhaps because of a trick of echo, the Abercrombie's guns did not sound as though they were being fired simultaneously. They seemed to go off a split second apart, bang-bang, like a colossal double-barreled shotgun.

As the Germans retreated, the skipper of the gallant crate, Captain G. V. B. Faulkner, was so eager to keep pounding them that he contrived a way of remaining in action long after the Germans were out of sight. He shifted ballast: emptied water tanks in the bow and filled tanks in the stern so that the vessel leaned back into the water. This gave added elevation to his guns, increasing their maximum range to about 36,900 yards (almost 21 miles). When Americans got far enough inland, they found that the Abercrombie had scored a lucky hit on an enemy headquarters.

The Italian heavy-gunned ships of Mussolini's battle fleet never did come out to dispute the Abercrombie or anyone else. They remained in port, carefully watched at long range by British battleships and aircraft carriers deployed to intercept them. However, the Luftwaffe and the Italian Air Force did their best to sink the invasion fleet, penetrating the Allied air screen repeatedly. Because Allied air-surface coordination was almost nonexistent, the German pilots enjoyed a kind of field day in spite of their inferiority in numbers. Off Gela, German planes badly damaged several ships and sank the destroyer U.S.S. Maddox and an LST (Landing Ship, Tank) carrying a precious cargo of antitank guns. The Robert Rowan, a Liberty ship loaded with ammunition, went up with a spectacular explosion that hurled flames, smoke and debris hundreds of feet in the air.

Apart from the direct harm the Luftwaffe did, the constant presence of the planes over the landing area had one indirect—and, for the Allies, disastrous—consequence. A German raid that took place almost simultaneously with a drop of badly needed American airborne reinforcements in the Gela beachhead contributed to one of the most tragic blunders of World War II.

On the night of July 11, after attacking the convoy off Gela throughout the day, German bombers again appeared in force over the Seventh Army landing area and supporting fleet anchorage. They dropped strings of parachute flares, illuminating the ships with a brilliant blue-white glare, and circled overhead picking out their targets.

The gun crews on the ships, half-blinded by the flares, fought back as best as they could, filling the air with an umbrella of tracers and scrap iron. The German planes were invisible; the Navy could not see what it was shooting at. But shortly after 10:30 p.m. it suddenly appeared to the gunners on the ships and to the crews of Army antiaircraft batteries on shore that the Germans had made a bad mis-

The Allied forces that invaded Sicily on July 10, 1943, sailed from Great Britain and ports (inset) scattered along the Mediterranean all the way from Oran to Beirut. The British Eighth Army landed with four divisions on the southeastern corner of the island (bottom map), while the American Seventh Army hit the southern coast with three divisions. After the Allies landed, the Germans counterattacked the Americans at Gela, then began a gradual withdrawal to the island's northeastern corner, taking full advantage of natural avenues of retreat through the mountains. Along the eastern coast, the Germans concentrated their forces to block the narrow corridor running from Catania to Messina. To the west, by blowing up bridges, mining roads and defending mountain passes, they wheeled back in the direction of Messina and made their last big stand at the Etna Line while ferrying their forces across the strait to the mainland of Italy.

take. The planes were coming in low, only a few hundred feet above the water, so low that their blue exhaust flames could be seen. More than 5,000 guns of all calibers opened up on them in an almost volcanic blast of fire and smoke.

Cheering, the gunners watched a number of the planes crash into the water or onto the beachhead. Out of other planes came parachutes from which dark objects dangled. Were the Germans dropping mines into the anchorage? The gunners cursed and fired at the dark objects to explode them in the air. When one of the planes crashed close to the destroyer U.S.S. *Beatty,* the gunners took no chances; they pounded the wreckage with streams of 20mm cannon fire

until at last the plane was recognized for what it was—an American C-47 transport.

In fact, all of the low-flying planes were American—144 of them—carrying 2,000 paratroopers of the 82nd Airborne Division. Six planes were shot down before the paratroopers could jump. When a final tabulation was made it turned out that 229 paratroopers were killed, wounded or missing; 23 of the planes were destroyed, and 37 were badly damaged. One of these, which somehow limped back to its base in North Africa, had 1,000 holes in it.

What had gone wrong? When Patton decided to bring in the paratroopers to reinforce the beachhead on the night of

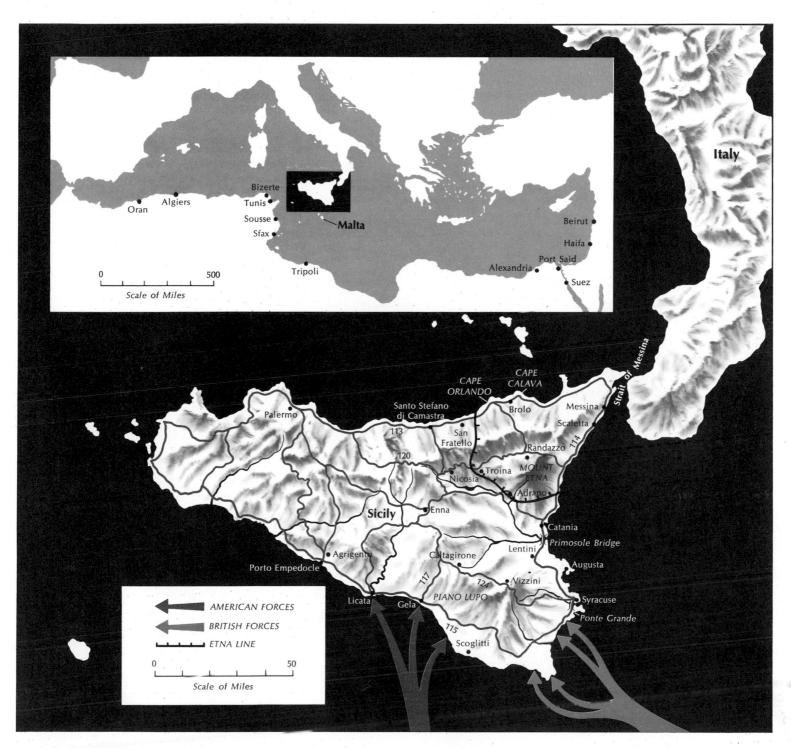

July 11, he gave an order that all units should be notified. Major General Matthew B. Ridgway, commander of the 82nd Airborne, flew to Sicily from North Africa to make sure that the warning order had been properly disseminated. Ridgway had previously obtained assurances from the Navy commanders that the planes would not be fired on if they flew through a narrow corridor along the beachhead. The planes flew along the prescribed corridor. But some units never got the message.

As General Eisenhower pointed out in a post-mortem dispatch, the course that the transports were ordered to fly "followed the actual battlefront for 35 miles; and the anti-aircraft gunners on ship and shore had been conditioned by two days of air attacks to shoot at sight." With or without adequate warning, the gunners very probably would have fired at the transports, even though the planes were displaying the proper amber recognition lights (some planes actually made it to the drop zone before the firing started). But by arriving on the heels of a German air raid, the transports virtually guaranteed themselves a violent reception. Later, after studying the disaster, General Ridgway came to the conclusion that the responsibility was "so divided, so difficult to fix," that no disciplinary action should be taken. "The losses are part of the inevitable price of war in human life," he said.

The night after this disaster the Germans made an airdrop of their own farther to the east, opposite the British Eighth Army. The uneventful arrival of parts of the 1st Parachute Division on the airfield at Catania signaled the beginning of a German build-up that would ultimately bring the number of German troops on the island to more than 50,000. The build-up had been personally ordered by Adolf Hitler—who wanted to gain some time for his faltering Italian partner, Benito Mussolini.

Earlier in the day, Kesselring had flown to Sicily to look into the situation for himself. Far more than most of the high-ranking German officers, Albert Kesselring liked and respected the Italians. But he could see that even with German support the Italians had failed to throw the Allies back into the sea. Still, Kesselring believed the Axis forces would be able to delay the Allied advance and halt it along a defensive line in the mountains of northeastern Sicily. As he and Hitler saw it, the next phase of the battle would be a German effort, with the Italians—still nominally in charge—providing the support.

Over the following days, additional troops from the 1st Parachute Division arrived from the mainland, as did the 29th Panzer Grenadier Division. General Hube's XIV Panzer Corps headquarters also transferred to Sicily, and Hube assumed combat command of the German troops on the island. According to the Axis strategy, all German forces, particularly the 15th Panzer Grenadier Division, were to abandon western Sicily (despite lingering fears of renewed Allied landings in the area), and they and the best remaining Italian troops would pull back to a defense line anchored on Catania on the eastern coast and running around Mount Etna's rugged western base to Santo Stefano di Camastra on the Tyrrhenian Sea in the north.

As the Axis forces withdrew, the roles of the Allied armies in pursuit theoretically remained the same: the British Eighth Army was the battering ram, the American Seventh Army the guard dog, protecting the British rear and flank. But as the campaign unfolded, the battering ram got stuck, and the guard dog turned tiger. Part of this evolution, of course, was caused by the always unpredictable fortunes of battle; a good deal of it, however, must be attributed to the personalities of the respective Army commanders, Patton and Montgomery. Although both were outstanding soldiers, and both were prima donnas, two more different men can hardly be imagined.

Their antagonistic styles came through clearly in their attitudes toward proper uniform. In the swelter of the Sicilian summer, Patton insisted on the wearing of helmets and even of neckties, at least in rear areas; Montgomery could not have cared less. Driving up to the front one very hot day, the Eighth Army comander's jeep passed a truck driven by a man wearing nothing but a silk top hat, which he swept off in a gallant salute to his general. Montgomery laughed heartily, and later dictated a jocular order: "Top hats will not be worn in the Eighth Army."

In battle, however, Patton's rigid attitude toward dress was offset by qualities of flexibility, boldness and cunning. Montgomery's casual attitude about uniforms belied his customary caution and orthodoxy in battle. He was a master of the conventional, set-piece engagement, one who wanted to have every bullet—some said every shoestring—in place before he moved.

As the month of July wore on, an intense rivalry began to develop between these two strikingly different commanders. That rivalry, which would continue until the end of the War, stemmed in part from Montgomery's low opinion of the fighting abilities of American troops, and from Patton's determination to demonstrate the worth of Seventh Army units. It stemmed also from the fiercely competitive natures of the two commanders. One British general, wise in the ways of military commanders thrust into the limelight, suggested another reason. "This may seem rather childish," he said, "but fighting men live for the glory of great achievements which make world headlines. Generals hope for personal victory."

Over in the Eighth Army sector, Montgomery drove two corps forward abreast. The XIII Corps, under Lieut. General Sir Miles C. Dempsey, moved up the east coast road toward Catania; the XXX Corps, commanded by Lieut. General Sir Oliver W. H. Leese, advanced inland on the right flank of the Americans—primarily men of Bradley's II Corps. The British XIII Corps launched an attack on the new German defense line below Catania, running inland to Enna, but the attack started badly, faltered, and then stalled. The flawed beginning involved a simultaneous Commando and airborne assault on two important bridges. The Commandos, too few and too lightly armed, were driven off their bridge by strong German counterblows.

The parachute troops—in the third airborne tragedy of the campaign—ran into Allied antiaircraft fire on their way to their objective, and then landed almost on top of the machine-gun battalion of the German 1st Parachute Division dropped earlier the same day. Of the 1,856 British paratroopers who had set out from North Africa, only 295 reached their bridge; they seized it and managed to hold on until relieved by XIII Corps ground troops.

As German resistance near Lentini slowed the main XIII Corps advance along the road to Catania, Montgomery conceived a new plan. He would swing Leese's XXX Corps around the base of Mount Etna and assault Messina from the west, while maintaining XIII Corps' pressure along the east coast road. But in order to push Leese in this new direction, Montgomery would need the use of Route 124, running west from the town of Vizzini through Caltagirone. This part of the road was in the sector originally assigned to the Americans, the only major highway in this part of the island then available to them.

For the victor of El Alamein the wish was father to the command. Montgomery launched Leese's men up Route 124—without telling the Americans, or at first even his superior, General Alexander. The American soldiers pushing northward toward Enna suddenly found themselves competing for the same objectives with British tankmen and foot soldiers of the Highland Division. For the American commanders and soldiers in the area the situation seemed somewhat confusing, but not completely illogical. Asked for assistance by some Highlanders who were trying to take Vizzini—one of his own objectives—Colonel Charles M. Ankcorn of the U.S. 45th Division's 157th Regimental Combat Team did not object; he even dispensed with normal field routine to save time. Ankcorn tore a shipping ticket off the side of an abandoned railroad car and scribbled an order on the back to one of his battalion commanders: "Murphy, go help the British."

When General Alexander finally learned of Montgomery's unsanctioned move to take over Route 124, he gave it his wholehearted blessing. And he warned Patton, in person as well as in writing, that it was now all the more important for the American Seventh Army to continue to play its passive role as guardian of Montgomery's rear and flank; there was to be no question of American participation in the assault on Messina.

Patton had been angry about his army's supporting role all along, and now he was even angrier—although he was not as furious as he would become later. For the moment, he held his temper in check and his fuming corps and divisional commanders as well. He did so out of respect for a direct order, of course. But he may also have seen that the Eighth Army's troubles in the east and Montgomery's peremptory response along Route 124 could give the Seventh Army a glorious opportunity.

As a matter of fact, Patton had his eye on Palermo, the largest city on the island. The capture of Palermo would enable him to cut off the western part of the island, to grab some headlines, and above all, to control a major port from which he could launch his own drive on Messina along the northern coast.

Patton did not share this ambitious—and still highly tentative—plan with Alexander just yet (perhaps hoping he could match Montgomery's *fait accompli* with one of his own). But he did seek and get verbal permission for a probe westward toward Agrigento; Porto Empedocle, Agrigento's satellite harbor, would come in handy for landing supplies needed in a drive on Palermo. Patton told Alexander he simply needed the port so that he could stop the cumbersome landing of supplies over the beaches.

It was a subsequent directive from Alexander that really caused Patton to erupt. The order was innocuous enough on its face: it merely confirmed everything that had happened since Montgomery's seizure of Route 124; as before it made no mention of any Seventh Army mission beyond that of a supporting role.

Patton had suffered in silence up to this point. But the thought that his army might be permanently assigned to protect Montgomery's rear made his blood boil. Alexander's order appeared to make that role official for the duration of the campaign.

Infuriated, Patton flew to Tunis to confront Alexander over what he regarded as a gross insult to American fighting capabilities. Alexander, who had assumed the Americans were reconciled to their role, was startled by Patton's vehe-

mence. "General," said Patton, "I am here to ask you to take the wraps off me and change your orders to read, 'The Seventh Army will drive rapidly to the northwest and north and capture Palermo.'" Alexander promptly agreed.

As it turned out, Palermo lay ripe for the plucking, and the lightning campaign that followed was to pay a rich dividend by clearing the western half of the island and delivering a major port into Allied hands. Patton swiftly organized a provisional corps under his deputy commander, Major General Geoffrey Keyes, for a drive on the city. Jumping off in the early hours of July 19, the 2nd Armored Division and the 3rd Infantry Division covered 100 miles in four days, encountering only token resistance along the way. Roads were mined occasionally. On the way to Palermo an Italian 75mm antitank gun held up the armored column briefly, but the gun was quickly put out of commission. The worst enemies that the Americans confronted were the scorching summer heat and the choking dust that rose from the parched gravel roads.

Foot soldiers of the 3rd Division covered 54 miles in one 36-hour stretch and arrived in Palermo in time to greet the tankers of the 2nd. The streets were lined with bedraggled Italian soldiers waiting for someone to surrender to. The Germans were gone and Palermo had long since been abandoned by most of its civilian population, who had fled

the city to escape the pulverizing Allied bombings. In the evening of July 22, General Keyes rolled into the city, and accepted its surrender from General Giuseppe Molinero.

True it may be (as Patton's many critics have pointed out) that the Palermo expedition was largely a road march, that opposition was slight, and that American casualties were low, with only 57 killed, 170 wounded and 45 missing. True also that the Germans had rendered the port of Palermo unusable by sinking 44 ships there. But U.S. Army Engineers, working at a feverish pace, would have the port operating at 60 per cent of its capacity in just seven days, giving the Americans their own port, close to the action to come. Moreover, Palermo's capture demonstrated to all the world, including the British, the talent that Patton and his subordinate commanders possessed for modern mobile warfare.

With Palermo in American hands, the Seventh Army was able to turn to the east, and begin a drive toward Messina. The competition between Patton and Montgomery to see who could get there first was now really on. "This is a horse race in which the prestige of the U.S. Army is at stake," Patton said; "we must take Messina before the British."

Patton now had two key roads, one of them leading along the coast directly to Messina, and the other slicing through the mountainous interior and running around the northern slope of Mount Etna to the island's east coast. The Seventh Army was to be a battering ram now, operating in the north as an equal of the Eighth Army, which continued hammering at the gates of Catania in the east and pushing into the interior against the left and center of the German line.

The Americans now faced a dual enemy: the terrain and the resourceful Germans, who were providing most of the opposition to their advances. The roads in the mountainous regions of northern Sicily were narrow, twisting and steep, punctuated by tunnels and bridges that could be easily defended and then effortlessly blown up by a few Germans equipped with an automatic weapon and some demolition charges. The only way to knock these positions out was to get off the road, climb the hills on either side and outflank the enemy—who usually withdrew to a similar stronghold around the next bend or at the top of the next hill. With the temperature hovering in the 90s most days, water was often in short supply in this rugged conutry, and the work of repairing bridges and roads would have been punishing even without the effect of accurate and persistent German fire from small arms, mortars and artillery.

In early August, with the 45th Division pushing eastward along coastal Highway 113 and the veteran 1st Division advancing in a parallel direction in the interior along Highway 120, progress was slow. Both routes were narrow and winding, and the Germans were mining the roads and blowing up the bridges and tunnels with fiendish effectiveness.

Patton—impatient at best, and highly emotional—was irritable. His temper was to give rise to an episode that would matter more at home than the capture of Palermo, and almost cost him his career. Daily he prowled the front to urge his men forward. As was his habit, Patton visited a U.S. field hospital near Nicosia to talk with wounded soldiers; according to General Omar Bradley, "few commanders spent more time touring the wards than George did, for he found in the bandaged wounds of those soldiers the recognizable badge of courage he respected most."

After congratulating several of the wounded men, Patton came to a soldier who had no bandages. "What's wrong with you?" he asked.

"I guess I can't take it, sir," the soldier said.

Patton exploded with rage. He slapped the man across

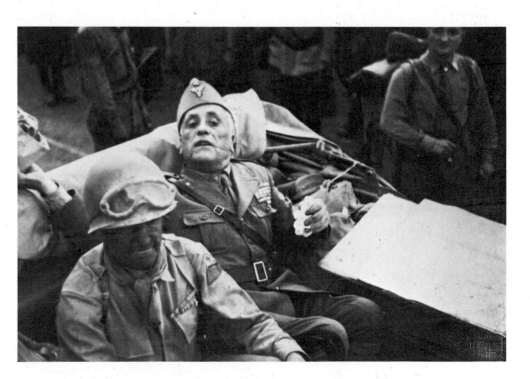

Jubilant Sicilians welcome liberating Americans in the village of Monreale, on the road to Palermo. The enthusiastic crowds showered the soldiers with flowers and fruit. Following Sicilian custom, most of the women remained indoors, leaving the celebrating to the men.

Scar-faced Italian General Giuseppe Molinero rides through Palermo with American Major General Geoffrey Keyes, whose face is covered with dust from the armored advance over Sicily's unpaved roads. The two generals were on their way to Palermo's royal palace, where Molinero surrendered the city to Keyes.

the face with his gloves and then violently shoved him out of the tent, calling him a coward and a disgrace. It later developed that the soldier was running a high fever caused by chronic dysentery and malaria.

One week after this incident Patton visited another hospital and encountered a soldier whose case was diagnosed as severe shell shock. "It's my nerves," the man said. "I can hear the shells come over, but I can't hear them burst."

"Your nerves, hell! You are just a goddamned coward, you yellow son of a bitch!" cried Patton. He then drew his pistol and waved it in the soldier's face. "You ought to be lined up against a wall and shot. In fact I ought to shoot you myself right now, goddamn you!"

The soldier began to weep and Patton struck him in the face so violently that the man's helmet liner was knocked off and rolled outside the tent. At that point the medical-

En route to Messina, American infantrymen struggle over the rocky remains of the blasted cliffside road at Cape Calavà in Sicily. The retreating Germans blew up a 150-foot section of the highway to bottleneck the advancing U.S. 3rd Division. Yet within one day, the 10th Engineer Battalion constructed a cable-and-timber bridge across the blasted stretch (inset) that could accommodate jeeps and trucks.

corps colonel in command of the hospital placed himself between Patton and the soldier and persuaded Patton to leave the tent.

General Bradley, reflecting on these incidents long afterward, felt that Patton's behavior could be understood if not condoned. "To George war was not so much an ordeal as it was the fulfillment of a destiny to which he shaped his life," wrote Bradley. ". . . Exhilarated as he was by conflict, he found it inconceivable that men, other than cowards, should want no part of war." Patton himself felt that in striking the soldiers he had been doing them a favor. He had been trying to rouse them and restore to them their self-respect, and "after each incident I stated to officers with me that I felt I had probably saved an immortal soul."

Word of Patton's actions soon reached Allied Commander in Chief Eisenhower. According to military regulations, Eisenhower would have been more than justified in relieving Patton of his command and sending him home. But Eisenhower recognized that Patton, whatever one thought of him, was a brilliant fighter who should be "saved for service in the great battles still facing us in Europe." Patton may not have been lovable but he was indeed a terrible swift sword, one of the most aggressive combat leaders the U.S. has ever produced, and it would have been a tragic waste to relieve him. Eisenhower retained him, but sent him a fierce letter of reprimand and obliged him to make public apologies to all concerned.

In any case, there were a good many soldiers who did love Patton. In his first public appearance after the scandal he spoke briefly to a theater full of GIs in Palermo and began his remarks with: "I thought I'd stand up here and let you fellows see if I am as big a son of a bitch as you think I am." The soldiers shook the roof with their cheers.

Impatient to reach Messina, Patton drove his army relentlessly. But he found himself stalled at Troina, a mountain town barring passage along Highway 120. Troina, along with the towns of Adrano and Catania in the British sector, was a vital underpinning of the German position. The German ground commander, General Hube, still had no orders to evacuate Sicily. But Hube, a master of defense and rearguard actions, needed to make sure he could pull out on an orderly timetable if he had to. He knew that if Troina fell too early a lot of German troops might get trapped in Sicily.

Perhaps Hube worried too much. In a countryside studded with natural defensive positions, Troina was almost in a class by itself. Built high on a beetling cliff, the town not only dominated its own approaches, but was solidly wedged into a system of ridges and peaks that blocked the way to the east. The ground was precipitous and broken, cut by mountain streams that the Germans lined with mines.

At first, however, the task of dislodging the Germans from the ridges around Troina did not look terribly hard to the Americans; Troina and the surrounding hills appeared to be held by a skeleton garrison intent on fighting a brief delaying action and then pulling out. But then the distress calls began coming in. One commander reported "a hell of a lot of stuff up there near our objectives" and questioned "whether we have strength enough to do the job." The job, judged at the outset well within the capabilities of a single regiment—about 3,000 men—eventually engaged a whole division plus a regiment.

The Germans, members of the 15th Panzer Grenadier Division, not only put up a stubborn defense from their fixed positions, they also counterattacked, sometimes after infiltrating between American units in the broken terrain, and always inflicting heavy casualties. However, they suffered a great deal themselves—losing some 1,600 troops in this battle alone, many of them to American bombers and artillery. U.S. intelligence officers found a letter on the body of a German soldier who had been writing to his brother stationed on the eastern front: "These astonishing Americans," it said. "They fight all day, attack all night and shoot all the time."

By dawn on August 6, after heavy air attacks, and with the Americans threatening to encircle the town, the Germans pulled out. The first GIs to enter Troina encountered only sporadic rifle fire, but they did find many bodies and a 200-pound dud bomb in the middle of the church. Similar scenes awaited the British who entered the towns of Adrano and Catania, pushing through streets choked with rubble and breathing air chalky with plaster dust and redolent of death. The Germans' Etna Line was broken.

But the Germans were still fighting hard, to make sure they would have time to get off the island. The rear guard of the 15th Panzer Grenadier Division held up the Americans at the key road junction of Randazzo, using thickly sown mines, skillfully sited artillery and demolitions.

Meanwhile, along the coastal highway, the Germans had set up defenses behind a series of fortified positions at Santo Stefano, San Fratello and along the Naso ridge, inland from a rocky promontory known as Cape Orlando. The U.S. 45th Division slugged its way through the first defensive position at Santo Stefano, then was relieved by the 3rd Division, which in turn came up against another tough defensive position at San Fratello. Determined not to get bogged down in the drive toward Messina, Patton ordered the 3rd Division to organize an amphibious force for an end run around the Germans. A reinforced battalion under Lieut. Colonel Lyle A. Bernard was loaded on a small flotilla of landing craft and came ashore in the rear of the Germans. Although the landing was a surprise, and may have forced the Germans to pull back a few hours earlier than they would have otherwise, they escaped the trap.

When the next German defensive position, at Naso ridge, was reached, Patton called the corps commander, Bradley, and ordered another end run. But the division commander, Major General Lucian K. Truscott Jr., normally an aggressive

troop leader, objected. He agreed with the plan, but he wanted to put off the operation long enough to give his main force time to push farther east and assure a quick linkup with the amphibious troops.

Patton was adamant. "Dammit," he said, "the operation will go on." Accordingly, Bernard's battalion was loaded up once again, and landed behind the Germans close to the town of Brolo. Bernard's troops pushed up the slopes of Monte Cipolla, a dominating ridge 450 yards inland from the beach. They came under artillery fire, but beat off a German infantry attack with machine guns and mortar fire. The U.S. cruiser *Philadelphia* sailed up the coast and helped out by firing on prearranged targets and by pounding German vehicles and infantry.

Meanwhile, the main body of 3rd Division troops attacking eastward was having such a hard time breaking through the German defenses that Bernard's battalion was in danger of being wiped out before the linkup could be effected. Truscott was getting radio messages from Bernard saying, "situation critical," and the general and his staff were growing more and more worried.

When the main force finally broke through to Bernard, he

had lost 167 men out of his force of 650. The Germans had escaped, and about all that had been accomplished was to force their withdrawal a day earlier than planned.

Later Patton attempted the amphibious end run a third time, landing troops of the 45th Division's 157th Regimental Combat Team at Bivio Salica, about 25 miles west of Messina. But once again the Germans escaped to the east.

As if spurred by Patton's example, Montgomery embarked two Commando forces on end runs up the east coast of Sicily, but at the last moment called off both operations before the landings were made, because of the risks involved. He decided instead to slug it out along the coastal road, challenging the defensive skills of the Hermann Göring Division, whose men holed up in stone farmhouses and on rocky hillsides until it was time to move out to Messina. Later, the frustrated Eighth Army commander finally did order a seaborne landing of Commandos. Landing south of Scaletta, the troops were held up by the Hermann Göring Division's rear guard and forced to halt the next day at a bridge that had been blown up two miles short of Messina.

It was an American patrol that first entered that city on August 17, cautiously picking its way around mines and booby traps, to find that the last of the Germans were gone. A couple of hours later a column of British tanks arrived.

"Where have you tourists been?" yelled an American.

The Americans had won the race to Messina—but only in the headlines. The Germans were gone by now, having crossed the Strait of Messina to the mainland.

As far back as August 8, Kesselring had given the order for German troops to evacuate the island via the Strait of Messina; he did not wait for instructions from Hitler, who he knew hated to give up any territory. The German ferry system was a marvel of cold efficiency. Unlike the Italian system, from which it was completely separate, the German ferry operation gave no boat room to civilians or men on leave. The able German ferry commander, Colonel Ernst-Günther Baade, disposed of 33 barges, a dozen Siebel ferries (motor rafts originally designed to invade Britain in 1940), 11 landing craft and 76 motorboats. These were protected from air and naval attack by as many as 500 guns, most of which were emplaced on the mainland side of the strait and were dual-purpose pieces that could fire at both air and ground targets.

Protected by this mass of guns, and by dwindling rearguard detachments, the Germans began ferrying troops and equipment across the two- to five-mile-wide strait on the night of August 11. The Italians had started pulling out as early as August 3, even before Kesslering's orders to the Germans. The Allies were aware of movement. On August 3, the day the Italians began their evacuation, General Alexander's headquarters picked up signs of ferry activity in the strait, and the general called on his naval and air counterparts in the Mediterranean to do something about it.

In response to Alexander's request, Admiral Cunningham explained that he could not bring large warships into the strait until the Air Force had knocked out the fierce direct gunfire from the shore. Air Marshal Tedder assigned some bombers to hit the evacuation. The Allied planes sank nine ferries and landing craft and succeeded in interrupting the Italian ferry service, but never seriously disrupted the German evacuation.

The Allies, of course, had gained their strategic objective by capturing Sicily in the 38-day campaign, and the Americans had shown their mettle in both mobile and mountain war. But Allied tactics had, by and large, been uncoordinated and discordant. Most important, despite all the planning, the use of naval and air superiority, and of an almost 2-to-1 advantage over the Axis forces on the ground, the Allies had been unable to prevent the enemy's escape.

Taking the island cost the U.S. Seventh Army 7,500 casualties, the British Eighth Army 11,500. Twelve thousand Germans were killed or captured; most of their 4,500 wounded were evacuated. Almost 40,000 German troops, 9,600 vehicles, 47 tanks, 94 guns and almost 18,000 tons of supplies and ammunition reached the mainland. The Italians lost 145,000 in captured and dead. They evacuated from 70,000 to 75,000 troops and between 75 and 100 guns. All of the Germans, their equipment and much of the better Italian matériel would be in place to confront the Allies on the mainland when the time came to make a new landing there.

The last Germans to leave Sicily in the massive Axis withdrawal across the Strait of Messina brazenly load their landing craft in broad daylight. Allied air forces trying to halt the fleeing troops claimed to have scored direct hits on 43 boats and to have destroyed 23 more. Actual losses were six German boats, one Italian boat and seven or eight others damaged.

ROME UNDER THE GERMAN HEEL

The tension between Germans and Romans during the city's occupation permeates Pio Pullini's watercolor of a sentry eyeing pedestrians near St. Peter's.

FROM ALLIES TO OCCUPIERS

His face to the sun, a German soldier on an off-duty tour of the ruins of the Forum strikes a conqueror's pose while a comrade snaps his picture.

When Italy announced the armistice with the Allies on September 8, 1943, the streets of Rome rang with cries of "Viva la pace!" (Long live peace!) The celebrations proved to be premature. Within hours, the Germans were taking over the city. Enraged by what they considered to be their former ally's betrayal, they gave their troops authorization for 24 hours of pillage. It was a foretaste of what was to come. Rome remained in German hands for nine months; during that time the suppression of its people was rigid and often brutal.

Certain groups—anti-Fascists, royalists, Jews—were special targets for persecution. The Vatican became a controlled enclave, with Wehrmacht sentries posted at the entrance to St. Peter's Square. No segment of the populace was spared indignities, harassment or, as the Germans requisitioned food and fuel in ever-larger amounts, deprivation. And always there was an undercurrent of panic, the fear of being arrested on the street and taken away, to be pressed into service as a laborer, sent to prison as a hostage, or worse.

Newspaper censorship was strictly enforced and, after an intrepid foreign news correspondent took photographs of military depots, the Germans imposed a ban on cameras. But one man kept a biting pictorial record. The watercolors on these pages were painted by Pio Pullini, a well-known artist who before the War had decorated palaces and government buildings. When the Germans moved in, Pullini, then 56 years old, was teaching art in Rome, where he lived with his wife and three children. It became his habit to wander about the streets of the city, observe the passing scene, return home and in the next few days paint whatever he had seen. Then he concealed the paintings behind a heavy bookcase, pulling them out only to show them to friends.

After the War, Pullini sold the sketches to Rome's municipal museum and to private collectors. Published here for the first time, they present a bitter testament to what life during the Occupation was like for the average Roman.

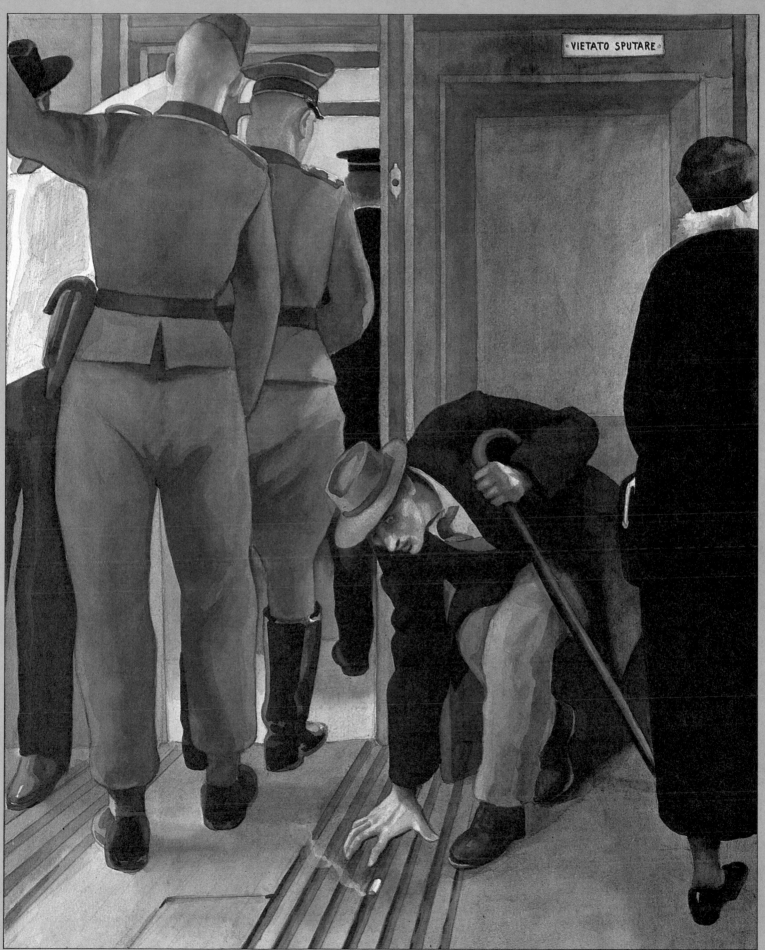

A streetcar passenger furtively retrieves a half-smoked cigarette tossed away by a German soldier. Smokers were allowed to buy only three cigarettes a day.

Attracted by a lissome young Italian girl, a German officer stops his camouflaged vehicle, opens the door invitingly and flashes his most ingratiating smile as he offers her a lift.

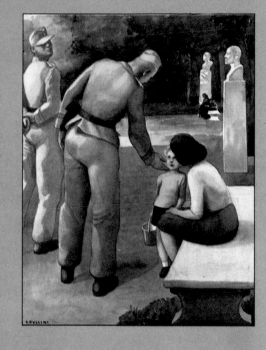

Staggeringly drunk, three off-duty soldiers lurch down a street after leaving a wine cellar in the hills above Rome. The Germans would sometimes go to a restaurant, eat and drink to their heart's content, and then tear up the bill.

Drawn to an appealing Italian youngster, a soldier chucks the boy under the chin. Weary after five years of fighting, enlisted men often admitted to the Romans that they wanted the War to end so they could return home.

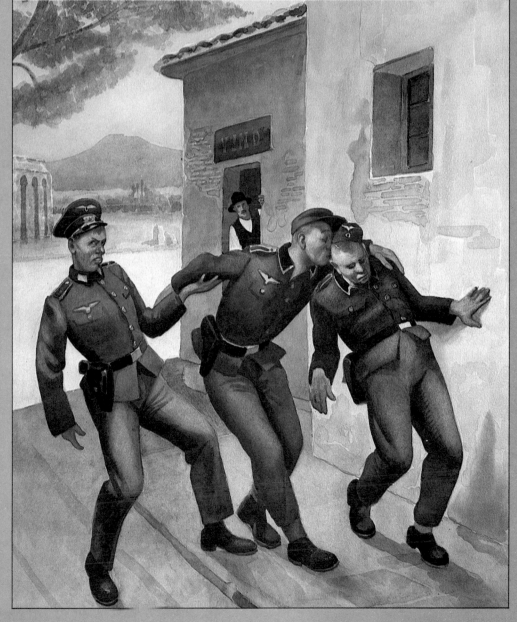

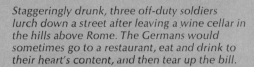

A FRUITLESS SEARCH FOR PLEASURE

Occupied Rome swarmed with Germans—infantrymen, tankers, SS men, even engineers brought in to drive locomotives because the Army Command did not trust Italian trainmen. On duty, the Germans drove around in armored cars, with their machine guns pointed menacingly at passersby, or careered their trucks down the thoroughfares, heedless of pedestrians.

Off duty, they tried to sample the pleasures of the Eternal City. But they were hampered in their efforts by the community's antagonism, which was so great that Germans were ordered to wear their guns wherever they went and never to walk the streets alone. Sometimes, soldiers out for a stroll on their Sunday passes picked up local girls, but more often they passed the time with one another.

The Occupation's martial law also made fraternization difficult. Even on such a festive holiday as New Year's Eve, all civilians were at home by 9 p.m., in obedience to the curfew. Denied any opportunity to find girls with whom to dance the new year in, young German soldiers spent the night carousing at local bars, then going out around midnight to fire rifles, revolvers and machine guns into the air until the small hours of the morning.

Hurrying past a menacing tank, a mother drags her child after her as a tankman grins down at them. Sometimes the Germans drove their armor slowly through the streets in a show of strength that was meant to cow the Romans.

While his terrified wife clutches a crucifix and watches from the doorway, a professor at bay tries to convince some Germans who have come to requisition his car that he has already turned it over to the authorities.

A German sentry has a Roman street all to himself as curfew begins while it is still daylight. In retaliation following incidents of sabotage and bomb-throwing by partisans, the Germans advanced the curfew hour to five o'clock.

A DAILY PLAGUE OF GERMAN INTRUSIONS

In the first week of occupation, angry Germans took jewelry and money from pedestrians at gunpoint, or flagged down motorists and drove off in their cars. So great was the banditry that some Romans wryly suggested that the Germans would soon leave the city, having stripped it of almost everything they wanted.

Although the looting subsequently became less open, the Germans continued to conduct searches for weapons or cars. Shoppers were barred from clothing stores while the shelves were systematically emptied and supplies carted off. Bicycles were banned after a series of incidents in which cyclists fired weapons at German soldiers and then fled. Taxis were prohibited, and on occasion the electric current for buses and streetcars was halted, bringing virtually all transportation to a stop. Telephones were cut off to prevent spies from tapping the wires, and gas for cooking was made available only for 90 minutes at midday and half an hour at night. As winter neared and the weather grew colder, there was no fuel for Italian houses, and vexation mounted as truckloads of coal arrived for hotels where the Germans were staying.

A black marketeer arranges his wares: lira notes. After spreading a false rumor that counterfeit 1,000-lira notes were circulating, black-market dealers did a brisk business buying up 1,000-lira notes for 900 lire apiece.

Gaunt-faced and dressed in clothes that are too big for their now-meager frames, two elderly Romans glance wistfully at the eggs a black marketeer is peddling from her satchel. The going price was one dollar an egg.

Peering at the scales, an anxious father checks his son's weight while a wide-bottomed German buys stamps in a post office. Loss of weight was so prevalent among the Romans that it became impolite to mention it.

THE CONSTANT PRESENCE OF WANT

As the Occupation dragged on, and autumn gave way to winter, the Romans suffered severely from the lack of twin essentials: fuel and food. By November, the German's habit of commandeering truckloads of coal to keep their own hotel billets warm had depleted the city's supplies. The unheated Roman houses, with their marble floors, high ceilings and enormous windows, became so chilled that the tenants had to dress more warmly indoors than out. Furniture, books and plates were icy to the touch, and aristocrats and slum dwellers alike developed chilblains.

Even worse was the shortage of food. Strict rationing allowed each Roman only three and a half ounces of bread per day and that same amount of meat per month.

Yet shops often did not have enough provisions to fill even these minuscule allotments. In some instances, entire monthly supplies of pasta, the staple on which Italians depended more than they did on bread, were confiscated by the Germans.

Faced with near starvation, those who could afford to traded on the black market. Here they could buy flour, rice and occasionally potatoes, at a price—$175 for a sack of rice. The German High Command ordered that black marketeers be punished by death or imprisonment, and periodically staged raids on their premises. But it was common knowledge that the raids were faked. A few days later the Germans, who were known to be the greatest profiteers in the black market, would sell the seized stocks back to the dealers.

Roused from bed, a frail old man is ordered out to join other hostages during a house-to-house roundup. Many Roman families devised hideaways, in basements or behind sliding panels, where able-bodied men hid from raids.

Brutally manhandled, a terrified elderly Jew is hustled toward a waiting truck. Roundups were customarily staged at 5:30 in the morning so that most victims would still be too heavy with sleep to make any attempt to get away.

A motley crew of labor conscripts—a glum student, an aproned worker and two cheerful South African prisoners of war—is driven through the streets, bound for duty mending roads and bridges or laying train tracks.

THE TERROR OF THE SUDDEN ROUNDUP

Behind the resentment the Romans felt toward the German occupiers lay the fear of a real danger: the massive manhunt. On any day, the Nazis would unexpectedly throw out a net across any quarter of the city, arrest every able-bodied man they found and cart him off to work on defense projects, either locally or in Germany.

There were more sinister motives behind other roundups. After acts of sabotage were committed, the Germans would surround neighborhoods thought to be havens for partisans, enter each house and drag off the men, young or old, to be imprisoned as hostages. On October 16, troops stormed the Roman ghetto, picked up more than 1,000 Jews and deported them to Auschwitz where, a week later, most of them died in the gas chamber.

For a while, partisans and Jews found shelter in Rome's religious schools, which were protected as the Pope's property. But by late December, even these premises were subject to raids. Dread of the roundup further heightened the Romans' eagerness to see an end to the Occupation, and by midspring of 1944, speculation about when the Allies would arrive and drive the Germans out was so rife that Romans could think of little else.

Seeking an answer to the question that torments them, Romans at a séance listen hard for a response from the attendant spirit to the medium's suggestion: "If the war will end within the month, knock once."

The end came on June 4, 1944. Here, a dejected German rides out of town in the cavalcade of defeated troops who left Rome that day. They withdrew in disorder, many frightened, under the silent gaze of the Romans lining the road.

WH
5787

"Then my ruin is complete," he muttered hoarsely.

That old dog of a sentence, which might well have come from *Uncle Tom's Cabin* or *The Perils of Pauline,* has a more recent pedigree. The speaker was Mussolini; he was muttering to Victor Emmanuel III, King of Italy; and the recorder was Field Marshal Pietro Badoglio, who on the 25th of July, 1943, fifteen days after the Allied invasion of Sicily, was appointed by the King to succeed Mussolini as head of the Italian government.

Having been dismissed by the King, Mussolini went out of the Villa Savoia in Rome and looked for his car. It was gone.

"Where is it?" he asked an officer.

"It is standing in the shade at the side of the villa," said the officer, pointing.

Mussolini walked in the direction indicated and found himself surrounded by police, who told him to get into an ambulance. "But can't I use my own car?" he asked sadly. "And where are you taking me?"

"To a place where you will be quite safe."

Mussolini was hustled off under arrest, and so the 21 years of his dictatorship came to an end.

The Italians had grown weary of the War and of two decades of Fascist rule. The disintegration of the country's military position was paralleled by a deterioration of the home front. The economy was in a shambles, industry was crippled and rations had been cut to 900 calories a day so more food could be sent to Germany. By the summer of 1943, the situation was ripe for the overthrow of Mussolini.

Two dramatic developments, coming in quick succession, precipitated his downfall. On the 19th of July the Allies dropped bombs on railroad-marshaling yards in Rome, killing and wounding 4,000 civilians, hitting the venerable basilica of San Lorenzo, plowing up graves in the Campo Verano cemetery and severely damaging the intended target. The second event, even more compelling, was the success of the Allied campaign in Sicily; by mid-July it was clear that nothing could prevent the American and British armies from overrunning the island. Mussolini had to be deposed and the alliance with Germany dissolved, or Italy would be dragged down to utter ruin. Accordingly, the Grand Council of the Fascist Party passed a vote of no confidence in him and the Duce was finished.

Field Marshal Badoglio announced that Italy would re-

2

CLOSE CALL AT SALERNO

main in the Axis camp, but no one took him seriously, least of all the German hierarchy. Back in Berlin, Dr. Joseph Goebbels, Hitler's Minister of Propaganda, noted in his diary with characteristic venom, "The Duce will enter history as the last Roman, but behind his massive figure a gypsy people has gone to rot." Hitler himself was so outraged by Mussolini's dismissal that his first impulse was to order his troops to seize Rome, the King, the Royal Family, the Badoglio government and even the Pope and "the whole swinish pack" of diplomats attached to the Vatican. His generals dissuaded him from this, but Hitler instructed them to find out where Mussolini was imprisoned and to rescue him. He also ordered the generals to stand by to execute *Plan Achse* (Axis Project), a scheme whereby German soldiers, at any clear sign of Italian defection, were to disarm the military and take over the coastal defenses to repel an anticipated Allied landing on the Italian mainland.

Mussolini's sudden removal from power not only had surprised the Allies, but also had signaled to them that Italy was ready to call it quits. Until now they had been proceeding cautiously. General Eisenhower, Allied Commander in Chief, was instructed in May merely "to plan such operations" in the aftermath of the Sicilian invasion "as are best calculated to eliminate Italy from the war and to contain the maximum number of German forces." But while the Allied strategists had given Eisenhower a good deal of latitude in planning, they had also proposed to take away much of his strength. Seven battle-tried divisions—four American and three British—were to be withdrawn from the Mediterranean in the month of November and sent to England to prepare for the Normandy landings scheduled for the following spring. With them would go many of the theater's landing craft, while others were ticketed for amphibious operations in Burma.

In view of these limitations, Eisenhower at first thought that the best he could do might be to seize the German-occupied islands of Sardinia and Corsica. Their capture would not represent a great triumph, but at least it could be accomplished with the resources available, and the islands could serve as bases for an intensification of the bombing attacks on central and northern Italy. Another possibility might be to invade the toe and heel of the Italian boot and then probe cautiously to the north. No really bold campaign against the Italian heartland was deemed possible.

When it was evident that the Sicilian campaign was going well, however, the strategists raised their sights. On July 16 they suggested that Eisenhower think about an amphibious assault on the Italian mainland near Naples, and on the 23rd they told him to prepare a plan for this operation "as a matter of urgency." When Mussolini was deposed on the 25th, the urgency was heightened and the Allies were filled with optimism.

Winston Churchill was delighted with this shift of strategy. The capture of Rome—one of the world's great cities, and the seat of the Fascist government—would offer important political and psychological rewards. Churchill had not been impressed with the notion of taking Corsica and Sardinia, nor did he care for a mere nip at the Italian toe. "Why crawl up the leg like a harvest bug from the ankle upwards?" he said. "Let us rather strike at the knee." Churchill was pleased to find himself seconded in this view by General Marshall, U.S. Army Chief of Staff, who previously had insisted that the Mediterranean was a sideshow and a drain on resources needed for the invasion of Normandy. In fact, Marshall had not changed his opinion at all, but had come to believe that if Churchill was not soon given his dearly desired prize of Rome he might insist on keeping major British forces in the Mediterranean until he did get it, thus impeding a cross-Channel invasion.

While the Allies hurried ahead with a variety of plans to exploit Mussolini's fall from power, Field Marshal Badoglio, who had announced on July 26 that Italy would continue resolutely in the War, sent emissaries on July 31 to make a secret deal for peace. An Italian representative contacted British diplomats in Lisbon to begin what Eisenhower described as "a series of negotiations, secret communications, clandestine journeys by secret agents, and frequent meetings in hidden places that, if encountered in the fictional world, would have been scorned as incredible melodrama." Churchill was skeptical. "Badoglio admits that he is going to double-cross someone," he observed grimly, and he indicated that he had no intention of being the victim.

Behind the furtiveness of the Italians lay a deeply held fear of German retaliation for Italy's defection. It was possible, indeed likely, that the Germans might shoot or imprison a good many people, including Badoglio and the Royal

AN IGNOMINIOUS END FOR THE DUCE'S SON-IN-LAW

Waving from the steps of the family home, Edda Mussolini stands next to her groom, Count Galeazzo Ciano. Her father wears a top hat at left.

When the Italian Grand Council of the Fascist Party voted to censure Benito Mussolini on July 25, 1943, thereby precipitating his downfall, one of the leaders of the coup was the dictator's own son-in-law, Count Galeazzo Ciano, who had served as Foreign Minister in the Fascist regime.

Then Mussolini returned—and, as head of a puppet state set up by the Germans, had Ciano seized and tried for treason in January 1944. Even the pleadings of the Duce's favorite daughter Edda, who had married Ciano amid great fanfare in 1930, could not save the count. He was convicted and sentenced to death.

At the appointed hour, Ciano was tied to a school chair with his back to the firing squad. He cried out, "Long live Italy!" Before the riflemen fired, Ciano managed at the last moment to slip his bonds and gain his last wish—to face his executioners.

The Duce's son-in-law, executed by a firing squad, receives a final blessing from a priest.

Family, if the surrender negotiations became known. Consequently, the Italians tried to extract from the Allies an assurance that British and American troops would invade the mainland of Italy in force sufficient to protect them from their former friends.

Badoglio thought 15 divisions, landed within striking distance of Rome, would be about right. He also wanted the United States to drop an airborne division on the city to help Italian troops hold it against the Germans.

Later, on the eve of the invasion of the Italian mainland, Eisenhower went so far as to send General Maxwell A. Taylor on a clandestine mission to determine the feasibility of a plan to drop the 82nd Airborne Division into Rome. Taylor moved past German positions by PT boat, landed at Gaeta and slipped into Rome on September 8. But he reported that Italian troops would not be able to secure the airfields and recommended against the drop.

Badoglio's scheme for a 15-division assault near Rome was out of the question. The Allies did not have the men or the sealift to put more than five or six divisions ashore—two in the toe and the rest on the beaches in the Gulf of Salerno, 30 miles south of Naples.

Moreover, the Allies, having fought the Italians for several years, were not full of solicitude for them. On a take-it-or-leave-it basis the Italians on September 3 were obliged to sign surrender terms without knowing when, where or with how many troops the Allies were going to invade. The surrender was to be kept secret until 6:30 p.m. on September 8, when it would be announced simultaneously by Eisenhower in Algiers and Badoglio in Rome. The timing was nicely calculated: the Allies intended to land at Salerno early on September 9, and they hoped the announcement would cause great confusion among the Germans.

The Germans were neither surprised nor confused by the announcement. They had already anticipated the possibility that Italy might drop out of the War. Realizing that they could not hold the entire peninsula by themselves, they had decided to sacrifice much of it and retire to a line in the north running from Pisa to Rimini, where they could defend the approaches to the German homeland. In the summer of 1943, when the fall of Sicily became imminent, they stationed an army group of eight divisions in this area under Field Marshal Erwin Rommel. If the Allies made a powerful amphibious assault on the lower part of the boot, German troops in the south would make their way north to the Pisa-Rimini Line before the invaders cut them off.

The German commander whose jurisdiction extended south from the Pisa-Rimini Line was Field Marshal Kesselring. The American press fastened on Kesselring the nickname "Smiling Albert," but he was by no means the affable boob that the name implied. He may have been too trusting—"That fellow Kesselring," Hitler said, "is too honest for those born traitors down there"—but he was a first-rate military leader and a shrewd strategist. He was convinced that he could beat back an Allied attack on the Italian mainland, particularly if a couple of Rommel's divisions in the north could be sent down to help him.

Kesselring hated to give up the excellent defensive terrain to the south. As Commander in Chief, South, Kesselring had eight German divisions already at his disposal, two of which were kept in the neighborhood of Rome. The other six were deployed around Naples and to the south as far as the heel and toe, and were organized as the German Tenth Army under Colonel General Heinrich von Vietinghoff genannt Scheel. General von Vietinghoff, an old and expert Prussian infantryman who was described in an American intelligence report as "the most capable officer on this front and the driving power behind Kesselring," was an exceedingly tough commander who, as the Italian campaign unfolded, would win the respect of everyone who fought him.

The invasion plan decided upon by General Eisenhower called for General Montgomery's British Eighth Army to cross the Strait of Messina sometime between August 30 and September 4. The timing was left to Montgomery, although Eisenhower hoped the crossing would be made as soon as practical. On the 9th of September the U.S. Fifth Army, comprising both British and American troops, would make the main assault at Salerno. On the same day British troops would land at Taranto, on the heel of the Italian boot, to secure that port and drive toward Naples. Although Montgomery and Lieut. General Mark W. Clark, commander of the U.S. Fifth Army, would be much too far apart (approximately 200 miles) to support each other at first, it was hoped that Montgomery could come up fairly rapidly to help Clark if the Salerno landing ran into trouble.

To the disappointment of several of his fellow commanders, both American and British, who thought he might perhaps have crossed the narrow strait by September 1, Montgomery waited until the 3rd. When he did move, it was
behind a barrage that seemed intended not merely to soften
up the opposition but to blow off Italy's toe. British and
American bombers plastered the opposite shore of the strait
in repeated strikes: the great guns of the battleships H.M.S.
Nelson, Warspite, Rodney and *Valiant* pulverized the landscape; three cruisers, three monitors, six destroyers and two
gunboats hammered away; and more than 600 fieldpieces
of assorted calibers threw thousands of shells into possible
enemy defense positions. But when the 5th British and the
1st Canadian infantry divisions made their crossing, they
encountered no Germans, only some bedraggled Italian
troops who volunteered to help unload their landing craft.
The Germans had withdrawn to the north, and the Italians
in the area welcomed the British. Responding to Montgomery's landing, some got hold of a press and printed a leaflet
written in English by veterans of the First World War:

> *Brothers,*
> *After thirtynine months of war, pains and grieves;*
> *after twenty years of tiranny and inhumanity, after*
> *have the innocent victims of the most perverce gang at*
> *the Government; today, September 8, 1943, we can cry*
> *at full voice our joys our enthusiasm for your coming.*
> *We can't express with words our pleasure, but only*
> *we kneel ourself to the ground to thank Good, who*
> *have permit us to see this day.*
> *With you we have divided the sorrow of the war,*
> *with you we wish to divide the day of the big victory.*
> *We wish to march with you, until the last days*
> *against the enemy N. 1.*
> *We will be worth of your expectation, we will be*
> *your allied of twentyfive years ago.*
> *Hurra the allied*
> *Hurra the free Italy*
> *The committee of antifascist ex fighters of the big war*

Despite the ease of Montgomery's landing, the immensely
capable, battle-tested Eighth Army faced no casual march to
the north. The country was mountainous, the roads narrow
and winding, with many bridges, viaducts, culverts and
tunnels. A handful of German engineers skilled in demolition could hold up an army in that region—a notion that
had already occurred to Kesselring and Vietinghoff, who
gave orders for demolition on the widest possible scale.

In contrast to this forbidding country, the area where the
Fifth Army was to land almost a week later would seem, to
almost anyone except an invading soldier, to be one of the
most beguiling spots in the world. Described by Longfellow
as "the blue Salernian bay with its sickle of white sand," the
Gulf of Salerno presents a magnificent panorama from the
sea. At the northern end of the gulf, the steep-walled, blue-
green Sorrento peninsula juts out, with the small jewel-like

*On his first journey outside the Vatican since
the beginning of the War, Pope Pius XII
blesses throngs of anxious Roman citizens after
the Allied bombing of military targets in
the Italian capital on July 19, 1943. Although the
pilots were carefully briefed and the raid
was carried out in daylight in an effort to limit
the damage to the surrounding buildings,
thousands of civilians were killed or injured.*

town of Salerno at its base, and southward from Salerno pale-gold beaches stretch for nearly 30 miles through Paestum to the town of Agropoli.

Inland from the beaches there is a half-moon-shaped, gradually rising plain that is encircled and overlooked by a jagged wall of mountains. The plain is watered by several streams and two sizable rivers, the Sele and its tributary, the Calore, which in many places are too wide and deep to be forded by vehicles. In 1943 the plain was intensively cultivated, with truck gardens, fields of tomatoes, tobacco and melons, and groves of walnuts and olives.

As a location for a major amphibious assault, the Gulf of Salerno presented the invaders with some definite advantages. The steep gradient of the beaches would make it possible for landing craft to run up on the sand and land troops directly on the shore, and the small harbor at Salerno, if seized intact, could handle a modest tonnage of supplies. Not far inland there was a railroad and a main coastal highway running from Agropoli north through Salerno to Naples and, eventually, to Rome. Another critical advantage for the Allies lay in the fact that fighter planes flying out of Sicily could provide air cover over the Salerno beaches, although the planes would be working close to the limit of their range. Furthermore, within the beachhead area there was a good airfield at Montecorvino that could be captured and put to use.

Salerno also had its drawbacks. The valleys of the Sele and Calore rivers form a low corridor that divides the plain into two sectors. Sand bars along the coast prevented landings near the Sele's mouth. Allied forces landing on either side of the corridor would be separated by about eight miles. Moreover, the mountains that enclosed the beachhead would pose a major obstacle. Enemy artillery in the mountains, trained on Allied troops, might do grievous damage. Field Marshal Kesselring, looking with satisfaction at these commanding heights, called them "God's gift to the gunners." After consolidating the beachhead, Allied troops would have to make their way north to Naples through the Sorrento hills, in which there were only two narrow, easily defended gorges.

As the invasion fleet approached Salerno on the calm, lovely evening of September 8, thousands of soldiers who had heard it somewhere turned over in their minds the Italian proverb "See Naples and die." Its innocent meaning now had an ironic ring.

At 6:30 p.m., when the sun was still up and the fleet was about 20 miles offshore, came the radio announcement of Italy's surrender. Almost instantly the British and American troops on the invasion ships, who had been wrapped in the silent, thoughtful loneliness of men on the eve of battle, erupted in celebration. Shouting with joy, they burst out of their individual solitudes and began to leap and dance on the steel decks. Men of the York and Lancaster Regiment, the Sherwood Foresters, the Coldstream Guards and the King's Own Yorkshire Light Infantry pounded one another on the back and yelled, "The Eyeties have jagged it in! It's all over bar the shouting!" They reached for what little beer and sharp North African wine they had at hand, while their officers opened bottles of Scotch and gin.

On an LCI (Landing Craft, Infantry) crammed with 200 soldiers of the 2nd Battalion Scots Guards, officers told the piper to leave off celebrating and compose a tune called "The Scots Guards' March through Naples." On an American attack transport a major looked at the cheering soldiers of the 36th Division. "I never again expect to witness such scenes of sheer joy," he wrote later. "Speculation was rampant, and it was all good. . . . We would dock in Naples harbor unopposed, with an olive branch in one hand and an opera ticket in the other."

Senior officers, who knew the Germans would fight stubbornly no matter what the Italians did, took to the ships' loudspeakers to try to dampen the celebrations, but with little success. Admiral Cunningham, commander of the Allied naval forces in the Mediterranean, observed dryly in his report afterward: "Many took no heed of these warnings and viewed the proceedings with a sense of complacency."

For the Allied troops, the timing of the announcement was "a psychological disaster," one historian would write.

As for the Germans, though taken aback by the news, they were ready. Kesselring, the Italophile, was hurt and felt personally betrayed by the surrender. He sent a brisk message to his field commander, Vietinghoff, saying that the Italians had "committed basest treachery . . . behind our backs." But he also said that "if we retain our fighting spirit and remain dead calm, I am confident that we will continue to perform the tasks entrusted to us by the Führer. Italian troops will be asked to continue the fight on our side by appeals to their honor. Those who refuse will be ruthlessly disarmed. No mercy must be shown the traitors. Long live the Führer." Actually Kesselring cared little for Hitler and did not wish him a particularly long life. He merely couched his orders in an acceptable form, knowing that they would be read in Berlin. Moreover, he was aware that he might later need reinforcements from the north, and this would depend on Hitler.

Throughout Italy, Italian soldiers threw down their weapons and sloped off into the night. German gun crews quickly took over Italian artillery. At Salerno one unhappy Italian officer removed the breechblocks from his guns and buried them, but most of the artillery pieces were taken over by the Germans intact.

Some Italian commanders, however, were disgusted by the surrender and the German take-over of their weapons. General Don Ferrante Gonzaga, commanding the 222nd Italian Coastal Division at Salerno, refused to hand over his pistol when a German major named von Alvensleben stormed into his headquarters and demanded it. Gonzaga, whose family had long been prominent in Italian military service, was an old soldier who had been awarded several decorations for valor in World War I. He stood up at his desk, trying to yank his gun out of its holster so he could put a bullet into the German. "A Gonzaga never lays down his arms!" he shouted, whereupon he was cut down by bursts from Schmeisser machine pistols. Von Alvensleben was impressed, and he later remarked that Gonzaga had died as "a great soldier." Posthumously the Italian government awarded Gonzaga another medal.

The invading U.S. Fifth Army had been formed in North Africa in recent months and was commanded by an officer who had not yet been tested in combat in World War II. Lieut. General Mark Clark had fought in France in World War I as a young West Point graduate and had recently served as deputy to Eisenhower in North Africa. Tall and slim, with a flair for public relations, he was 47 at the time of Salerno, one of the youngest men of his rank in the Army.

General Clark's army was divided into two corps. The U.S. VI Corps, under Major General Ernest J. Dawley, included the 36th and 45th divisions, with the 3rd and 34th divisions in reserve in North Africa. The British X Corps, under Lieut. General Sir Richard L. McCreery, was composed of the 46th and 56th divisions, with the 7th Armored Division in reserve offshore.

The initial assaults would be made by four divisions totaling approximately 70,000 men, considerably fewer than had hit the beaches in Sicily. Clark's plan (map, pages 58-59) called for three battalions of American Rangers and two British Commando units to secure his left, or northern, flank by taking strong positions in the mountains at the base of the Sorrento peninsula and by seizing the two gorges that led north to Naples. To the right of the Rangers and Commandos the 46th British Infantry Division was to take the town of Salerno. Still farther to the right the 56th British Infantry Division was assigned the tasks of seizing the road and rail junction of Battipaglia and the airfield at Montecorvino. Then there was the gap around the mouth of the Sele River, on the other side of which the U.S. 36th Infantry Division, under Major General Fred L. Walker, would come ashore. The Americans were to capture the main roads, secure the right flank of the beachhead and send patrols to the south, hoping to make contact with Montgomery's army coming up from the toe. In immediate reserve offshore, ready for action where needed, were two regiments of the U.S. 45th Infantry Division.

After taking their initial objectives, the British and Americans were to push speedily inland to establish a firm, semicircular defensive position on the arc of high hills and mountains that overlooked the beaches. They were aware of the weak spot in their beachhead, the low-lying flood plain of the Sele and Calore rivers. If German troops and tanks got into the corridor between the rivers in force, they could drive a wedge between the British and Americans and perhaps compel their surrender or reembarkation. But if the British could seize the heights around Eboli to the left of a bridge at the head of the corridor, the Ponte Sele, and if the Americans could take a village called Altavilla and a position to the right designated on Allied maps as Hill 424, they would command the entrance to the corridor and thus pinch it off. That was the plan.

As for the Germans, they had only one division—the 16th Panzer—immediately available to oppose the Allied landing, but other divisions to the north and south could be brought into action when needed. The 16th, the only fully equipped armored division in southern Italy, had 17,000 men, more than 100 tanks and ample artillery, and was primed for combat, having held anti-invasion maneuvers in the beachhead area shortly before the Allies arrived. Because the front covered by the 16th was nearly 30 miles long, no continuous defensive system could be set up along the beaches. Instead, between Salerno and Agropoli the Germans had constructed eight strong points—bearing such names as Moltke, Scharnhorst, Lilienthal and Schlieffen, after famous German military heroes—and had manned them with platoons of infantry supported by heavy machine guns, mortars and artillery. They had also established observer squads and signal stations at intermediate points, and on the eve of the landing German troops had taken over six Italian coastal batteries in the line. At 3:40 p.m. on September 8, the 16th Panzer Division got word that an Allied fleet was headed in its direction, and the Germans gave their guns a final check, laid out their ammunition and waited.

There was no possibility of surprise at Salerno, although great emphasis had been placed on security throughout the planning stages. Speculation and gossip had been rampant, and there were information leaks in spite of determined efforts to stop them. One particularly zealous effort resulted in a change in command just two weeks before D-day, with Major-General John Hawkesworth replacing Major-General H. A. Freeman-Attwood as commander of the British 46th Division. In a letter to his wife from North Africa, Freeman-Attwood had written: "I hope I shall be drinking a bottle of champagne somewhere in Italy on our wedding day." A censor had reported the letter, and Freeman-Attwood was removed overnight and sent back to England as an example to others.

By September 8 the lumbering Allied fleet—some 500 vessels covering 1,000 square miles of sea—had long since been spotted by German planes. Under the circumstances the British in the northern sector asked for a preliminary bombardment and the Navy happily obliged. But General Walker, commanding the U.S. 36th Division in the southern sector, did not ask for any. He did not think much of the proposed target list submitted by the Navy; he feared that his men might be hit by short rounds from ships; and in any case he felt that at least some measure of surprise might yet be achieved. His memoirs would later record his reasons, revealing a sensitivity not always present in combat generals: "There are a few old emplacements back from the beach, but there are no appropriate targets for navy gun fire, and I see no point to killing a lot of peaceful Italians and destroying their homes."

Walker's decision (authority to make it had been delegated to him by Clark) may have been reasonable, but it deprived the men of the 36th of the psychological lift that would have been provided by thunderous naval salvos. The soldiers of the 36th, many of them from the Texas National Guard, were brave and well trained, but had not been in combat before. They began landing on the Salerno beaches at 3:30 a.m. on September 9, and made for cover behind dunes and patches of scrub. They had to crawl through barbed wire and work their way past enemy tanks and machine guns while behind them their wrecked boats and equipment floated among geysers from exploding shells.

As Sergeant Manuel S. Gonzales of Company E, 141st Infantry Regiment, crept toward a German emplacement, with machine-gun fire whistling just over his head, a tracer bullet hit the pack on his back and set it afire. He slipped out of the pack and kept crawling. A grenade fragment wounded him, but still he kept going until he was close enough to wipe out the gun crew with his own grenade. Sergeant James M. Logan shot several Germans who were coming at him through a hole in a rock wall. Then he

The Italian Premier, Field Marshal Pietro Badoglio, consults with General Maxwell Taylor, U.S. representative on the Allied Military Commission to Italy, prior to announcing Italy's declaration of war against Germany on October 13, 1943. Badoglio, 72, had served as Chief of the Armed Forces General Staff under Mussolini and then succeeded him as Premier in July of 1943. After serving 11 months, Badoglio was replaced by Ivanhoe Bonomi—the man Mussolini ousted when he came to power in 1922.

dashed across open ground, killed the crew of an enemy machine gun, swung the gun around and opened fire on the Germans. Gonzales was later awarded the Distinguished Service Cross, Logan the Medal of Honor.

While the build-up on the beaches continued, assault teams trying to get inland were pinned down by artillery and mortar fire, and by machine gunners and snipers firing from buildings, concealed positions behind sand dunes and clumps of small trees. Boat schedules were disrupted and some of the troops waited vainly for supporting weapons. Radio teams and gun crews had difficulty operating effectively. Yet through it all, men and equipment continued to pour ashore.

Then at 7 a.m., while the troops were still scattered and disorganized along the beaches, the 36th Division was hit by its first large-scale tank attack. From the moment the first assault units had come ashore, enemy tanks had been able to take pot shots at them from scattered positions, but now, on the beaches northwest of Paestum, the 16th Panzer Division assembled 15 or more Panzer IVs and hurled them against elements of the 141st Regiment. Helped by machine guns that had been set up behind four-foot stone walls and inside farm buildings, the tanks moved back and forth, pouring their fire into the regimental line strung out across the flat terrain.

The battle raged past noon of D-day before the main tank assault on the southernmost beaches was brought to a standstill. It was fought mainly by infantrymen using infantry weapons, and there were heroic actions up and down the line. On the left flank, Captain Hersel R. Adams of the 141st Regiment's 3rd Battalion was wounded while leading a charge against oncoming Panzer IVs. After urging his men to leave him and carry on the fight, he was killed when the tanks regrouped and came back with their guns blazing. Private First Class Edward L. Rookey and Private First Class Lavern Counselman crawled within 30 yards of four approaching tanks, dragging a bazooka they had obtained from a wounded man. Their fire and that of others in their squad forced the tanks to withdraw.

In the center of the line, men of the 2nd Battalion also fought back fiercely. Private First Class Ramon G. Gutierrez, after being wounded in the arm while firing his automatic rifle, located a German machine gun and knifed the gunner to death. Private First Class Salomon Santos Jr. and Private First Class Abner E. Carrasco, while under enemy machine-gun fire, installed their machine gun on top of a wall and fired on the Panzer IVs that threatened the frontline position, forcing the tanks to withdraw.

As the fighting raged throughout the first day, the 36th Division finally sorted itself out on the beaches, made its way as much as four miles inland and seized its initial objectives. The division took a large stretch of Highway 18, the main road along the coast, established itself on the approaches to Monte Soprano and by 4 p.m. was able to report that the Germans had fallen back. A foothold had been gained, but there was virtually no communication with the British X Corps and the dangerous gap remained.

In the northern sector, following a 15-minute barrage by the Royal Navy, British troops had landed against only light opposition. Flanked on the far north by American Rangers, whose job was to secure the Chiunzi mountain pass of the Sorrento peninsula beyond the town of Maiori, British Army and Marine Commandos went ashore at Vietri, just north of Salerno, under covering fire from the destroyer H.M.S. *Blackmore*. A crisis developed after the landing when German mortars and guns turned their attention from the fleet to the assault craft bringing in reinforcements and supplies. In the resulting confusion it was falsely reported that the Germans had retaken the beach. But in fact the British prevailed.

In the area around the Montecorvino airport, the landing of the main British forces was proceeding on schedule, but confusion and turmoil developed here also. The British troops were using rocket-firing landing craft called "Hedgerows," for the first time. With a capacity to launch almost 800 three-inch rockets simultaneously, the Hedgerows were murderously effective, but blueprints for the new weapons had never arrived from England. The Hedgerows had been hastily assembled, and some of the early rounds were wildly off target. One spectacular rocket blast was almost a half mile from where it should have been; the troops of the 56th Division were under orders to follow the rockets, and the first waves, misled, went ashore on the wrong beach. There they became entangled with troops of the 46th Division in a chaotic mix-up that lasted several hours and was aggravated

A COVETED PRIZE: THE ITALIAN NAVY

British sailors on the Warspite eye their former enemies on the horizon—Italian battleships being escorted to North Africa after the Italian Navy surrender.

Italy's Army and Air Force virtually melted away when the armistice was announced on September 8, 1943, but no one could forecast what the Navy might do. Italian warships had been skittish about engaging the Allies in battle before the surrender, and although they had seemed not to pose any real threat at the time, they had had to be watched by sizable numbers of Allied ships and planes. Now there was the danger that some, if not all, of the 206 Italian ships might put up a fight, be sabotaged or, more likely, fall into German hands.

According to the terms of the truce, warships on Italy's west coast, most of them at La Spezia and Genoa, were to steam south for Corsica, past Sardinia, and then proceed to North Africa to await orders. The ships at Taranto, in the heel of the Italian boot, were to sail for British Malta.

At 2:30 a.m. on September 9, three battleships, the *Roma, Vittorio Veneto* and *Italia,* shoved off from La Spezia escorted by three light cruisers and eight destroyers. German troops stormed into the town to try to stop them. Enraged by the escape, they rounded up and summarily shot several Italian captains who, unable to get their vessels under way, had scuttled them.

That afternoon, the ships were attacked off Sardinia by German bombers. Several suffered damage and the *Roma* was sunk, with a loss of nearly 1,400 men. The remaining ships made it to safety, the majority reaching North Africa, while three destroyers and a cruiser, which had stopped to rescue survivors, docked in Minorca.

With the turnover proceeding smoothly in most places, an Allied naval force headed for the big Italian naval base at Taranto. The Italian ships stationed there steamed out of the harbor. There were moments of agonizing tension on the Allied vessels before the Italians' intentions became clear. Would they fire? Sailing closer, they headed for the Allied flotilla—and then sailed right through it. They were on their way to surrender at Malta.

by the fact that all of their vehicles and heavier weapons had been landed on the correct beach and did not reach them before night.

Meanwhile, on a beach near the Montecorvino airport, a more ludicrous snarl developed as a landing craft was unloaded and one of the first items to be disgorged proved to be a piano. An irate officer wanted to throw the piano into the sea, while a noncommissioned officer, charged with the responsibility for its safe delivery to the sergeants' mess, valiantly protected the instrument. The noncom's mission was accomplished when some gunners rushed the piano up the beach while the officer's attention was diverted.

In other areas of the beachhead, British assault forces beat off numerous counterattacks by tanks and infantry, with the aid of accurate naval gunfire. Troops of the 9th Battalion Royal Fusiliers, shortly after landing at 3:45 a.m., spotted a German rocket battery and signaled its position to a headquarters ship. A destroyer moved close to the shore, turned broadside and fired. "The shells almost parted our hair," a Fusilier wrote. "The rockets were wiped out but a machine gun nest, spared in the barrage, had to be taken by the troops." Lieutenant David Lewis, a Welsh Rugby player, was killed when he led a platoon armed with grenades and bayonets in a charge that not only silenced the guns but yielded 25 prisoners.

Around the vital Montecorvino airfield, fighting raged inconclusively all day. British machine gunners reached the edge of the field early enough to shoot up two enemy fighters and a bomber as they roared down the runway trying to get airborne. A British plane came in for a landing, its pilot believing the field was in friendly hands, and was destroyed by counterattacking Germans. At nightfall the field was a no man's land as tanks and patrols of both sides struck at each other.

In spite of all the confusion, British troops had established a shaky hold on the town of Salerno and had seized a beachhead. But they had been so heavily engaged that they had not been able to reach out toward the Americans on their right, and they, too, were concerned about the gap.

On the other side of the lines, the German commander, Vietinghoff, saw no reason to be discouraged, in spite of the Allies' initial successes. He had managed to contain the invaders within a small area with only one division, the 16th Panzer. Now, if he could bring up reinforcements quickly enough, he might be able to throw the Allies back into the sea. He ordered the 19th Panzer Grenadier and the 26th Panzer divisions to break off what little contact they had with Montgomery's advance troops, and, leaving only small rear guards and demolition teams behind, rush to Salerno at top speed.

North of Naples the Hermann Göring Division and the 15th Panzer Grenadier Division were licking their wounds from the Sicilian campaign. Both had taken severe losses, but they could count 27,000 tough, seasoned troops between them. Vietinghoff directed the two divisions to hurry south, and overnight they began to make their presence felt on the British sector of the beachhead. In the meantime,

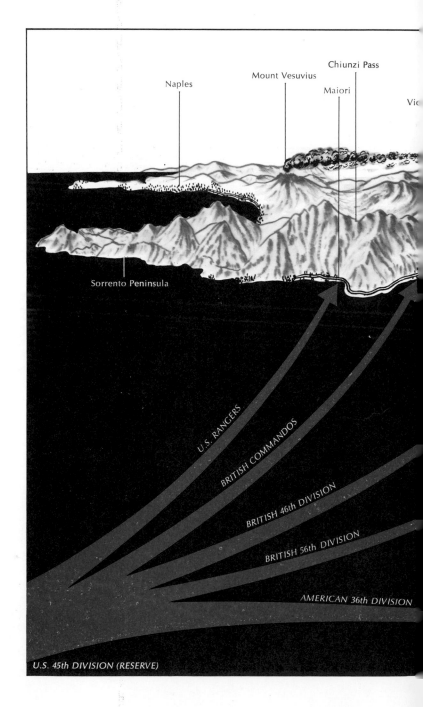

The crescent-shaped Salerno beachhead stretched from the rugged Sorrento peninsula in the north to the town of Salerno, then south nearly 30 miles through Paestum to Agropoli. When the Allies came ashore at five different points, they found themselves hemmed in by mountains that rose more than 4,000 feet in the north and from 1,500 to 4,000 feet in the center and south. The British 56th Division was separated from the U.S. 36th Division by the Sele River and a treacherous sand bar at its mouth. With the roads leading northward from the beachhead easily defended by the Germans, the Allies faced a tough drive toward their primary objective—the city of Naples, which appears to be closer in this foreshortened drawing than the actual distance of 30 to 40 miles.

Vietinghoff's superior, Kesselring, urged the German High Command to let him have two of Rommel's armored divisions in northern Italy to throw against the Allies. The request was turned down. Kesselring later said his proposal "might have led to a decisive German victory if Hitler had acceded to my very modest demands." He may well have been right, but Hitler was determined not to commit more troops to the south, where they might be cut off by another Allied landing.

While the Germans were attempting to build up their forces opposing the beachhead, the Luftwaffe was making a major effort against Allied shipping in the Gulf of Salerno. During the first three days of the invasion, German pilots, who seemed unaware of the Allied domination of the air, launched almost 550 sorties by fighters, fighter-bombers

and heavy bombers. They also launched a new weapon that had been used tentatively against the invaders at Sicily, but was now to be utilized with a vengeance: a remote-controlled glide bomb. Two types had been developed, both fitted with fins and rocket boosters. One had a range of about three and a half miles and a speed of 660 miles per hour, the other a range of eight miles and a speed of 570 miles per hour; both carried war heads packed with 660 pounds of explosive. They were released from high-flying planes and guided by radio to their targets.

The distance traveled by the glide bombs was so great that when the British cruiser H.M.S. *Uganda* was hit by one in midafternoon on September 13, off Salerno, no air alert was on and the attacking plane was not even seen. The bomb penetrated seven steel decks and exploded beneath

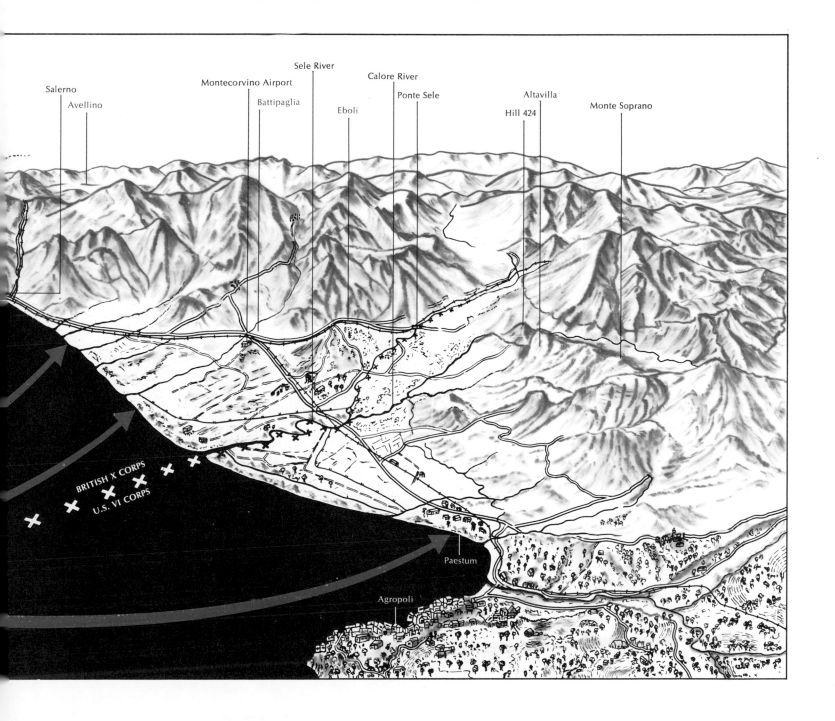

the ship. Although she was flooded with 1,300 tons of water, the *Uganda* remained afloat and was towed out of the combat area. The battleship H.M.S. *Warspite* was also put out of action by a glide bomb, as was the cruiser U.S.S. *Savannah*. With this weapon or with conventional bombs, the Luftwaffe managed to sink four transports, one heavy cruiser and seven landing craft, meanwhile inflicting varying degrees of damage on other ships.

The Allies had had scarcely time even to guess at a defense against the glide bomb. A radar expert on board the British headquarters ship came up with the notion that perhaps the bomb's delicate guidance controls might be upset by interference from the tiny motors of electric razors. Accordingly a dead-serious signal was sent to all ships in the fleet directing that all electric razors be turned on whenever a glide-bomb attack was thought to be imminent. The effect of this was never discovered.

To counter the German build-up on the ground at Salerno, General Clark put ashore his floating reserve, two regiments of the U.S. 45th Infantry Division. Their goal was to move inland and plug the gap between the Allied sectors. But because transports were in short supply and the time required for voyages from Sicilian and North African ports was long, no additional reinforcements could be brought in by sea in time to meet a major enemy assault.

The only hope for further immediate help lay with the British Eighth Army in the south, but the rugged terrain and German demolitions were posing serious problems for Montgomery. "The roads in southern Italy twist and turn in the mountainous country and are admirable feats of engineering," he later wrote. "They abound in bridges, viaducts, culverts and even tunnels, and this offers unlimited scope to military engineers for demolitions and roadblocks of every conceivable kind. The Germans took the fullest advantage of this fact, and our advance throughout was barred and delayed by demolitions on the widest possible scale." On September 10, Montgomery found it necessary to "have a short pause" because his army was "getting very strung out." He gave his men two days of rest, while he awaited a new supply of bridging materials. On the 13th of September, the day the Germans launched their counterattack against the Salerno bridgehead, Montgomery's advance elements were still about 120 miles from the beachhead, and his main body was 40 miles farther down the peninsula.

Meanwhile, a critical situation was developing for the Allies on the Salerno beachhead as the tempo of the fighting increased. The heaviest blows were falling on the British

Royal Fusiliers, who had occupied Battipaglia. On September 10 the Germans forced the Fusiliers out of the town, inflicting heavy losses and taking nearly 1,500 prisoners. For the next two days, in the hills north of Salerno fighting raged between British Commandos and a parachute battalion of the Herman Göring Division. Casualties were heavy for both sides. Among the British troops killed was Captain the Duke of Wellington, fifth lineal descendant of the victor at Waterloo.

After two days of combat in this sector, the heights at Eboli and Altavilla on both sides of the Sele-Calore corridor remained in German hands. On September 11, American tanks and infantry made a major effort to take these objectives. Although they were stopped short of Eboli, they were able to seize Altavilla and Hill 424, gaining domination of the corridor from the south. But on the following day the Germans counterattacked and threw the Americans back with heavy losses.

Rolling down the corridor, the Germans overran the 2nd Battalion of the U.S. 143rd Infantry Regiment and destroyed it as a fighting unit. More than 500 officers and men were lost, most of them captured, while the survivors reeled back out of control. With scarcely a pause the attack swept on and German tanks reached the juncture of the Sele and the Calore, a scant two miles from the beach.

"At this point," said Clark, "we were almost certainly at the mercy of Kesselring, provided he massed his strength and threw it at us relentlessly." Between the German spearhead and the water stood only a handful of American infantrymen and some 105mm guns of the 189th Field Artillery Battalion, under Lieut. Colonel Hal L. Muldrow Jr., and the 158th Field Artillery Battalion, under Lieut. Colonel Russell D. Funk, both of the 45th Division.

By now, Clark had come ashore and his command post was only a few hundred yards behind the artillery pieces. He made arrangements to evacuate his headquarters on 10 minutes' notice, intending to take a PT boat to the British sector, and went out to have a look at the action. To protect their guns Muldrow and Funk were putting out a forward line of improvised infantry—clerks, cooks, drivers, mechanics and other miscellaneous headquarters troops. On the roads nearby, officers were "stopping trucks, jeeps and everything else that came along. Every soldier who got

out of the vehicles was given a gun and put in the line." Clark noticed "a hill on their flank that might have offered the enemy a vantage point . . . so I ordered a regimental band armed and sent there immediately. The hill didn't have any name so I told them to call it Piccolo Peak."

The German tanks were advancing toward a ford beside a burned-out bridge on the Calore when the American artillerymen opened fire. Funk's and Muldrow's men, stripped to the waist and sweating in the September heat, slammed shell after shell into their pieces. Soon the guns of the two battalions, as nearly hub to hub as modern war allows, were firing eight rounds per minute per gun, a rate perhaps unsurpassed by any artillery in World War II. "The ford beside the bridge and the road leading to it simply went up in dust," said Clark, who moved along the gunners, encouraging them—and in the process exposing himself to enemy fire. "The fields and the woods in which the enemy tanks took cover were pulverized."

The enemy wavered, fell back and at sunset retreated up the corridor. The American gunners had fired 4,000 rounds of ammunition on the narrow front, stopping the most serious threat against the beachhead.

Despite the enemy's retreat, Clark thought the worst was yet to come. He was, however, receiving occasional word from General Montgomery in the south. "He was coming up, well, I won't say 'leisurely' but it sure wasn't as fast as I had hoped," said Clark. "In the meantime I was really having a rugged time and in the middle of it I kept getting these messages from Monty: 'Hold on—we're coming up' and then, later, 'Hold on—we've joined hands.' I remember sending one message back where I said, 'If we've joined hands, I haven't felt a thing yet.'"

On the night of September 13, while the exhausted artillerymen slept beside their guns, it occurred to Clark that he might have to pull out of his beachhead or drastically consolidate it. He sent a message to Vice Admiral H. Kent Hewitt asking him to prepare plans to evacuate Americans south of the Sele River and remove them to the British sector. Hewitt thought this was a poor idea. When landing craft come in empty to a beach and are then loaded with men and equipment, it is often hard if not impossible to get them off the beach again. Hewitt's British colleague, Com-

Striding along the pebbly shore at Salerno, British General Sir Harold Alexander (left), commander in chief of Allied land forces in Italy, visits the tenuous Allied beachhead with U.S. Lieut. General Mark Clark (center), commander of ground forces at Salerno, and British Lieut. General Sir Richard McCreery, commander of the X Corps. In a dispatch written shortly after his visit, Alexander, reporting on the counterattack by the Germans, said: "By the use of every reserve, the enemy was held. It was an impressive example of stubborn doggedness in defense."

modore G. N. Oliver of the Royal Navy, was horrified and remarked coolly that that sort of thing was "simply not on." Nonetheless plans were made.

While the Navy reluctantly got ready for a small-scale Dunkirk, Allied reinforcements arrived on the beachhead. Responding to a rush order from Clark, a battalion of the U.S. 82nd Airborne Division, based in Sicily, dropped inside the American lines. The 82nd's commander, General Ridgway, had first made it emphatically plain that he did not want a repetition of the fiasco at Gela, in Sicily, where his paratroopers had been shot at by their own countrymen. Accordingly a strict "guns tight" order was enforced before the airdrop, and there was no foul-up German night bombers in the neighborhood were even allowed to carry out a raid without challenge.

The number of paratroopers who came in—1,300 men of the 2nd Battalion, 504th Parachute Infantry—was relatively small, but their arrival gave a disproportionate boost to the morale of the beleaguered Allies. Soon afterward in daylight the remaining regiment of the U.S. 45th Division came in by sea, as did part of the 7th British Armored Division.

Because the Allied troops were scattered and extended over a wide area, Clark prudently shortened and reinforced his lines during the night of September 13-14, pulling them back at several points to improve defensive positions. In the next day's fighting the Germans lost as many as 30 tanks when they attacked without realizing the new American arrangement. Now the lines, better integrated and stiffened at many points by artillery, held everywhere. The artillery of the 36th Division fired more than 4,100 rounds, that of the 45th Division 6,687 rounds, a one-day record for the Salerno struggle.

Although under direct artillery and small-arms fire most of September 14, the 636th Tank Destroyer Battalion defended the line effectively. Five Panzer IVs were disabled by Company B near the junction of the Calore River and La Cosa Creek. Company C's score was seven tanks and an ammunition carrier, most of it credited to the crew of a tank destroyer named "Jinx," commanded by Sergeant Edwin A. Yost. Their first shot, fired from a ridge that overlooked approaching enemy armor, missed the target by 200 yards; the next set fire to a tank; the third blew up the ammunition vehicle. In all Yost and his men accounted for the ammunition truck and five tanks—in 30 minutes' fighting.

In the British sector, the X Corps had also encountered heavy opposition. The 46th Division was dug in among the hills near Salerno. On the 13th the Germans shelled that area and sent tanks against the 56th Division, which was spread out on the open plain southeast of Battipaglia. The

battle raged for three hours, but the Coldstream Guards of the 201st Guards Brigade and the 19th Royal Fusiliers of the 167th Infantry Brigade held their positions.

Often the pressure on Allied troops was so intense that only the weight and accuracy of naval gunfire tipped the balance. The Germans, who had nothing to match it, were frequently intimidated by shelling from the sea and spoke of it with wistful resentment. "The attack this morning pushed on into stiffened resistance," wrote Vietinghoff, "but above all the advancing troops had to endure the most severe heavy fire that had hitherto been experienced; the naval gunfire from at least 16 to 18 battleships, cruisers and destroyers lying in the roadstead. With astonishing precision and freedom of maneuver, these ships shot at every recognized target with overwhelming effect." During the entire action at Salerno the Navy delivered more than 11,000 tons of shells on the beachhead.

Help also arrived from the air. Eisenhower had ordered Air Chief Marshal Tedder to throw the whole weight of the Northwest African Air Forces into relief of the ground forces in the Salerno action, and on the 14th of September, hundreds of bombers, including B-25s, B-26s and B-17s, passed over the beaches to blast targets at Eboli, Battipaglia and other key positions.

Now reinforcements were coming in, and the situation of the Fifth Army at Salerno was greatly improved. As the VI and X corps moved inland, the left flank of the VI Corps linked up with the right flank of the X Corps southeast of Battipaglia. By the 15th, the 180th Infantry Regiment of the 45th Division had moved into the area near Monte Soprano; the 505th Parachute Regiment had dropped near Paestum; the ████h Glider Regimental Combat Team had arrived by LCI; ████ the rest of the 7th British Armored Division was landing. (The experience of the 509th Parachute Battalion was an exception to the brightening picture. Dropped behind the German lines on the night of September 14 at Avellino, the battalion was dispersed over such a wide area that it was unable to accomplish its mission of disrupting enemy communications.)

Although the mere presence of General Montgomery's Eighth Army moving up from the south had its effect on the Germans—Vietinghoff was always obliged to keep looking nervously over his shoulder—Montgomery did not make an effective linkup with the beachhead troops until most of the fighting was over. "Some would like to think—I did at the time—that we helped, if not saved, the situation at Salerno," later wrote Major-General Sir Francis de Guingand, Montgomery's chief of staff. "But now I doubt whether we influenced matters to any great extent. General Clark had everything under control before the Eighth Army appeared on the scene."

On September 18, after nine days of fighting, the Germans pulled back from the beachhead. Although they had yielded the Allies a lodgment, they had not been defeated. Indeed, their withdrawal was part of the established plan to fall back to positions in the northern Apennines. It was no headlong retreat toward Rome and the north but a calculated action that established a succession of defensive lines across the peninsula. Fierce fighting lay ahead for the American and British forces; they would face rugged rain-swept mountains and a tough and determined enemy who was skilled at delaying tactics in mountain warfare. But by establishing a firm beachhead at Salerno, the Fifth Army had achieved its first objective in the Italian campaign.

In the nine-day period, the Americans had suffered 3,500 casualties—500 soldiers killed, 1,800 wounded and 1,200 reported missing. Moreover, they had come perilously close to being pushed back into the sea. Visiting the VI Corps headquarters a week after the Salerno landing, General Eisenhower took the corps commander, Dawley, to task for the near debacle in the Sele-Calore corridor. "How'd you get your troops into such a mess?" he asked. A few days later Dawley was relieved.

The British, in the heavy fighting around Salerno, the Montecorvino airport and Battipaglia, had suffered even heavier casualties: a total of 5,500 killed, wounded and missing in action. But the successful conclusion of the first large-scale opposed landing on the European continent, the Salerno operation, which had almost collapsed when the Germans came within two miles of pushing the Allied Army back into the sea, now meant that they were in Italy —and Europe—to stay, and control of the Mediterranean was in their hands.

Raising a cloud of dust on a country road, a U.S. Sherman tank rumbles toward Naples, forcing Italians in a horse-drawn gig to pull to the side. After Italy surrendered, the inhabitants tried to carry on as best they could, but the fighting between the Germans and Allies, with shellings and bombings, took a heavy toll. The War claimed 146,000 civilian casualties.

HEADING 'EM OFF AT THE PASS

A Ranger half-track, mounting a 75mm cannon, poises at the crest of Chiunzi Pass before dashing into the open to fire on German positions on the Naples plain.

HOLDING THE HIGH GROUND FOR THE ALLIES

While the main Allied offensive against the Italian mainland unfolded at Salerno in September 1943, U.S. Rangers under the leadership of Lieut. Colonel William O. Darby were entrusted with the vital task of securing the westernmost section of the Allies' beachhead. After landing on the narrow shore at Maiori, 12 miles west of Salerno, they dashed six miles inland and seized the strategic 4,000-foot-high Chiunzi Pass, overlooking the plain of Naples.

By occupying these commanding heights, the Rangers could prevent the Germans from mounting a flank attack on the Salerno beachhead through the pass. They could also direct disabling fire on German strongholds in villages below, and on troops and supplies bound for the enemy's beachhead forces via Highway 18, the major coastal artery linking Naples and Salerno. And, when the time came for the big Allied push to Naples, the Rangers would be in a position to spearhead the drive from Chiunzi Pass.

Darby's three battalions of hand-picked volunteers were well suited to the demands of this difficult assignment. While undergoing training by British Commandos in Northern Ireland and Scotland, they had practiced amphibious landings under live mortar and machine-gun fire, and had been tested by instructors who lobbed live grenades alongside assault boats. They actually suffered more casualties in training than they would on some of their combat missions.

Battle-hardened by participation with British and Canadian commandos in the ill-fated raid on Dieppe in 1942 and later in the landings in North Africa and Sicily, the Rangers were to experience some of their most harrowing action at Chiunzi Pass. For nearly three weeks Darby's men fought as many as six close-range actions a day and endured relentless shellings. Exhausted, outnumbered, weakened by illness—many were felled by a recurrence of malaria contracted in Sicily—the Rangers still managed to cling to the crucial heights, justifying the confidence of Colonel Darby, who had radioed Allied headquarters on the first day of the operation: "We have taken up positions in the enemy's rear, and we'll stay here till hell freezes over."

Lieut. Colonel William Darby (left), commander of the Rangers, confers with battalion commander Major Roy Murray in the hills west of Salerno.

The town of Maiori, where the U.S. Rangers landed, lies at the foot of the mountains on the Sorrento peninsula. The road at center leads to Chiunzi Pass.

TENACIOUS DEFENSE OF A MOUNTAIN REDOUBT

The Rangers had to endure 18 days of rugged fighting at Chiunzi before the Allies could begin their main drive through the gap toward Naples. Outnumbered 8 to 1, they beat back seven large-scale German counterattacks and held out against round-the-clock mortar and artillery barrages that forced them to live in cramped foxholes hacked in mountainsides.

They also engaged in sharp, small-scale fire fights with waves of tough German mountain fighters and SS troops who were trying to pierce their lines. Although they were strung across a nine-mile front normally allotted to a battalion, the Rangers successfully repelled each assault.

"We held on by our fingernails," recalled one of the Rangers later. "We were spread so thin that we had a hell of a time stopping the Germans, but we did—thanks to our speed, versatility and rugged training. When the Germans came up the hill, we'd all rush over to plug the gap and let them have it."

The Rangers managed, however, to accomplish a great deal more than merely withstand attacks. They had with them four half-tracks that became locked in a deadly game of cat and mouse with German artillery and 88mm guns. The half-tracks would dart, one or two at a time, to the crest of Chiunzi Pass, fire off several rounds, then "get the hell outta there" under heavy retaliatory fire. At night the Rangers dispatched four- to seven-man patrols to gauge the enemy's strengths and weaknesses and to bring back prisoners for interrogation.

So effective were the Ranger operations in the pass that captured Germans later said their officers had estimated that a full division of Americans held the heights.

Rangers take cover in mountainside foxholes while a half-track retreats to avoid German counterfire.

With shell casings littering the ground, a half-track blasts away as German rounds land nearby. Each of the vehicles sustained hundreds of shrapnel hits.

Under a smoke screen, a Ranger patrol clambers up a hillside near Chiunzi Pass. Patrols sneaked into towns to take prisoners and set off demolitions.

Crouching in a rocky crevice, a Ranger Tommy gunner sprays bullets at the advancing German force.

White phosphorous shells fired from 4.2-inch chemical mortars at Chiunzi Pass cast smoke to obscure the view of German mortar men in the town of Sala.

BULL'S-EYES FROM A MOUNTAINTOP FARM

In addition to their close-range combat with the Germans, Darby's Rangers made full use of the commanding view of the valley from Chiunzi Pass to pinpoint en-

emy targets for Allied artillery, mortars and naval gunfire. And to hamper the Germans' own fire the Rangers lobbed smoke shells from mortars onto the enemy gun positions below.

The Rangers called in the barrages from a forward command post, a thick-walled stone farmhouse near the crest of Chiunzi

Pass. Darby's troops nicknamed the building "Fort Schuster," in honor of an American captain who had set up a medical aid station there on the first day of the battle. Even though it was pounded by the Germans, the command post was sturdy enough to survive hundreds of direct hits by artillery and mortar fire.

From their observation post in "Fort Schuster," American and British spotters direct artillery fire against the German defenses in the valley below the pass.

A U.S. light 105mm howitzer, emplaced in a rear area near Maiori, is fired by 82nd Airborne Division artillerymen, who were supporting Darby's Rangers.

An American sergeant steadies two wounded soldiers being trucked to the makeshift hospital in Maiori.

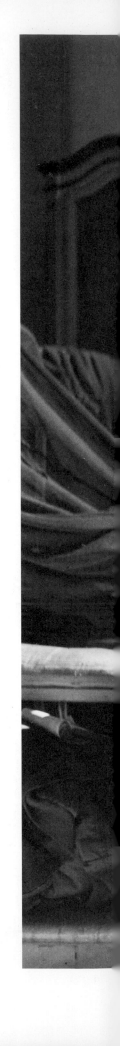

CARING FOR THE WOUNDED IN A MAKESHIFT HOSPITAL

The price of the heroic 18-day defense of Chiunzi Pass came high. The Rangers suffered heavy casualties—up to 30 per cent in some units.

The wounded, many of them shrapnel victims, were carried in the back of a jeep or truck down the steep slopes to Maiori. There, in the chapel of a Catholic monastery, the Allies had established a makeshift hospital. Pews were pushed up against the walls to make way for two long rows of beds that had been hauled in from a nearby orphanage. At a portable operating table lighted by a gasoline lamp, British doctors performed surgery 24 hours a day. Because of the heat and poor ventilation, they toiled shirtless, wearing only masks and caps, short pants and white rubber aprons. After emergency treatment by the doctors, the wounded Rangers were cared for by Italian nuns and nurses. Most were then ferried down the Italian coast in landing craft and shipped to big medical bases in North Africa.

For some of Darby's Rangers, the monastery at Maiori was the last stop. In one of the rooms an Italian carpenter constructed dozens of simple pine coffins. Working as fast as he could, he was unable to keep pace with the mounting toll of dead.

In front of the altar of the temporary hospital, an Italian nurse changes the dressing on an American soldier's head wound as he cheerfully enjoys a cigarette.

The Italian campaign was a creature of improvisation. It did not spring full-blown from the mind of a military genius; it just grew. Sicily was invaded, and when that operation went well the planners decided to invade the mainland. Then, as the investment in men and equipment increased, so did the temptation to push farther north to reap larger dividends. And thus the campaign gradually escalated into one of the most grinding and protracted struggles of the entire War.

When the beachhead at Salerno had been secured, the drive for Naples began. The objectives of the campaign still were limited: the U.S. Fifth Army would secure the port of Naples and advance as far north as the natural barrier of the Volturno River. Meanwhile, the British Eighth Army would capture the airfields around Foggia, near the east coast.

The main effort in the drive toward Naples was to be made by the British 46th Infantry and 7th Armored divisions. They would fight their way through the passes in the Sorrento hill barrier, sweep past the ruins of Pompeii and the great bulk of Mount Vesuvius and approach the city from the south. The British 56th Division would also attack through the mountains, but bypass Naples, and head directly for the Volturno River. At the same time, two American infantry divisions, the 3rd and the 45th, would hook inland through the mountains to threaten Naples from the northeast.

It was a sound plan of battle and—given the terrain and the limited road network—one that was clearly apparent to Kesselring and Vietinghoff. The Germans were obviously determined to delay the British and Americans as much as possible, and to make them pay in sweat and blood for every mile of advance. They were also bent on wrecking the port of Naples so thoroughly that it would be a battered prize when the Allies finally took it.

As the Americans set forth on their flanking march beyond the beachhead on September 20, they found themselves surrounded by jagged mountains that were gashed by ravines and streams and split by cliffs. Movement was restricted to narrow roads with innumerable hairpin turns. Tanks and artillery were nearly useless—and the enemy took pains to place obstacles in their way.

Between the ancient city of Paestum on the sea and Oliveto, only about 25 miles inland, the Germans blew up more than 25 bridges. U.S. engineers replaced some of these with Bailey bridges, made of prefabricated steel parts

"SEE NAPLES AND DIE"

that were bolted together like Erector Sets. Other demolished bridges had to be replaced with rock-and-earth ramps and causeways carved out by explosives or built up by bulldozers. "There was no weapon more valuable than the engineer bulldozer," said General Truscott, commander of the U.S. 3rd Division, "no soldiers more effective than the engineers who moved us forward."

But as a rule the Germans were not content with demolition alone. By positioning a few machine guns, a tank or self-propelled gun to cover the site of a wrecked bridge, they forced American infantrymen to drag themselves for miles up steep, trackless slopes to work their way around enemy strong points. When that was done, the Germans merely withdrew to the next good defensive position and set up their weapons again.

Bulldozers, working close to the front and at times even ahead of it, were a favorite German target. As Eisenhower noted, the Germans used "hidden machine guns and other long-range light-caliber weapons which, from the safety of a thousand yards distance, picked off operating personnel and often destroyed the machines themselves." But help was on the way in the form of a hybrid but very effective contraption called a tankdozer. "Some imaginative and sensible men on the home front," continued Eisenhower, "hearing of this difficulty, solved the problem by merely converting a number of Sherman tanks into bulldozers. These tanks were impervious to all types of small-arms fire and could not be destroyed except by shells from large-caliber guns or by big mines. From that time on our engineering detachments on the front lines began to enjoy a degree of safety that actually led them to seek this kind of adventurous work. None of us could identify the individual responsible for developing this piece of equipment but had he been present he would have, by acclamation, received all the medals we could have pinned upon him."

As they penetrated deeper into the mountains, where they were forced to operate more and more off the roads, the Americans were obliged to rely on packtrains of mules to carry food and ammunition up and down the steep hills. Soldiers ransacked the countryside for mules—300 to 500 were needed per division—and urgent requests were sent back to the U.S. not only for animals, but also for mule shoes, nails, halters, packs and, above all, for people: mule skinners who knew how to manage the beasts; packers who understood the proper rigging and loading of packs; blacksmiths, harness makers and veterinarians.

The search for men possessing such skills, which were no longer officially recognized by the U.S. Army, was a frustrating one. In the 1930s, the Army had included two cavalry divisions, a number of mule-pack artillery battalions and a Quartermaster Corps packtrain battalion, and all of these outfits had included experts of the sort now in such desperate demand in Italy. However, in their zeal to modernize the Army, the authorities not only had abolished the actual units, but also had converted to infantrymen and truck drivers the soldiers who were skilled in dealing with animals and with their equipment—and had sent most of these retreads to the Pacific.

In addition to the packtrains, the Americans improvised cavalry units, primarily for reconnaissance. These impromptu horse outfits employed commandeered animals and volunteers who knew something about riding. Boots, breeches and saddles were scrounged from local sources. In roadless areas, the soldiers could maneuver with greater flexibility mounted than on foot, and they could make relatively fast cross-country movements in terrain where tanks and trucks could not operate at all.

The rest of the troops had hard going. The terrain south of Naples was so rugged that it took the British several days to get through the Sorrento hill passes and onto the plain where they could deploy their tanks, and it was not until October 1 that their advance units entered the city. That same day elements of the U.S. 82nd Airborne Division occupied Naples. The British swept on for another 20 miles against stubborn opposition until they reached the Volturno River six days later, where exhaustion—and the Germans—brought them to a halt. For two weeks the Germans had been preparing a defensive line along the Volturno, and they were ready to contest any attempt to cross it.

The Germans had also had two weeks to work on Naples. Kesselring had been explicit in his demolition instructions: spare the monasteries and churches, including the cell where Saint Thomas Aquinas lived while teaching at the University of Naples. Spare the museums, historic buildings and hospitals. But beyond that, leave nothing that might benefit the Allies. He ordered Vietinghoff's Tenth Army to dismantle and remove the machinery from the Alfa Romeo plant as well as the equipment from all factories that could produce typewriters, accounting machines and manufacturing tools. The Tenth Army was to remove all railroad rolling stock and demolish tracks, switches, power plants and water lines. Trucks, buses and cars were to be evacuated or destroyed, as were canning plants, warehouses, food stocks, wineries, radio and meteorological stations. Above all, the port of Naples was to be made useless.

The Germans worked with brutal thoroughness, so frightening the civilians who remained in the city that they holed up in their houses and stayed indoors for days. When General Clark entered Naples on October 1 with an armed escort, he reported that he had the "eerie sensation" of being watched by "eyes that peeked out at us from behind the closed shutters of every house and every building. It was still that way when we drove out of Naples; I had a feeling that I had been seen by millions of persons, although I hardly glimpsed a civilian during the entire trip."

Smoke drifted everywhere. Furniture and bedding had been heaped up in the courtyards of the major hotels and set ablaze. One German demolition team, exceeding Kesselring's orders, had found the city's archives in a villa, soaked them with gasoline and burned them. Near the docks huge piles of coal smouldered so stubbornly that it took Army engineers three days to put out the fires.

The streets were obstructed in more than 200 places by mountains of rubble from dynamited buildings. The Napo-leonic aqueduct that brought water into Naples had been destroyed and the sewers blown up at more than 50 points. Administration buildings at the university were on fire. Booby traps had been hidden in innumerable places, particularly in houses or hotels the Allies were likely to occupy. Delayed-action bombs, some of them with as much as 42 days' time set on their clockwork mechanisms, had been bricked into the walls of public buildings. Six days after the Allies entered Naples, the post office was wrecked by a massive explosion that killed or wounded 70 people. Four days later a time bomb went off in an Italian Army barracks, killing 18 men of the U.S. 82nd Airborne Division.

By far the worst damage was in the port. Intensive Allied bombing over the previous weeks and months had made a mess that the German demolition teams needed only to refine. The harbor was clogged with the half-visible or submerged wrecks of more than 130 ships. Oceangoing liners, tankers, destroyers, floating cranes, tugs, trawlers and lighters had been scuttled helter-skelter, and on top of them the Germans had piled locomotives, trucks, oxygen bottles, ammunition and mines—smothering all under a thick scum of oil. The 73 electric dockside cranes that once had served the port had all been dynamited, as had piers, wharves, grain elevators and office buildings.

Although the Allied had not anticipated the extent of the damage, they were prepared to cope with it—the Germans had previously wrecked Bizerte in North Africa and Palermo in Sicily. British and American salvage experts had quickly

A trio of young Italian snipers—the youngest one only nine years old—stands ready for action after an outbreak of street fighting in Naples. Before the Allies captured the city, hundreds of Neapolitan youths took up arms and harassed the Germans for four days. Many died in the skirmishes; one school lost 20 boys between the ages of 14 and 20.

put those ports back in order, and now they moved into Naples on the heels of the combat troops. Two regiments of U.S. engineers cleared the streets, repaired the sewers and the aqueduct, and set up an ingenious electric-power system that linked a trolley substation and the generators of three captured Italian submarines. In the port a salvage team under Commodore William A. Sullivan used British heavy-lift crane ships, American tugs, divers, welders, mechanics and bomb-disposal experts to such good effect that in only four days the first cargo-carrying Liberty ship was able to enter the harbor and unload. To discourage looters and souvenir hunters the salvagers erected signs: DANGER: POISON GAS! And to give the signs authority they set off stink bombs on every wreck.

Within two weeks the Allies were unloading 3,500 tons of cargo a day in the port, and within a month 7,000 a day (the prewar average had been 8,000). The smaller satellite ports of Salerno, Torre Annunziata, Castellammare di Stabia and Pozzuoli were also quickly opened to traffic, while still more cargo was discharged over the Salerno beaches. So many tons of supplies were pouring in that, at least from a military point of view, the great German demolition effort had turned out to be only a passing nuisance.

Apart from the booby traps, the mines and the delayed-action bombs, Naples posed a threat of quite a different sort. When Allied troops finally got into the city after hard fighting, they celebrated their accomplishment in the way of all soldiers in all wars. They quickly found themselves beset by that age-old enemy of invading armies: gonorrhea. Allied authorities were concerned: a soldier hospitalized with gonorrhea was removed from combat just as effectively as if he had been struck by gunfire.

The Allied medical corps were amply supplied with condoms. (They were used not only for their intended purpose but for keeping rain and dirt out of rifle barrels. One American colonel, whose troops were operating in a wild, mule-train-supplied area where the presence of Italian women was unlikely, put in a requisition for 1,728 condoms and promptly got them: military necessity.) But in spite of the ready availability of these items, soldiers often failed to use them in the customary manner.

In 1943, sulfanilamide had recently come into widespread use in both the Allied and German armies. A potent anti-infectant, it was commonly dusted directly from a packet onto open wounds and was, as a rule, the first medication a casualty received. Sulfanilamide was also used in pill form for the cure of numerous diseases, including gonorrhea. But unfortunately the soldiers had contracted a virulent strain of the disease that did not easily yield to sulfanilamide. Prophylactic stations were set up around the city—and finally the brothels in Naples were put off limits to the troops.

As the Fifth Army swept through and past Naples, General Montgomery's Eighth Army on the east coast captured the large airfield complex at Foggia and pressed on another 40 miles to the Biferno River. The Allies were now established in Italy beyond possibility of being thrown out, and from Foggia their heavy bombers could attack southern Germany, Austria and the Balkans—particularly the vital oil fields and refineries at Ploeşti in Rumania.

The prospects now seemed bright for the Allies. Four months before the landing at Salerno, the Combined Chiefs of Staff, the principal British and American military advisers of President Roosevelt and Prime Minister Churchill, had given the invading forces two tasks: to drive Italy out of the War and to involve and tie down as many German troops as possible so that they would be unavailable to counter the projected Allied attack in Normandy. Both tasks had been accomplished. Germany had been forced to deploy substantial forces in Italy to confront the British and Americans. German divisions were being tied down in Yugoslavia, Albania and Greece to meet the constant threat of Allied amphibious attacks from the Italian heel, and to police local guerrilla forces, which were much encouraged by Allied success in Italy. Moreover, the Germans had withdrawn from Corsica and Sardinia following the Allied landing at Salerno, and now they would need more troops in southern France to counter any assault from these islands.

Encouraged, Eisenhower decided on September 26 to raise the stakes of the Italian campaign by going for the glittering prize of Rome.

Throughout the fighting in Italy, the terrain proved to be an enemy every bit as formidable as the Germans. The Italian boot is about 750 miles long, but in places it varies from 120 miles to only 85 miles wide. A dorsal range of mountains, the Apennines, runs down its center, forming a barrier from

2,500 to 6,000 feet in height that is tipped with snow as early as October. From this central spine a series of ridges runs down like the bones of a fish toward the coast on either side. Between the ridges there are deep valleys and rivers. The only flat land, south of the broad plain of the Po River, lies in narrow coastal strips perhaps 25 miles wide on the west and only 10 on the east. There is little room to deploy masses of tanks. It is infantry country. Two armies fighting their way north, such as the British Eighth on the coast and the U.S. Fifth on the other, would be separated from each other by the Apennines, and each would have to slog from ridge to ridge, river to river. There are few major roads. The weather can be abominable: rain, fog and freezing sleet in muddy winter and blinding heat in dusty summer.

The Germans, to be sure, were well aware of the advantages held by a defender on the ground in Italy. But they feared the Allied capacity to make amphibious end runs. As soon as they settled into a good defensive line, the Germans believed, the Allied would hook around them by sea and

attack in their rear. For this reason the Germans planned to retreat to the Pisa-Rimini Line or even to the Alps, where they could not be outflanked. However, the events of September 1943 brought about a change of mind.

Kesselring and Vietinghoff's defense at Salerno had been exemplary, suggesting that it might not be quite so easy to outflank able generals. The evacuation of Corsica and Sardinia had brought nearly 40,000 more German troops to the Italian mainland. Moreover, after his arrest by Italian authorities, Mussolini had been rescued by the Germans *(pages 190-203)*, and Hitler wanted to restore him to power. Should not such a government embrace as much territory as possible, including particularly the capital of Italy?

There were also psychological factors favoring a German stand in southern Italy. On the Soviet front Germany's armies were falling back from Orel and Kharkov toward the Dnieper River, the last good defensive position in Russia. In the Mediterranean the Germans had been in steady retreat for nearly a year since the Battle of El Alamein; they—and

Germany in general—were in need of a morale-building stand. Most important of all was the mood of Hitler himself. He had become obsessed with real estate. He was no longer willing to yield an inch anywhere. Suddenly the optimistic counsels of Kesselring, who had always maintained that he could stop the Allies south of Rome, seemed sound and attractive to the Führer. On the day after the Salerno landings, Kesselring had drawn several possible defense lines on a map, indicating where he thought he could fight strong delaying actions while the main force of Germans withdrew as planned to the north. Might he be able to hold one of these lines, not for a few weeks, but for months?

On October 4, Hitler instructed Kesselring to make a stand on a line drawn across Italy between Naples and Rome, and by the 9th of October, Hitler was speaking of "the decisive importance" of that line and had ordered Rommel in the north to send Kesselring two infantry divisions and some artillery. The Germans would hold south of Rome; Kesselring would command all German troops in Italy; and Rommel, who disapproved totally of this development, would be sent to France to prepare defenses against an Allied invasion of Normandy.

The Allied planners had not reckoned on the new German attitude. They had been reading intercepted messages from the German High Command that had led them to believe that the enemy would withdraw steadily to the north, doubtless making temporary stands along the way. A few days after ordering the capture of Rome, Eisenhower had said that he hoped to be north of Rome in only six or eight weeks. He had thought of moving his headquarters from Algiers to Naples; now he thought he could wait until he could "make the jump straight into Rome."

But on October 7, having got word that German divisions were coming down from northern Italy to reinforce Kesselring, Eisenhower informed the Combined Chiefs of Staff that "clearly there will be very hard and bitter fighting before we can hope to reach Rome." Well then, inquired the Combined Chiefs, would it be better to cancel the offensive and keep the Fifth and Eighth armies where they were, north of Naples and Foggia? Eisenhower did not think so. He felt now that it was necessary to keep the pressure on and go north of Rome. Also, if the Rome airfields and those

of Ancona could be taken, the air forces would have bases even closer to Germany. Eisenhower believed too that nothing could help the forthcoming Normandy invasion—code-named *Overlord*—so much as a simultaneous landing in southern France launched from the north of Italy. Even if that goal could not be achieved, the enemy must still be contained, and the best way to accomplish this was to attack him. "If we can keep him on his heels until early spring, then the more divisions he uses in a counteroffensive against us the better it will be for Overlord and then it makes little difference what happens to us."

Psychological factors also influenced the Allies. It was not just that Winston Churchill kept insisting that "nothing less than Rome could satisfy the requirements of this year's campaign," or that "whoever holds Rome holds the title deeds of Italy." Though none of them was explicit about it, thoughts of taking the Eternal City were surely in the minds of all the Allied generals. What soldier since Hannibal has not wished to have listed among his achievements: "Took Rome!" Even sober-thinking General Alexander, commander of all Allied ground forces in Italy, was not immune. "A stabilized front south of Rome cannot be accepted," he said, "for the Capital has a significance far greater than its strategic location. . . . This being so, the seizure of a firm defensive line north of Rome becomes imperative."

Thus, while the Germans were deciding to hold in the south the Allies decided to go north. But the American Joint Chiefs, still not convinced that the Germans could or would make a determined stand south of Pisa-Rimini, were firm in their resolve not to weaken *Overlord,* the Normandy venture, by funneling more resources into the Mediterranean. The seven experienced divisions that were to be withdrawn and sent to England in the month of November would be replaced in part by French, Moroccan and Algerian troops training in Africa, but the Allied divisions in Italy would total only 14 in early December. Against these, the Germans, who already enjoyed the defensive advantage, could throw more than 20. The Allied capacity to make amphibious end runs was to be further weakened by the withdrawal of more ships and landing craft for the Normandy invasion. Moreover, the bad winter weather, fast approaching, would handicap the Allies by drastically reducing the effect of their air supremacy. Drenching rain and ankle-deep mud

Smoke billows up from the main post office in Naples on October 7, 1943, after the explosion of a delayed-action bomb. Planted by the Germans before they evacuated the city a week earlier, the bomb went off on a busy afternoon when the building was crowded with Allied soldiers and Italian civilians. Seventy people were killed or injured in the blast, including one woman who was walking nearly 150 yards away.

would cancel their superiority in motorized equipment.

Altogether, it was not a bright prospect. The U.S. Army's official history of World War II would put it thus: "Whether the Allied forces, against increased German opposition, had enough troops, equipment and supplies to drive north in Italy fast enough to make the campaign worthwhile was a moot question, but they were going to try."

What this meant in immediate terms was the crossing of the Volturno River. In early October, the Fifth Army confronted that task, the first of many bitterly contested river crossings in Italy. The Americans of the VI Corps, on the right of the Fifth Army forces, faced many problems on both sides of the river that were already drearily familiar: steep hills, and narrow, winding roads punctuated by easily demolished bridges and culverts. In the British X Corps sector, on the left, the terrain was relatively flat. However, on the south side of the river it was not only flat but open, offering very little cover from German fire or concealment from observation.

Both the British and Americans, of course, had to cope with the Volturno itself—in flood after weeks of rain. In the X Corps stretch, the river was 250 to 300 feet wide, and the waters rampaged from one to five feet above their normal six-foot depth. Farther upstream in the American area, the river was more negotiable; there were even fordable stretches where the river depth was as little as three feet, and it varied in width from 150 to 220 feet. Moreover, in the American sector the Germans had problems of their own. The Volturno was deeply cut in a few places, creating a kind of trench that served as a protective wall against German fire for U.S. troops crossing the river. In other places, the Allied-held south bank was higher than the north bank, affording good observation of the German defenders. But Vietinghoff knew that his defensive positions were solid. He also knew that he had only to hold on to the river line until October 15; after that date, he had permission from Kesselring to fall back to an even stronger defense line.

The Fifth Army's assault plan called for the action to begin on the far right, in the sector assigned to the American 45th Division, which had orders to advance northwestward down the valley of the Calore River—a tributary of the Volturno. The role of the division in making this maneuver was to protect the flank of the main VI Corps

crossing of the Volturno, which was to be mounted by the 3rd and 34th divisions to the west. The 45th Division began moving down the Calore valley on the 9th of October, pushing along a narrow corridor that cut through the mountains but that was obstructed by rugged hills and deep ravines. Through the terrain wound the predictably miserable roads.

Major General John P. Lucas, the VI Corps commander, felt that the first day's progress by the division along the

Military vehicles cross a pier built on top of sunken ships by U.S. Army Engineers in the wreckage-strewn harbor of Naples. After the Germans demolished the port, 30 major hulks could be seen poking out of the water while more than 100 others lay submerged. Using the sunken vessels as bases for their improvised piers, the engineers made it possible for landing craft to dock in the harbor only three days after the Germans left.

Calore was too slow, and he called for more speed. The division commander, Major General Troy H. Middleton, pointed out that his men had been in continuous action for a month—they were exhausted. Lucas doubted that they were that tired, but he told Middleton that the outfit could figure on a rest after the Volturno crossing had been accomplished. Thus encouraged, the men of the 45th Division made much better progress in the next few days.

The 3rd and 34th divisions attacked together on the night of October 12-13, crossing the Volturno along the stretch to the west of its confluence with the Calore. Assaulting the river line on the right, the 34th Division had a relatively easy crossing, at least at first—largely because the 3rd Panzer Grenadier Division, defending the north bank, was only partly in place; the troops that were there had only just arrived. But the 34th Division's crossing operation almost died for lack of supplies, because the Germans had all the good bridge sites—including those where existing bridges

had been blown—under observation by artillery spotters.

Trying to construct bridges, engineers of the 34th Division had a grim time of it. At one site, having inflated their rubber bridging pontoons in advance so as to speed things up, an engineer column drove up to the river in trucks. German shells promptly knocked out three of the vehicles and punctured the inflated pontoons, many beyond repair. The engineers unloaded 12 trucks and salvaged three of the floats. Within seconds, a single artillery round destroyed all three pontoons, caused heavy casualties and brought the whole enterprise to a halt.

Later in the day, the engineers managed to cart their remaining equipment away from the river and out of German eyeshot. They patched up the salvageable pontoons, set out smoke pots to screen the site and tried again. But the artillery fire was simply too heavy and too well aimed. Finally, a reconnaissance party found another bridge site—one that was protected from fire by a high riverbank. However, the approach roads were even worse than usual, and the river was 70 feet wider than at the first site.

With equipment borrowed to replace their losses, the engineers began work at 3 a.m., and by 10:30 a.m. they had finished a bridge. Then, once the approach roads had been fixed up, and as soon as the mines that the Germans had strewn on the far bank had been cleared, trucks loaded with food and ammunition could start rolling across the river. By October 14 the bridgehead was four miles deep, and the 34th Division was planning its pursuit of the enemy.

On the left flank, General Truscott determined that sur-

prise was a crucial ingredient for the success of the 3rd Division's attack on the river. And once the assault got started, he was insistent that it keep moving. "We must have the men imbued with the idea that they have to get to their objective and they won't stop," he said.

To conceal preparations for the attack from the Germans, the artillery fired occasional rounds throughout the evening of October 12, and the usual patrols went down the river-bank. In the rear, the assault battalions fussed with special equipment for the crossing: rope lines to be used as guides for wading men and for assault boats; kapok life preservers—of which 1,000 had been found in a nearby Italian warehouse; rubber life rafts borrowed from the Navy and rafts improvised from logs.

The job of selecting and marking the crossing sites was carried out by a few very brave engineers who plunged into icy waist-deep water in the pitch dark, and waded through 200 feet of flood-swollen stream in the knowledge that they might plunge into a hole in the bed and sink over their heads at any moment or die in the fusillade of rifle and machine-gun fire that sprayed the water at most crossing sites. These were men, according to one intelligence summary, "who had to lie helpless and shivering on a muddy bank and watch a comrade be shot as he struggled with the current," and who were still capable of wading out into the river themselves. On the opposite, precipitous bank, which was up to 15 feet high and slick with mud, they clambered out and fixed guide ropes for the assault battalions.

At 1 a.m., the entire weight of division and reinforced

corps artillery opened fire on the north bank and the hills behind it. Later, shells that contained smoke for screening the crossing sites were fired. Steered to the riverbank by the surviving engineers, the men assigned to the main attack had their own problems: Guide ropes that had been tied to trees on the banks collapsed when the trees, their underpinnings weakened by days of rain, tore loose and fell into the water; the improvised rafts broke up. In places where the river was deeply cut, it was relatively safe on the water. But as dawn approached, the Germans adjusted their fire, which became more accurate and heavy; the last assault boat to leave the south bank at one site took a direct hit from an artillery shell.

Throughout the morning of October 13, infantrymen of the 3rd Division got across in sufficient strength to take important high ground north of the river, get rid of some of the machine-gun nests and hold on. However, they felt the lack of support from tanks and tank destroyers, which had been waterproofed to make the crossing, but could not negotiate the steep banks and get down into the river. Bulldozers were sent forward to break down the banks so that the armored vehicles could enter the water, but German artillery drove them back. Then an intercepted radio message gave Truscott a scare; the Germans, it seemed, were about to counterattack. Truscott ordered the tanks and tank destroyers across no matter what. Since no tank-dozers were available, engineers on foot, with picks and shovels, had to cut down the banks under fire.

By early afternoon on October 13, the armored combat vehicles were on the north side of the river; by late afternoon, the 3rd Division bridgehead was too deep for the Germans to pinch off, and divisional bridges were carrying supplies and heavy equipment forward. Artillery and tank destroyers broke up the German counterattack before it could do any damage.

The British, in the westernmost sector of the Volturno, had drawn the hardest job of all. The three divisions of the X Corps—the 46th near the coast, the 7th Armored in the center and the 56th on the right, next to the American 3rd Division—had very little bridging equipment. The river was so swollen with floodwater that fording was unthinkable. The Germans had all possible bridge sites not only under

observation, but within range of mortars and even small arms as well as artillery. Incessant rain had created virtually impassable quagmires of mud on nearly all approaches to the river except the main roads leading to Capua, Grazzanise and Cancello.

As it turned out, the best—at any rate, the least awful—place for the British to attack was on the left near Cancello and the coast. There the German troops seemed less numerous, and the Navy could help from offshore. The X Corps commander, General McCreery, made his main crossing with the 46th Division, supported by tanks that he arranged to have ferried around the mouth of the river in landing craft. Meanwhile, farther inland, the other two divisions fired their weapons in a feint to draw the Germans away from the main attack. Elements of the 56th Division then attempted to cross the river near Capua and were stopped cold. At Grazzanise, the 7th Armored made three attempts, and succeeded on the third bloody try in getting a handful of men dug in on the north bank.

The main attack also ran into heavy going. One battalion of the 46th Division paddled over the river in assault boats, landed on a dangerously exposed stretch of riverbank and was overrun after a daylong fight. Farther downstream, two more battalions crossed in the same way, hung on and waited for the tanks to arrive by sea. When the armor landed, several tanks promptly bogged down in soft sand; others were held up by mines—nonmetallic charges that were hard to detect and were only cleared after a whole day's slow, dangerous work. On October 14, the British were able to reinforce the troops in this tenuous bridgehead, and ferry across artillery and other heavy gear under cover of naval gunfire, a big factor in the qualified success of this enterprise.

The X Corps took heavy losses: 200 captured, 400 killed and wounded. Figuring that the British would be sluggish in exploiting their bridgehead on account of their casualties, the Germans held firm in the X Corps area, but began a gradual withdrawal in the American sector on October 14. The Germans speeded up their pullback on Kesselring's schedule in succeeding days, and by October 19 the Allies had complete control of the Volturno River line. Thereafter, as the Fifth Army advanced, the German Tenth Army begrudged it every turn in the muddy, tortuous road to Rome.

A Bailey bridge, assembled on shore, is shoved across the Volturno River. By using pin joints to link steel beams, engineers could build an 80-foot, 21-ton-capacity bridge in two and a half hours. With additional sections, a bridge could be made to span gorges as wide as 240 feet. Praising this British invention, General Alexander once said, "Whatever the valor of the fighting troops, without the 'Bailey' to bridge the rivers and ravines of Italy, the campaign would have been abortive from the outset."

FRIENDS AMONG THE FOE

As villagers look on sympathetically, a U.S. Army medical corpsman administers a bottle of blood plasma to a soldier who was wounded in action on Sicily.

GESTURES OF KINDNESS IN A WAR-TORN COUNTRY

A thirsty American infantryman takes time out to gulp from a pitcher offered by a policeman in the rubble-strewn streets of a Sicilian village.

"Those people were our enemies," war correspondent Ernie Pyle wrote of the Italians. "They declared war on us. We went clear over there and fought them and when we had won they looked upon us as their friends." Indeed, many Italians seemed to regard the Allies as liberators rather than as conquerors, and received them accordingly: with fluttering American flags and gifts of wine and fresh fruit.

There were reasons for this warm reception. By the time of the Allied invasion, the War, which had never been popular with the majority of Italians, had become for them intolerable. Allied bombs had pulverized their towns and their resolve. Food shortages, mounting civilian casualties and war profiteering had sapped their morale. The German occupiers of Italy had proved ruthless, shipping precious Italian wheat and thousands of Italian laborers to their own beleaguered country. "Under these conditions," a woman wrote in a letter, "deprived as we are of everything and above all, of our liberty, all we can do is to stay in bed, and, if the Allies do not come in time—wait for death."

The armistice signed in September 1943 meant that the Allies were no longer at war with Italy—a welcome event for the many Italians who felt a special kinship with the United States, a favored destination for Italian immigrants before the War. "In the very remotest and most ancient town, we found that half the people had relatives in America," wrote Pyle, who traveled with the advancing Allies, "and there was always somebody popping up from behind every bush or around every corner who had lived for twelve years in Buffalo or thirty years in Chicago."

And so, as the Allied troops pushed northward, the Italians shared with them their homes, their songs and their knowledge of German defenses. The GIs reciprocated with gifts of rations and clothing, and gestures of special tenderness for the country's most pitiful victims, the children. They "adopted" hundreds of the orphaned and homeless, clothing them in cut-down Army uniforms, feeding them better than most had been fed in years and finding safe havens for them when it came time to go into action again.

A GI spoon-feeds an Italian waif found alone in the hills after the baby's two sisters were killed in the explosion of a mine planted by the Germans.

A military policeman with the U.S. Fifth Army (above) points out the safest route to an Italian couple trying to pedal their way out of the combat zone near the port of Anzio. Strapped to their bikes are their meager possessions.

Her bare feet cut and bleeding, an old woman (below) who has fled from combat through a rocky mountain pass gets a pair of new socks from an American private who had received them in the mail as a Christmas present.

Having complied with German orders to abandon

their homes and head for the Allied lines, refugees caught in the path of the fighting listen to instructions from two soldiers with the U.S. 88th Infantry Division.

A homeless orphan until "adopted" by GIs, this Italian youngster proudly wears his new outfit of modified Army issue as he directs traffic through the town of San Vittore in his new job—honorary MP.

While his playmates giggle at his discomfort, an Italian street urchin named Charleto stands amid artillery ammunition in Anzio and stoically allows an American soldier to bandage his cut finger.

A French-Canadian soldier attached to the U.S.

Fifth Army accepts a rose from a solemn child in exchange for a piece of candy. Other floral gifts sprout from the camouflage netting on his helmet.

During the U.S. Fifth Army advance toward Rome, two Italian women who managed to escape from the German-occupied city and reach the Allied lines collaborate with U.S. soldiers trying to pinpoint enemy defensive positions on a map spread out on the hood of the soldiers' jeep.

An Italian youth strains under the weight of an artillery shell as he lends a helping hand in stacking ammunition at a gun battery being set up by American soldiers beside the youngster's farmhouse north of Anzio.

High in the mountains above the valley Cassino, the wife of an Italian shepherd looks on dispassionately as an Allied soldier meticulously removes a German antipersonnel mine from a stone wall in her tiny village. Having watched the withdrawing Germans lay and conceal the mines, the old woman was able to point out their locations to the Allied troops.

Two Italian youngsters lighten the load of an American soldier by carrying his rifle and pack for him as they trudge up a steep hill near Salerno.

Near the ancient ruins of Paestum, south of Salerno, Italian women launder grimy fatigues for GIs.

Two footsore American soldiers rest and share a cup of cocoa at the hearth of their elderly hostess.

Fifth Army soldiers round up a pair of beef cattle they bought for their outfit's chow from an Italian farmer, who is helping push one reluctant animal from behind.

Obviously more interested in the woman than in the array of trinkets she is trying to sell, three American soldiers on leave cluster around an attractive street vendor. Above her table laden with ashtrays is a poster advertising a decidedly nonmartial pursuit—a competition for typists.

Backed up by an amused Italian squeezing an accordion, an enthusiastic American soldier entertains his comrades with a concert beside a truck.

"I hope I never see a mountain again as long as I live," General Lucas, commander of the U.S. VI Corps, confided to his diary as the Allies slugged and slogged their way northwestward after crossing the Volturno River. His sentiment was shared, no doubt, by many Fifth Army foot soldiers. And the farther they pushed, the more pronounced their dislike of the topography would become, for the Germans, who were determined now to stop the Allied advance south of Rome, had used the rugged terrain to create perhaps the most forbidding series of defensive positions that had yet confronted an attacking army in World War II. The mountains bristled with murderous, mutually supporting strong points, each of which the Allies would have to overcome or neutralize at bloody expense if the advance was to continue.

The German defenses beyond the Volturno, generally referred to by the Allies as the Winter Line, actually consisted of three different lines (map, page 105)—each a progressively tougher barrier than the one before it—prepared under the watchful eye of Field Marshal Kesselring himself. "With my constant inspections of the progress made in fortifying our rear positions," Kesselring wrote later, "I must have been a thorough nuisance to the senior engineer officer." The first defensive position, called the Barbara Line, was a series of strong points designed not to stop the Fifth Army but to delay its advance while the defenses beyond it were completed. The line stretched only part of the way across the Italian peninsula, from Monte Massico, just seven miles north of the Volturno River, in the west to the Matese Mountains of Italy's spine, running through the villages of Teano and Presenzano.

Approximately 10 miles behind the Barbara Line was a much stronger position, the Bernhard Line, running from the mouth of the Garigliano River in the west to the Matese Mountains in the interior. In a less defined form, this string of defenses extended eastward to the Adriatic along the Sangro River in front of the British Eighth Army. In the west, the Bernhard Line was developed in depth and bulwarked by some formidably fortified mountains whose names—Monte la Difensa, Monte Camino, Monte Lungo, Monte Sammucro—were to become familiar evocators of anguish to the Allies.

And finally, there was the most intensely fortified Ger-

4

Mountains bristling with deadly obstacles
"Bouncing Bettys" and vicious "Schu" mines
General Alexander's tribute to the Germans
The gauntlet of the Mignano gap
A polyglot army
Searching for an easier route to Rome
Upstairs-downstairs fighting in Ortona
A hair-raising climb to capture Monte la Difensa
Churchill's pneumonia gives Anzio a boost
A costly bridgehead over the Garigliano
Disaster on the Rapido

THE DEFIANT MOUNTAINS

man position, the position that Kesselring was determined not to yield: the Gustav Line. In the west, along the Garigliano River, the Bernhard and Gustav lines were one and the same. But farther inland the Gustav Line snaked some 12 miles to the rear, where it was anchored on a superb natural fortress whose name few Allied soldiers had ever heard: Monte Cassino. The Gustav Line then continued all the way across the boot of Italy, reaching the Adriatic coast some 20 miles to the northwest of the Sangro River. The Gustav was the strongest line of all—so strong, Kesselring believed, "that the British and Americans would break their teeth on it."

The German task in planning and constructing these defenses was made easier by the fact that there were so few well-defined corridors through which a motorized army could hope to advance. There were only two main roads from Naples to Rome, and it was along these—and on precipitous mountain tracks and trails close by—that the Fifth Army was obliged to attack. One of the roads was the ancient Appian Way, known in modern times by the less romantic designation of Highway 7. It approached Rome by way of the coast and from a military viewpoint was not the best way of getting there. Highway 7 was pinched between the Aurunci Mountains and the sea and, farther north, it ran through the Pontine Marshes, drained by Mussolini in the early 1930s and now open meadows. At both points the Germans could make it well-nigh impassable.

The second road, Highway 6, threaded its way north through the mountains about 35 miles inland from the coast. Built by the Romans 2,500 years earlier, Highway 6—the old Via Casilina—had been trodden by many marching soldiers, among them Roman legions striding south to confront Hannibal in the Third Century B.C., and the French and Spanish armies disputing control of Italy in the 16th Century. The latter clash was particularly fascinating to one scholarly German corps commander, Lieut. General Fridolin von Senger und Etterlin, because it had been played out near Cassino, in what was now his sector of the German defenses. In the winter of 1943-1944, Senger believed, it would be the turn of the Allies to attempt to force a passage on that road.

The virtue of Highway 6 to the Allies was that once the road passed Cassino, it led into the wide valley of the Liri River, the gateway to Rome. If the Allies could break into the valley, they could deploy their tanks and dash 80 miles northwest to the city. But to reach the Liri valley they first would have to overcome the Barbara Line, run the gauntlet of the Mignano gap, a narrow corridor dominated by mountains that were incorporated into the Winter Line, and then break through the main Winter Line fortifications at Cassino and along the Rapido River, a natural barrier that ran across the entrance to the Liri valley. Knowing full well the route that the Allies would take, the Germans concentrated their strongest defenses to block it.

The German field fortifications were constructed under the supervision of a brilliant engineer officer, Major General Hans Bessel. He was assisted by units of Organization Todt, a civilian group of German engineers named for its founder, Dr. Fritz Todt, a prewar minister of armaments. Much of the labor was performed by Italian civilians, who were paid good wages, plus bonuses of scarce food and tobacco. They did their work well.

Gun positions and command posts were blasted into solid rock in the mountains, their approaches guarded by barbed wire, booby traps and mines. Machine-gun emplacements, sited to provide interlocking fields of fire, were shielded on the top and the sides by armor plate. These emplacements were supplemented by portable pillboxes that encased machine guns and their crews in armor five inches thick and could be hauled from place to place by tractors. Mortars were dug in behind rock ridges or in deep gullies from which they could safely lob their projectiles onto pretargeted trails along which the enemy would have to advance. The mountainous terrain severely limited the mobility of tanks, so the Germans ingeniously sank some of theirs into the ground up to the turrets to take advantage of tank firepower while presenting smaller targets to the enemy. They concealed others inside houses in mountain villages, their guns positioned to cover the few possible routes of approach.

The minefields that the Germans prepared were not only extensive—some 75,000 mines were strewn before the Bernhard Line—but were filled with devices of a notably nasty sort. The antipersonnel S-mine, called "Bouncing Betty" by the Allies, would leap several feet into the air after it was stepped on. It would then explode a few feet above the ground, scattering metal fragments in every direction. Perhaps even worse than the Bouncing Betty was the vicious little *Schu* mine; its case was made almost entirely of wood and could not be located by the mine detectors used by the Allies, which responded only to metal. The *Schu* seldom killed a man outright; it blew off one of his feet if it was stepped on, or a hand if he set it off while crawling.

Most of the 11 divisions that made up the German Tenth Army assigned to these defensive positions were first-rate fighting units, although a couple were considered less than totally reliable. The 94th Infantry had almost no experience in combat before it came to the front, and its arrival sparked a wry exchange of messages. Vietinghoff, the Tenth Army commander, protested that "it is completely illogical to send us this division." To this Kesselring's chief of staff, Major General Siegfried Westphal, replied, "It is not illogical. Hitler has ordered it."

The 3rd Panzer Grenadier Division, which was also part of the Tenth Army, had a poor reputation as well. A British general noted that it was "composed of East Europeans with only a tenuous German ancestry who were not fired with the same determination that the native German divisions possessed." But among the other divisions deployed here by the Germans were some of the finest to bear arms in the War, notably the 15th Panzer Grenadier, the Hermann Göring and the 1st Parachute.

General Alexander, the Allied ground commander, visited an English hospital during the fighting and asked if there were any German wounded. Told that there were about 20 seriously wounded German soldiers from the 1st Parachute Division who were being looked after in a separate ward, he asked to see them. "When I appeared at the door of their ward," he later wrote, "the German *Feldwebel* (technical sergeant), who was very seriously wounded, called his men to attention: '*Achtung, Herr General!*'—and the wounded men all lay to attention in their beds with their arms outstretched stiffly over the sheets. I had to say: '*Machen Sie weiter*' (Carry on) or they would have kept their position until further orders.

"I mention this incident to illustrate the type of soldiers

we were fighting. Whatever we may feel about the Germans, we must admit that German soldiers were extremely tough and brave."

The armies that were trying to batter through the German defenses also had some tough troops—from many countries. As the winter of 1943-1944 settled in, the make-up of the Allied forces in Italy was becoming more and more multinational. Despite the widespread impression in the U.S., the Italian campaign was never primarily an American effort. The U.S. supplied, on the average, fewer than one third of the combat troops. The Allied divisions facing the German positions included Canadians, Indians and New Zealanders. Soon they would be joined by Poles, South Africans, Italians, and Free French divisions consisting mainly of Algerians and Moroccans. Later a Brazilian division would join the Allies in Italy.

The mix of nationalities caused some problems. In addition to the communications difficulties that were to be expected in such a polyglot force, differences in dietary customs put stress on the Allied supply system: Moslems from North Africa would not eat pork and required a great deal of mutton; Brazilians did not want American food; the French had to have their wine and brandy rations.

The soldiers of each nation also had their own characteristics and preferences in combat. The Gurkhas and Rajputs from India were awesomely brave, full of pride in their profession and willing to accept the worst hardships and risks simply because they were the Gurkhas and the Rajputs, and had a long tradition of valor to uphold. Among the Moroccans and Algerians were the fierce Goumiers, mountain troops who were not fond of complicated weapons but who relished fighting at night with knives. A French officer in Italy once asked a Goumier who was going out on a patrol in the dark to fetch back a German wrist watch if he chanced to run across one. The Goumier returned with a bloody, cloth-wrapped package containing a man's severed forearm, a watch still attached to it, and politely dropped the package at the flap of the officer's tent.

Men of the 2nd New Zealand Division were more sophisticated but equally rugged. Stubbornly independent, bold in action, they had no use for spit and polish. A British general who visited their headquarters complained to their commander, Lieut. General Sir Bernard Freyberg, "Your people don't salute very much do they?"

"You should try waving to them," replied the New Zealander. "They always wave back."

But even the combat-hardened veterans had a difficult time cracking the German defenses in the Barbara Line. Kesselring had ordered his troops there to hold the Allies away from the heart of the Winter Line until at least November 1, when stronger defenses would be completed, and his men did just that. They fought hard and then withdrew, for the most part adroitly, inflicting considerable damage on the Allies by their skillful rear-guard actions. The Fifth Army took more than two weeks to push through the Barbara Line and advance 15 to 20 miles from the Volturno along a 40-mile front. And then, at the beginning of November, the bruised and tired Allies found that the fight had barely begun; they faced an enemy who was still largely intact and well dug in along the main positions of the Winter Line.

The Fifth Army pressed on, almost without pause. The Germans had been right to expect that the Allies would try to pierce the Winter Line along the Highway 6 corridor. In early November, to the roar of their massed guns, the British and Americans made their first attempt to force their way through the Mignano gap.

The gap was not merely a notch in the hills but a winding six-mile passage between steep mountains that would have to be taken one after another. Several of them were more than 3,000 feet high, with rocky slopes that slanted up at angles of 30°, 45° or even 70°. On the upper reaches there was very little cover. There was no earth in which to dig foxholes, only rock. Attacking soldiers had to seek shelter in crevices or behind ledges or make pathetic little bulwarks of loose stones. Bursting mortar and artillery shells sent murderous fragments of rock flying in all directions. All the natural approaches to the mountaintops were booby-trapped and mined, so the attackers were obliged to seek routes that goats could scarcely manage—some Americans, indeed, drove little flocks of Italian sheep and goats in front of them to set off the mines.

Rations, water and ammunition were carried part of the way up the mountains by pack mules, and when the mules would not or could not travel any farther, the loads were taken over by soldiers who lugged them on packboards or

The blinding flash of a 155mm "Long Tom" artillery piece lights up the night as Allied forces pound the German defenses in the Mignano gap, south of the town of Cassino. Artillery was used so extensively by the U.S. Fifth Army that the Germans claimed the Americans never slept. In the course of one 24-hour period, 925 pieces fired a total of 164,999 rounds.

dragged them with ropes. Assault troops, who needed both hands for climbing, could carry so few supplies that at times half their number served merely as burden bearers for comrades clinging to the slopes above. At night the temperature fell below freezing; rain, sleet and fog shrouded the mountains. Sometimes when the fog momentarily lifted, Allied and German patrols found themselves within just a few yards of each other and fell into savage hand-to-hand combat. More than once, their ammunition gone, they threw rocks at each other.

The soldiers trying to penetrate the German defenses had at least one advantage over their entrenched enemy: a substantial superiority in artillery firepower. The Allied guns were employed lavishly—so lavishly that at times artillery ammunition had to be rationed as shortages developed. The VI Corps commander, General Lucas, was keenly aware of the brutal conditions his men were fighting under and felt that any expenditure in shells was more than justified. "I don't see how our men stand what they do," he wrote in his diary. "They are the finest soldiers in the world. My constant prayer to almighty God is that I may have the wisdom to bring them through this ordeal with the maximum success and the minimum loss of life. Hence my use of artillery ammunition. If the lives of American boys are of value, the ravenous appetite of the guns of the VI Corps is not in vain in spite of the tremendous cost in money and vital transport." Lucas' guns were indeed ravenous. In a single two-week period in November at the Winter Line the artillery of the U.S. 36th Division alone fired 95,000 shells at the Germans.

American war correspondent Ernie Pyle, whose reports from Italy were focused not on generals but on GIs in combat, spent some time with a battery of 155mm howitzers and described the artillerymen's role in the fighting. The guns were about 80 yards apart in a rough square. Each was planted in a three-foot-deep pit, ankle-deep in mud, and was protected by a shoulder-high breastwork of sandbags. On one side of each pit was a double row of big rust-colored shells, constantly replenished by an ammunition truck. On the opposite side were the powder charges in black cases three feet long, clipped together in clusters of three. Inside each case were three white cloth sacks,

the size of two-pound sugar bags. One to three sacks were used for one charge, depending upon the range of the target. After a shell had been manhandled into the breech of a gun, the sacks were shoved in behind it. Then a gunner yanked the firing lanyard and—*WHOOM!*—the projectile was on its way.

The gunners never saw what they were shooting at and rarely had even a notion of what the target was. An officer in the battery executive post gave firing directions to the chief of each gun crew by telephone, and he in turn got his orders from a regimental command post half a mile to the rear. Ultimately all the directions came from observers miles ahead in the mountains, who spotted the explosions made by the shells and called for adjustments in aim to the right, left, forward or rear.

Several of the men in Pyle's crew came from South Carolina; they called their gun "howzer" instead of "howitzer" and said "far" instead of "fire." They enjoyed a few creature comforts that were not available to frontline infantrymen. Occasionally, portable showers were set up in the woods nearby, and the gunners could go, a few at a time, in a truck to bathe, but most of the crew had not had a shower in more than two months. "Taking baths is just a habit," said one gunner. "If our mothers hadn't started giving us baths when we were babies we would never have known the difference."

Pyle was impressed with the cost of big guns and shells. "We were sitting around conjecturing how much it costs to kill one German with our artillery. When you count the great price of the big modern guns, training the men, all the shipping to get everything over, and the big shells at $50 each, it must cost, we figured, $25,000 for every German we killed with our shelling."

"Why wouldn't it be better," one fellow said, "just to offer the Germans $25,000 apiece to surrender, and save all the in-between process and the killing? I bet they'd accept it, too." Pyle did not think so.

"During one of my last nights with the battery we were routed out of our blankets an hour before dawn to put down a barrage preceding an infantry attack. Every battery for miles around was firing. Batteries were dug in close together and we got the blasts and concussions from other guns as well as our own. Every gun threw up a fiendish

When Allied troops reached the Cassino front north of Naples in January 1944, they attempted initially to skirt the hub of the powerful German defenses at Monte Cassino and break into the Liri River valley for a quick linkup with British and American forces landing at Anzio. Troops of the British X Corps succeeded in establishing a small bridgehead across the lower Garigliano River. But the British 46th Division was thrown back when it attempted to cross the river farther upstream. On the U.S. II Corps front two regiments of the 36th Division were repulsed in their bloody struggle to get across the Rapido River at Sant'Angelo. The fighting at Cassino and Anzio then developed into a long and costly stalemate.

flame when it went off, and the black night was pierced with the flashes of hundreds of big guns.

"Standing there in the midst of it all, I thought it was the most violent and terrifying thing I'd ever been through. Just being on the sending end was staggering. I don't know how human sanity could survive on the receiving end."

At the receiving end the Germans kept their sanity without difficulty because their well-prepared positions provided so much protection. In spite of the intensity of Allied artillery fire, the Fifth Army foot soldiers who tried to advance behind such barrages found the defenders of the Winter Line very much alive and resisting lethally. On the left of the entrance to the Mignano gap the 56th British Infantry Division, which had been in combat almost without letup since Salerno, fought for eight days to take Monte Camino and failed. Nearby the U.S. 3rd Infantry Division struggled for 10 days to drive the Germans off the well-named Monte la Difensa and was repulsed with heavy losses, on slopes so precipitous and slashed by ra-

vines that it took six hours to get a wounded man down off the mountain.

This first attempt to penetrate the Mignano gap was not a total failure. On the right the U.S. 34th and 45th infantry divisions advanced a few miles and took some high ground, including Monte Rotondo, which loomed over the right-hand side of the gap's entrance. But it was not enough to worry Vietinghoff, who noted that "enemy gains constituted no great threat and every step forward into the mountainous terrain merely increased his difficulties." On November 15, General Mark Clark, acknowledging that his Fifth Army troops were on the verge of exhaustion, called a halt to offensive operations. For the next two weeks the army would rest and refit for a renewed attack.

Meanwhile, Allied planners had been applying themselves urgently to the problem of getting to Rome by some means easier than mountain climbing.

The easier means, as General Eisenhower had long been

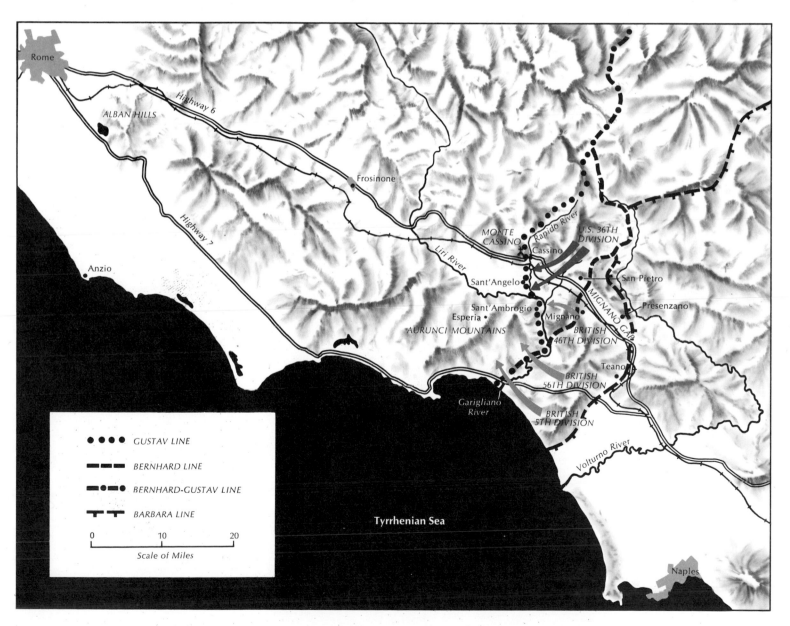

thinking, was to make an amphibious end run around the enemy's lines in order to threaten the Germans from the rear and cause them to abandon their defensive positions south of Rome. But at least one and preferably two divisions would have to land in the enemy's rear to have any effect, and initially that seemed out of the question. There were not enough transports, particularly LSTs. In the global strategy of the Combined Chiefs of Staff, the Mediterranean theater had a low priority, and it was getting lower as the time approached for the Allied invasion of Normandy. Most of Eisenhower's landing craft were scheduled to be withdrawn to England in the early part of December, which would not leave enough time to plan and execute a major attack by sea.

But the idea of a landing was too attractive for the Mediterranean commanders to dismiss. They were well aware of the danger. Any landing would have to be made close enough to the main battlefront so that the seaborne forces could quickly link up with the troops advancing overland. Otherwise the landing force could be penned in its beachhead and perhaps wiped out. Eisenhower and his planners thought the linkup could be managed.

Accordingly, Eisenhower asked the Combined Chiefs for permission to retain 56 British and 12 American LSTs in the Mediterranean until December 15. When he got their approval—later extended to January 15—Eisenhower ordered General Alexander to go ahead and capture Rome. Implicit in the order was a call for a major amphibious landing. Alexander issued instructions for the offensive.

In Alexander's plan the Eighth Army, under the command of General Montgomery, would attack first on the east coast, breaking through the German defenses at the Sangro River and driving northwest through the Winter Line to Pescara. There the Eighth Army would wheel to its left along the Pescara River valley and threaten Rome from the east. This, in view of the swollen rivers in its path, the poor roads and stout German defenses, was a very large order for the Eighth Army to carry out—and that attack was only a diversion. The main effort was to be made by the Fifth Army.

The Fifth Army's job was to break through the Mignano gap, advance a dozen miles to the Rapido River, cross it, reduce the German defenses at Cassino and drive 30 miles up the Liri valley to Frosinone, a town some 50 miles southeast of Rome. When the main body of the Fifth Army reached Frosinone, a two-division amphibious landing was to be made at Anzio, 35 miles south of Rome. The two segments of the army would then be in a position to link up within a few days, and the Germans, afraid of having their supply and escape routes cut, would doubtless retreat north of Rome—if indeed they were not trapped, as Alexander hoped. The assigned task was not merely large, it was stupendous. But somehow, Mark Clark thought, he could get through the whole series of German fortifications in the short time remaining before the landing craft had to be sent to England. "Don't worry," he said, "I'll get through the Winter Line all right and push the Germans out."

The Allied Fifth and Eighth armies would be brought up to their anticipated strength of 14 divisions by early December—and recent shifts of bombers and fighter planes from North Africa to Sardinia and mainland Italy promised increased air support for the ground troops. Even so, all of the top Allied commanders—Eisenhower, Alexander, Clark and Montgomery—were remarkably optimistic in their estimate of what their soldiers could do, especially considering the firm rebuff the Allies had just been dealt at the Mignano gap. But it was necessary to keep pounding at the Germans, to keep them off balance, to deny them time to build more formidable fortifications. If the Germans were allowed to become impregnably entrenched, they could release several divisions from the Italian front and send them to Russia or to Normandy. The basic aim of the Allied Italian campaign now was to prevent this. If the campaign was to achieve such an objective, a gamble had to be made while the Mediterranean commanders still had the resources, however slim.

The Allied offensive began on November 20 on the Adriatic side of the boot, when General Montgomery's Eighth Army began fighting its way across the Sangro River. The Sangro was in flood, overflowing its banks, and the approaches to the river were soft as pudding. At one crossing point sappers—engineers—of the British 78th Division had to build a road through half a mile of ooze to the water's edge, dumping tons of bundled tree branches, railroad ties and steel matting ahead of them. They threw a Bailey bridge across the river and then on the other side poured load after

Soldiers of Canada's Loyal Edmonton Regiment push an antitank gun, used to blast German-held buildings, over a rubble-strewn street in the town of Ortona on the eastern coast of Italy. The house-by-house advance through the labyrinth of German booby traps and snipers was agonizingly slow—in one day, only 200 yards were covered. The Canadians finally captured the small town on the 28th of December, 1943, following seven days of fierce fighting that cost them 650 men and the Germans 455.

load of stone into mud that seemed to have no bottom. But in two days of working under enemy fire they made a road bridge that supported guns and trucks. The British pouring across the river chewed up the German 65th Infantry Division so thoroughly that Kesselring's chief of staff, General Westphal, found that the unit "to all intents and purposes no longer existed."

But then the Sangro, glutted with still more winter rain, rose even higher and washed out all of the British bridges. Montgomery was obliged to pause until the 27th of November, when improved weather enabled him to get the 8th Indian Division and the 2nd New Zealand, recently added to his army, across the river. With support from more than 4,000 Allied aircraft, the attack resumed.

The delay gave the Germans time to bring a division from the Mignano area and another from northern Italy to plug the breach in their defenses. They soon slowed the British advance to a crawl. After a month of hard fighting the

Eighth Army had gained less than 15 miles and was stalled on the coast outside the town of Ortona, where the Germans were making a determined stand. The 1st Canadian Infantry Division pounded its way into Ortona on December 21 and for seven days battled the Germans at close range in the streets.

In Ortona the Canadians became, among the Allied soldiers, the acknowledged masters of house-to-house fighting. When the Germans dynamited buildings to block the streets with mountains of debris, the Canadians used fieldpieces to blast the crests off the rubble so that tanks could climb over it. In solidly built-up blocks, where enemy snipers and machine gunners picked off every man who ventured into the street, the Canadians advanced by "mouseholing." They climbed to an upper floor of the first house in a block and attached a delayed-action explosive charge to the wall that separated it from the adjoining house. Then they retired downstairs, waited for the charge to blow a

hole through the wall and rushed back up to storm through the still-smoking breach. They then repeated the process, blasting their way from the second house to the third, the third to the fourth, and so on until they had mouseholed their way through the entire block.

During the night of December 27 the Germans, in danger of being cut off by a Canadian flanking movement to the west of the town, pulled out of Ortona. But by that time the Canadians and the Eighth Army in general were bone tired. Montgomery called a halt. He had inflicted heavy casualties on the Germans and had siphoned some of their strength away from the west as intended, but he had not made the breakthrough to Pescara and the left wheel toward Rome that General Alexander had hoped for.

The Fifth Army, after waiting 10 days for Montgomery's drive to pull German troops over to the Adriatic and thin the defenses at the Mignano gap, had launched its main attack on December 1. The initial objective was to try once again to take the rugged mountains at the left of the entrance to the gap: Monte Camino and Monte la Difensa. Allied aircraft and artillery did their work: during the first two days of battle 900 bombing runs softened enemy defenses, and in a single hour the big guns laid down 22,000 rounds on Monte la Difensa alone.

Again the British 56th Division stormed Monte Camino,

and this time, after five days of bitter fighting in which the men twice reached the summit and were pushed off by German counterattacks, they took the mountain. Simultaneously, a remarkable unit called the 1st Special Service Force, which had arrived at the front only a few days before and had not yet been in combat, undertook the conquest of Monte la Difensa. The force was binational, composed of specially selected Americans and Canadians in about equal numbers, and its men had been trained in mountain climbing, to fight as ski troops and as paratroops, and to carry out demolitions and long-range sabotage operations. They were a deadly group; the Germans, after encountering them, called them "The Devil's Brigade."

Instead of attacking La Difensa along routes that had been tried earlier, the 1st Special Service Force took an approach that the Germans thought impossible. Silently at night, using ropes, 600 riflemen climbed the last 1,000 feet of the 3,000-foot mountain on a rocky, clifflike pitch that in places was almost perpendicular. Assembling just below the crest of the mountain, the Special Forcemen clung to ledges so narrow that soldiers had to lie on top of one another. They were so close to the Germans, who occupied a saucer-shaped depression on the summit about the size of a football field, that they could smell the cooking odors from the mess area. It was still dark. The officer commanding the lead troops told his men in a whisper to hold their fire until

Officers of the 1st Italian Motorized Group, the first Italian unit to join the Allies in combat, chat with an American officer (far left) near Monte Lungo. In the months following Italy's surrender, the Allies equipped 350,000 Italian soldiers as combat and service troops.

6. a.m. If a German stumbled into their position, they were to kill him silently with knives.

A clattering rockfall gave them away. In a moment brilliant magnesium flares illuminated the mountaintop and the Special Forcemen swarmed over the crest and fell upon the Germans. The wild combat that followed is best described by the random and fragmentary impressions of those who survived it.

"Deyette and I started to move up the side of the hill when he called, 'They're below here!' and then he went down. I found he had a bullet in his forehead and was sucking in his breath with a loud snoring sound. . . . I recognized Bernstein throwing a grenade and then turning away. . . . Sergeant Fisher, my Browning gun squad leader, was completely blind—struck by stone fragments. . . . Poor Casey, who could have stayed behind as a cook but insisted on going to a combat platoon, was killed by a direct hit of a dud mortar that cracked his skull. . . .

"When we first got up to the top and were pinned down I ran a little way and lay down beside a soldier and talked to him for a long time before I found out that he was dead. I wondered why he did not talk back to me. . . . I recall borrowing Captain Border's rifle when I came across him in a kneeling position observing the enemy through binoculars on the opposite ridge. When I returned with his rifle, some 30 minutes later, he was dead with a sniper's bullet in the head."

A Special Force captain and his men flushed some Germans out of a gun emplacement. One of them held a white flag, but when the captain went forward to take him prisoner another German shot the captain in the face. The captain's men opened up on the Germans with all their weapons and wiped them out. In later battles the 1st Special Service Force took no prisoners unless they were specifically ordered to capture a few for interrogation purposes.

Monte la Difensa was rapidly taken, though the Forcemen had to fight for several days to hold it. After a week of combat 511 men out of about 1,800 involved were casualties.

In the meantime, the 142nd Infantry Regiment of the U.S. 36th Division took Monte Maggiore with surprising ease, thanks at least partially to effective artillery support. Having captured Monte Rotondo on the right during early Novem-

ber, the Fifth Army now held both sides of the entrance to the Mignano gap.

But it was only the entrance. Behind every mountain in Italy there is another. Now the Allied soldiers faced Monte Lungo—a prominence right in the middle of the Mignano corridor, between the railway to Rome and Highway 6. To the right of the highway was Monte Sammucro, towering to almost 4,000 feet, with the village of San Pietro on its lower slope.

Allied commanders thought that Monte Lungo would be easy to conquer because they were already in possession of the dominating Monte Maggiore nearby. They also thought that a German withdrawal from the Mignano gap might already be under way and doubted that San Pietro was still occupied by the enemy. The 1st Italian Motorized Group, the first soldiers of liberated Italy to join the Allies in combat, was assigned the task of taking Monte Lungo; an easy victory on their debut in battle would lift the morale of the Italian troops. General Walker's 36th Division, with assistance from Rangers, would simultaneously capture the peaks of Monte Sammucro and sweep across its slopes through San Pietro. What the Allies did not know was that the 29th Panzer Grenadiers were firmly entrenched in these positions and that Hitler had personally ordered that there was to be no withdrawal.

The Italians, who wore Alpine uniforms with long feathers in their hatbands, were a colorful sight as they marched up Monte Lungo on the morning of December 8. Confident that artillery bombardment had already virtually eliminated the enemy, they moved in close formation, two battalions abreast, disappearing from the view of reserves and artillerymen into a low, thick mist that hung over the mountain. Soon the air exploded with the noise of German mortars and machine guns, and before long the Italians began reappearing at the foot of Monte Lungo, seeking refuge in Allied gun pits. By noon it was clear that the attack was a disastrous failure, and the Italians were officially permitted to withdraw.

The 36th Division's attack on Monte Sammucro that same morning fared better. A battalion of the 143rd Regiment seized the summit of the mountain before 6 a.m., surprising the few Germans posted there, and held it despite repeated fierce counterattacks. But the two battalions of the 143rd that were to sweep across the flank of Sammucro and through San Pietro advanced no more than 400 yards, being stymied by a hard German defense position of barbed-wire entanglements and pillboxes with slits from which poured streams of machine-gun bullets. The Germans were so well dug in that they could order their artillery to pour fire almost directly onto their own positions whenever the attacking Americans came close to them.

For more than a week the 36th Division tried to crack the stronghold the Germans had made of the village, fighting all the while to keep possession of the top of the mountain against enemy counterattacks. Casualties skyrocketed. During the fighting one regiment was reduced to 21 per cent of its normal strength and another to about half.

As was generally the case with National Guard divisions, many of the officers and men of the 36th came from the same towns (the 36th was from Texas) and had known one another before the War. This helped *esprit,* but it made casualties all the more difficult to take—at least at first. "At the terminal of the trail, the litters bearing the wounded and the dead would stop," a veteran of the battle later recalled. "The former would be hustled to the aid station, while the blanket-covered dead would lie stiffly lashed to their litters, with only their feet, with their frayed, muddy leggings or combat boots, protruding forlornly from under the blankets. Soldiers built up an immunity to such scenes. As long as the identity of the dead or the mark of a gaping wound were concealed, the living could almost ignore the dead."

The 36th Division made three desperate and costly attacks on the town, but no amount of sacrifice or heroism seemed sufficient to dislodge the Germans from San Pietro. The last attack, which began on December 15, was accompanied by another attempt on Monte Lungo, this time by the 142nd Infantry Regiment backed up by the Italians.

The Texans, despite their losses over the previous week, were still fighting hard. First Sergeant Joe W. Gill captured a German soldier and forced him to reveal all the camouflaged German positions, thereby leading to the capture of 15 more enemy troops. At the top of the mountain a private first class named Gordon Bondurant dodged the enemy machine-gun fire for an hour and a half while he carefully picked off eight Germans one by one with his rifle. His sniping kept 40 enemy soldiers pinned down until the rest of the company could surround them. By midafternoon on December 16, Monte Lungo had been cleared of Germans. Now the defenders of San Pietro, with the Allies occupying mountains on both sides of the village, were in danger of being cut off. That night, after launching a sharp, short counterattack, the Germans withdrew from the town.

The December offensive had been under way for half a month, and yet the Allies had not even reached the main German defense line at Cassino. The Fifth Army had fresh reinforcements—the 2nd Moroccan and 3rd Algerian divisions—to help make up for some of the heavy losses it had sustained to date, but General Clark recognized that his troops were much too far from Anzio to link up with an amphibious force landing there. On December 18, he reluctantly recommended that the Anzio landing be canceled. General Alexander agreed—and with that, the prospect of a quick capture of Rome went glimmering.

To all outward appearances the Italian campaign was stalemated and the Anzio project was dead. It might have remained so had it not been for one of the random, freakish events that sometimes affect one man and, through him, whole armies. Winston Churchill came down with pneumonia, and it can be argued that as a result the course of the war in Italy was dramatically changed.

In late November and early December the Allied political leaders—Roosevelt and Churchill at Cairo and then Roosevelt, Churchill and Stalin at Teheran—met to discuss world strategy. Churchill was not pleased with these meetings. He argued for increased Allied operations in the eastern Mediterranean, in the hope of luring Turkey into the War on the Allied side, and was turned down. He asked for a heavier effort to take Rome, and again he lost out. The major Allied stroke in 1944 was to be the cross-Channel invasion, and nothing was to be allowed to weaken it. Depressed and weary, Churchill left Egypt on December 11, intending to spend a night at Eisenhower's headquarters in Tunis and then visit Generals Alexander and Montgomery in Italy. But when he reached Tunis he found himself physically "at the end of my tether." He went to bed and was treated for pneumonia.

As he lay ill, Churchill had time to fret about the sad state of the Italian campaign—his campaign—and he became increasingly determined to redeem it from stalemate. He sent a telegram to his Chiefs of Staff in England, complaining that "the stagnation of the whole campaign on the Italian Front is becoming scandalous" and that no combat use of assault shipping had been made for three months, since Salerno. Soon he was calling meetings of the theater commanders and announcing flatly that "we must have the big Rome amphibious operation."

When Churchill was committed to a course of action, few men could withstand his cajolery, aggressive argument and special pleading. He instructed General Alexander to resume making plans for Anzio. "If this opportunity is not grasped," he said, "we must expect the ruin of the Mediterranean campaign of 1944."

Churchill had some new ground to stand on. As a result of the Cairo-Teheran decisions, there was to be a major change of command. Eisenhower would leave the Mediterranean to become Supreme Allied Commander in Europe, concerned mainly with the invasion of France. His replacement in the Mediterranean command would be a Briton, General Sir Henry Maitland Wilson, and thus Churchill and the British Chiefs of Staff were to be the prime Allied agents in the theater.

Knowing well that the Normandy landings scheduled for late spring, 1944, would reduce the Italian campaign to a sideshow, Churchill was bent on using what time he had to do something in his favorite theater. And as he raced ahead with his ideas, he found himself in an excellent psychological position. Now that he was ill, would Roosevelt, his old friend, deny him the use of a few LSTs for a few weeks? He sent a message to the President, asking that the LSTs—which had been scheduled to be moved to England—be kept in the Mediterranean until February 15. Whether out of sympathy for the ailing British leader or agreement with his aims—Roosevelt, too, saw the value of conquering Rome as a blow to Axis morale—he acceded to the request. The vessels would stay for a while in the Mediterranean; the amphibious operation would take place.

While Churchill convalesced at Tunis and later at Marrakech, plans for Anzio went rapidly ahead. General Clark had some momentary doubts—was there really enough shipping not only to make the landing possible but also to keep the beachhead supplied later? What would happen if he weakened his front line by withdrawing the necessary forces for Anzio? Would not the beachhead and the main battle line, at 70 miles' distance, be too far apart for mutual support? But Clark soon waved these questions aside. The notion of taking Rome was overpowering. By January 2,

Dressed in a striped burnoose, a Goumier sharpens his knife in preparation for battle. The Goumiers, or Goums as they were called, were Moroccan soldiers who had served as scouts in the Atlas Mountains in North Africa. Known for their ability to make their way through seemingly impassable mountain country, they were renowned also for their skill with knives, which they frequently used to cut off the ears or head of an enemy.

1944, he found himself "genuinely eager" for a landing on Anzio, only two weeks after he had recommended its cancellation. On January 14, Churchill, fully recovered, went happily home to England to await the success of his plan.

The Anzio landing was scheduled for January 22, allowing time—though not much—for the LSTs to make a few supply runs to the beachhead before their withdrawal on February 15. Before the landing, the Fifth Army was to launch a strong attack in the south with three aims: to tie down the enemy; to draw German reinforcements from the Rome area, so that they would be unavailable to counterattack at Anzio; and to break into the Liri valley and dash north to link up with the landing force.

In the first two weeks of January, American, British and French North African troops, by an extraordinary effort that cost them many casualties, overcame the last strong points before the main German line of resistance at Cassino. There the entrance to the Liri valley, about seven miles wide, was guarded by fortified positions along the Garigliano and Rapido rivers and on the commanding heights that stood like gateposts on both sides, at Sant'Ambrogio on the left, and above and behind the town of Cassino on the right.

Clark's battle plan called for the French Expeditionary Corps—Moroccans and Algerians—to capture the heights north of Cassino while the British took the high ground at Sant'Ambrogio. That done, the American 36th Infantry Division was to deliver the main stroke, an attack across the Rapido in the center of the valley's mouth. After the 36th had established a bridgehead across the Rapido, the U.S. 1st Armored Division was to cross the river, pass through the 36th Division and speed north on the relatively flat ground toward Frosinone and Anzio. All of this, it was hoped, would be accomplished before the amphibious landing took place on January 22, or at least soon after.

On January 12 the French launched their attack on the right, trying to break into the mountains behind and above

Field Marshal Albert Kesselring, commander in chief of German forces in Italy, holds a field marshal's baton, symbol of his high rank. In October of 1933, after 29 years of service as an artilleryman, the 48-year-old Kesselring transferred to the Luftwaffe and learned to fly. In December of 1941, Hitler sent him to Italy as Commander in Chief, South. At the time, Kesselring commanded little more than the Luftwaffe troops in Sicily, but by the next fall, his authority was extended to include nearly all German armed forces in the Mediterranean.

Cassino, but after four days of ferocious combat—much of it at short range with grenades and bayonets—they were exhausted and forced to halt. One gatepost to the valley remained in German hands.

On January 17, the 5th and 56th divisions of the British X Corps on the far left forced their way across the Garigliano River in the face of the German 94th Infantry—the division whose posting in the defense line had been judged "not illogical" because Hitler had ordered it. The Allied effort here was intended primarily as a diversion, but the British attack was so successful and the bridgehead the troops established so threatening that Kesselring felt the fate of the German right wing "hung by a slender thread." Knowing the weakness of the 94th Division, he played what one of his subordinates called "his trump card." Kesselring pulled in his only strategic reserves, two divisions from the Rome-Anzio area, to "clear up the mess." Thus, while Clark had no knowledge of it, his Fifth Army had accomplished one of its aims, drawing German forces from the area of the planned amphibious assault.

But then the British failed in their efforts to expand the Garigliano bridgehead to encompass the Sant'Ambrogio heights. The attempt hinged on another river crossing—by the 46th Division—some 11 miles inland from the first, and it broke down mainly because the strong current snapped the cables of rafts and ferries. General Clark noted that this "was quite a blow," since it meant the 36th Division attack across the Rapido would have to be launched without any flank protection on either side. But his conviction of the need for the Rapido crossing did not waver. "I maintain that it is essential that I make this attack fully expecting heavy losses," he noted in his diary. Only by attacking, he said, could he hold all the enemy troops on his front and clear the way for Anzio. "The attack," said Clark, "is on."

General Walker, commander of the 36th Division, had grave doubts about the operation. "The river is the principal obstacle of the German main line of resistance," he wrote in his diary. "I do not know a single case in military history where an attempt to cross a river that is incorporated into the main line of resistance has succeeded. So I am prepared for defeat."

The Rapido did not look impressive. It was only 25 to 50 feet wide, running between steep banks about four feet high. But the water was ice cold, fast-moving and 10 feet deep. The Germans had cut down all the trees on both sides of the river, denying any cover to an attacking enemy. On the American side the floodplain was more than a mile wide; the Germans, by manipulating power dams upstream, had turned much of it into a marsh. Everywhere, on the remaining patches of solid ground and among the reeds, they had sown mines. Because there were no roads across the muddy flatland capable of supporting heavy trucks, the assault troops would have to carry their boats, cables and bridges two miles or more to the crossing sites. And because any movement by day would have provoked an immediate storm of German artillery and mortar fire, the attack would have to be made under the cover of darkness. The 36th Division was now confronted with the most difficult operation in infantry warfare: a night crossing of a heavily defended river.

On the far bank the German defenses—a deep belt of dugouts, concrete bunkers and slit trenches protected by barbed wire, booby traps and thousands of mines—ran a zigzag course that would enable machine guns to pour enfilading fire into the flanks of assault parties. On a bluff about 40 feet above the Rapido was the shattered town of Sant'Angelo, long since reduced to rubble by Allied bombs and shellfire. The stone ruins provided excellent defensive positions for the Germans, who had turned the town into a major strong point of their line.

It did not take a general's military education to discern the problems that attackers would face. "Hell, we didn't hardly ever even get a patrol down the river in the nights before the crossing without its getting shot up," Billy Kirby, a staff sergeant from Gatesville, Texas, later recalled. "It was an ideal defense. Anybody who had any experience knew, this ain't the place to cross the river."

The task would have daunted an outfit in prime fighting condition. The 36th was not in such good shape. The division had been mauled at Salerno and shattered at San Pietro. It had been hastily patched back together with green replacements. A high proportion of its officers were new and did not yet know their men. Whether the troops had been infected by General Walker's pessimism or had simply made their own individual assessments of the undertaking,

"You'll get over it, Joe. Oncet I wuz gonna write a book exposin' the army after th' war myself."

Splattered with mud but amused, cartoonist Bill Mauldin sketches a Willie and Joe cartoon.

For thousands of GIs in Italy, the cartoons of Army Sergeant Bill Mauldin seemed to capture the essence of the infantryman's life at the front. Combining sardonic humor and pathos, Mauldin's realistic caricatures of GIs made him the champion of the enlisted man and the most popular cartoonist of the War. By the time he was 23, Mauldin, who learned cartooning through a correspondence course, had turned out more than 1,500 drawings and was syndicated in more than 100 U.S. newspapers.

Mauldin's main characters were Willie and Joe, baggy-eyed, unshaven, tattered foot soldiers who fought mostly in Italy. They sweated and shivered in foxholes and griped about food, MPs and rear-echelon "brass hats"—a tendency that got Mauldin into hot water with higher-ups.

Mauldin knew the source of his success with the fighting men. "I can't be funny about the war," he said. "The only way I can try to be a little funny is to make something out of the humorous situations which always accompany misery."

AND THE MAN WHO LIVED THEIR LIVES

"Let 'im in. I wanna see a critter I kin feel sorry fer."

"I'll let ya know if I find th' one wot invented th' 88."

a sense of futility prevailed. That most of the men resigned themselves to the job in spite of this is testimony to the quality of their soldierly character. "We had the feeling we were being sacrificed, a feeling that we couldn't win," said Staff Sergeant Kirby, "but we'd give it our damnedest." Technical Sergeant Charles R. Rummel, an acting platoon leader from Waco, Texas, put it this way: "We thought it was a losing proposition, but there ain't no way that you could back out."

General Walker planned to make his attack with two regiments of about 3,000 men each, the 141st Infantry crossing the river upstream, or north, of Sant'Angelo and the 143rd Infantry crossing south of the ruined town. After securing their bridgeheads they were to converge beyond the town, pinching it out. Accompanying the assault troops were several battalions of combat engineers who, having cleared mine-free routes through the approaches to the river and marked them with tapes the night before, were to guide the infantry to the bank and help launch the boats. They would then put up footbridges and, as soon as the riverbanks were no longer under enemy small-arms fire, build larger bridges on which heavy equipment might cross.

The attack began at 8 p.m. on January 20 in a heavy fog that cut visibility to only a few yards. The soldiers moved forward with fixed bayonets, lugging bulky 24-man rubber rafts and 12-man wooden assault boats that were 13 feet long, weighed 410 pounds and were wretchedly awkward to carry. Almost at once, while they were still a mile from the river, German shells began to fall among them. One infantry company lost 30 men in a single volley; the commander was killed and his second-in-command wounded before they had got halfway to the Rapido. Shell fragments punctured the rubber boats and splintered the wooden ones. The tapes that marked the safe lanes were torn up or buried in the mud. Some had been removed by Germans, who earlier that evening had crossed the river and laid new mines. In the darkness and fog, guides lost their way and stumbled into minefields. Bodies, wounded men and wreckage clogged the way.

By the time soldiers of the 141st Infantry Regiment got to their crossing site, about a third of their boats had been destroyed or abandoned. Of the four footbridges that the engineers were to install, one had been blown up by mines on the way, another was found at the water's edge to be defective and the remaining two were smashed by German shells as they were being put in place.

When the remaining boats were launched, several with holes in them promptly sank. Some were swept away by the current and others capsized because the troops did not know how to handle them. In the confusion, what had been low morale was transmuted into panic. Some men fell into the water deliberately and others refused to enter the boats at all. Fewer than 1,000 men managed to get across the river and dig in on the opposite bank, waiting for reinforcements to help them move forward.

By 4 a.m., using parts salvaged from the wrecked foot-bridges, engineers managed to complete one bridge—seven hours after the assault began. Although it was constantly under fire and slippery with water and blood, another 350 men crossed it. But soon after dawn, German shelling increased, knocking out the bridge and the remaining boats, and the men on the far bank were isolated. Their telephone wires were cut, their battery-powered radios failed and there was no communication with them. Only the sound of their weapons could be heard, diminishing as the Germans closed in on them.

Downstream from Sant'Angelo, the 143rd Infantry Regiment was initially more successful, getting one battalion of about 1,000 men across the river before daylight. But as dawn broke that group came under heavy artillery fire directed by observers on the heights on both flanks. The shallow bridgehead was ringed by German tanks and self-propelled guns pumping fire into the Americans. Foreseeing annihilation, the battalion commander, Major David M. Franzior, requested permission to withdraw, and by 10 a.m. all who were able to do so had made their way back across the Rapido.

Late that afternoon, under cover of a heavy smoke screen laid down by artillery, the Americans tried again. Neither the withering response from the defenders nor the horror of the experience for the attacking troops had abated. Staff Sergeant Kirby, then a 22-year-old machine-gun section leader in the 143rd's 3rd Battalion—which had not managed to get a single man across the river the previous night—described the January 21 crossing: "We were under constant fire. I saw boats being hit all around me, and guys falling out and swimming. I never knew whether they made it or not. I was in a rubber boat with three inflated compartments. One compartment was hit and deflated but somehow we stayed afloat.

"When we got to the other side it was the only scene that I'd seen in the war that lived up to what you see in the movies. I had never seen so many bodies—our own guys. I remember this one kid being hit by a machine gun; the bullets hitting him pushed his body along like a tin can.

"We had a new man, an old boy from west Texas, in our outfit. He was tough as a boot, wanted to win the war singlehanded. He had been telling us, 'When we get over there just keep the ammunition coming.'

"He got ashore, saw a body that had been blown apart, and fainted dead away. We revived him and he fainted again. I'm not saying he wasn't a good soldier, but you just never know how you're going to react."

Kirby's company, advancing at a slow crawl under the incessant fire, got through two barbed-wire obstacles. "We were close enough to hear the Germans talk," he said. "I don't know exactly how close, but I felt like they were as near as across the street."

By this time it was dark, and the units that had been able to get across the river had lost all touch with one another. Kirby's company commander told him to move off to the right to establish contact with whoever was there. "I was crawling around trying to find someone, when it felt like somebody hit me real hard in the shoulder with his fist. Then I felt the blood coming out and knew I'd really been hit. Another boy came along and got me down to the river. He found this rubber boat with one compartment still afloat and got me back somehow. I don't know how. I had lost a lot of blood and was pretty hazy." Kirby later learned that his company commander had been killed by a German shell only minutes after he had crawled away. "Just about everybody was hit," Kirby recalled. "I didn't have a single good friend in the company who wasn't killed or wounded."

Kirby's friend Sergeant Rummel was hit in the lower part of both legs at once by the low-grazing German fire. "I didn't feel any pain," Rummel said. "I was just scared to death. There was confusion all around. Two of the boys offered to carry me back but the fire was so intense I told them to get out the best way they could." He crawled around collecting packets of sulfa from "guys who weren't going to need it any more"—his dead comrades—and swallowed it. "I could hear my bones cracking every time I moved. My right leg was so badly mangled I couldn't get my boot off, on account of it was pointed to the rear." Mercifully, Rummel soon passed out.

In the appalling storm of fire one battalion lost all its company commanders. Another lost three successive battalion commanders in four hours; the first was wounded and the next two killed. Major Milton J. Landry, commander of a battalion in the 141st Infantry, was wounded three times in quick succession, the last time after he had been evacuated and was lying on a stretcher back on the American side of the river.

The battle raged on through the night and the next day, January 22. Most of the bridges the Americans had managed to establish were demolished one by one during the day. Small groups of shaken and wounded soldiers made their way back across the river. Many were drowned. As night fell again, the sound of American weapons on the far bank faltered and faded. By 11 p.m. there was silence. Every GI on the German side of the Rapido was either captured, wounded or dead.

For some the nightmare had not come to an end. For several days—"I was coming and going in and out of consciousness and didn't know how much time was passing"— Charlie Rummel dragged his shattered legs from foxhole to foxhole on the enemy's side of the river, eating whatever rations he could find and hiding from the Germans. "I often heard them talking but for a long time none came near enough to see I wasn't dead. I was constantly cold and wet. Every hole that I crawled into was filled with water."

At one time he waited out a two-hour Allied artillery barrage. "I was right in the middle of it. Our guns were firing white phosphorous shells and I expected any minute for one to drop into the hole with me." On January 25 the Germans observed a truce, allowing Americans to come across the river to recover dead and wounded, but Rummel, half-conscious, did not realize what was happening and was overlooked. Finally a party of German soldiers found him, offered him black bread "that I couldn't eat," and took him to a field hospital. Both of his legs were amputated before he was later repatriated in a prisoner exchange and sent back home to Texas.

In an action that lasted just short of 48 hours, the 36th Division had lost more than 1,000 men without making a dent in the German line. Bitter arguments about the wisdom of the operation arose immediately, and after the War the veterans of the 36th Division Association called on Congress "to investigate the Rapido River fiasco." They blamed it on Mark Clark, whom they called "inefficient and inexperienced." Congress duly investigated and found no reason to blame him. The Secretary of War, Robert P. Patterson, declared that the action "was a necessary one and that General Clark exercised sound judgment in planning it and in ordering it."

Clark himself remained steadfastly convinced that the attack was necessary to assure the success of the Anzio landing: "If we had to spill blood one place or the other, and we knew we were going to spill it, it was better to spill it where we were securely established than at the waterfront." According to German General von Senger, however, the Rapido crossings had no effect on Axis troop dispositions to the north. "The German Command paid little attention to this offensive," he said, "for the simple reason that it caused no particular anxiety. The repulse of the attack did not even call for reserves."

On January 22, as the last attempt at the Rapido was failing, the Allies were making their landing at Anzio. If any of the seaborne soldiers cocked their ears to the southwest, hoping to hear the distant rumble of the guns of their comrades coming up the Liri valley to help them, they were disappointed. There was only silence.

THE MENACE TO ITALY'S ART

German looters display Botticelli's Minerva and the Centaur for an art expert before carting it off to Austria. Pieces of tape protect cracking and flaking areas.

THE GALLERY THAT BECAME A BATTLEFIELD

In 1944, German Field Marshal Albert Kesselring remarked that he never realized what it was like to wage war in a museum until he came to Italy. Almost every Italian city, town and hamlet was crowded with religious and historical treasures—frescoes, statues, churches, medieval monasteries, Roman bridges and aqueducts, Baroque fountains and Renaissance paintings. When the Allies and the Germans began to battle their way along the corridors of this overstuffed museum, a major portion of Italy's—and the West's—cultural heritage was imperiled.

Italian authorities and the opposing armies went to considerable lengths to protect the country's artistic riches. The German Army's motor-transport section contributed valuable gasoline and trucks to the Italian effort to evacuate masterpieces to safety. The Allies, for their part, set up the Subcommission for Monuments, Fine Arts and Archives (MFAA), which briefed bomber crews and infantry commanders on monuments that should be spared if possible. Once a town was captured, the MFAA officers—nicknamed Venus Fixers by the GIs—traced lost works of art; they also helped the Italians erect scaffoldings to support shaken walls and build makeshift roofs to shield battered interiors from the elements.

But not all treasures could be saved or spared. As Allied bombs rained down on military targets in Italy's ancient cities, many priceless objects were destroyed. In the meantime, the retreating Germans—angered by the withdrawal of Italy from the War—took their pick of transportable paintings and sculptures. Then, after declaring Florence an "open city," they blew up all of the bridges except the Ponte Vecchio, which was Hitler's favorite. To prevent the Allies from using that bridge to cross the Arno, they dynamited the medieval buildings at either end.

What was surprising, however, was not the number of treasures damaged or destroyed. "Considering the intensity and scope of the military action," Lieut. Colonel Ernest T. DeWald, head of the MFAA, concluded after duty in Italy, "it is amazing that so much survived."

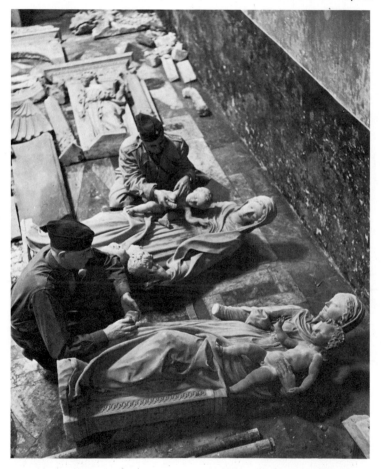

Lieut. Colonel DeWald (left) and a fellow officer examine statues salvaged from the ruins of the Church of Monteoliveto in bomb-shattered Naples.

The bridge of Santa Trinità in Florence—the most graceful and original bridge of the Renaissance—is shrouded with smoke as explosive charges go off.

A pyramid of sandbags provides protection for the 21-centuries-old statue of The Dying Gaul, displayed in Rome's Capitoline Museum.

A scaffold packed with sacks of pumice guards Rome's Arch of Constantine.

SHIELDING ANTIQUITIES AGAINST WAR'S RAVAGES

Long before fighting broke out on Italian soil, the country's officials began a program to protect as many art treasures as possible, with particular attention to those works that could not be moved to safety. They piled bags of pumice or sand around hundreds of monuments, ringed ancient columns with brick and concrete *(right)*, and braced fragile arches with brick piers.

Mosaics were covered with jute, to keep the pieces in place, and then wrapped in aluminum foil to counter the heat from bombs and fires. Frescoes were swaddled in glass wool and foil, with just enough room left between the covering and the painting so as not to mar the patina or encourage the growth of mold.

The Aurelian Column, erected in 176 A.D. in Rome, is partially sheathed with brick and mortar. It took masons months to cover the 97-foot-high monument.

Marcus Aurelius—removed from his horse on Rome's Piazza Campidoglio—lies sprawled on his back in a museum before being locked away in a special vault.

Carefully crated by Italian workers, two Florentine bronzes await transfer to a safe storage place.

HIDEAWAYS FOR PRICELESS PIECES

While many art treasures were sandbagged and covered with protective shields, almost anything that could be moved was stashed away in isolated villas, farmhouses, castles and abbeys, or even walled in under the arches of Roman aqueducts.

One of the largest repositories was the castle of Montegufoni outside Florence. Here, 246 paintings were stored. In 1944, Eric Linklater, a British essayist, and his companion, Vaughan Thomas, came upon the trove while idly exploring the castle. Inside a minor entrance, they discovered three or four pictures propped against a wall. Although they found the paintings to be good, they were certain that they were copies. The pair entered a room where other pictures had been stacked, some in wooden cases, some in brown paper, others exposed to view. Thomas went off to

explore the rooms beyond and returned, crying: "The whole house is full of pictures and some of the cases are labeled! They've come from the Uffizi and the Pitti Palace!"

In another chamber a battle scene and "an austere and tragic Madonna in dark raiment upon gold" stood together. Thomas shouted, "Uccello!" and Linklater, at the same time, cried, "Giotto!" The men stood "quite still," Linklater recalled, "held in the double grip of amazement and delight. Giotto's *Madonna* and Uccello's *Battle of San Romano,* leaning negligently against the wall, were now like exiled royalty on the common level. They had been reduced by the circumstance of war from their own place and proper height."

The castle's custodian, Guido Masti, received only 17 lire a day for guarding the paintings—valued at the time at $320 million. For Masti it was the honor, not the money, that mattered. "These pictures belong not to one nation," he said proudly, "but are the possession of the world."

CHAMPION LOOTER OF THE ITALIAN CAMPAIGN

As the Italian campaign wore on, looting became as much a threat to Italy's treasures as bombs and shells. Allied and German soldiers alike walked off with prized objects large and small, but the champion looter was the No. 1 Nazi himself. Adolf Hitler was determined to amass the most magnificent art collection in the world for display in his hometown of Linz, Austria. After the Germans took over in 1943, Italy became his happy hunting ground.

Hitler's primary agent was Colonel Alexander Langsdorff of the Kunstschutz, the German art-protection commission. In July 1944, Langsdorff's men requisitioned 297 paintings, including Bellini's *Pietà*, Botticelli's *Minerva and the Centaur* and Tintoretto's *Venus, Amor and Vulcan*, from a repository outside Florence. Langsdorff's men also made off with 58 cases of valuable works of sculpture while broadcasting appeals to the Allies not to bombard the villa where the pieces had been stored.

The bulk of Hitler's loot was stashed in South Tyrol—an Italian region under German rule—and in salt mines in Austria. Though the Germans filched thousands of art treasures from other occupied countries, the spoils from Italy were, in the opinion of one MFAA officer, more valuable than all the other loot combined.

Nobody knows the wartime fate of the three masterpieces at left—Paolo Veneziano's Madonna and Child, G. B. Utili's Saint Sebastian and Michelangelo's marble Mask of a Faun, sculpted, according to tradition, when the Florentine genius was only 15 years old.

The greatest art disaster of the Italian campaign occurred on the 11th of March, 1944, when an Allied bomb struck the Eremitani Church in Padua, destroying this series of frescoes by the Renaissance master Andrea Mantegna. The frescoes depicted the lives of the Apostles.

A prewar photograph shows the ornate interior of the Church of Santa Chiara, built in Naples in the 1300s and remodeled in the Baroque style in the 1700s.

In the fall of 1943, Allied incendiary bombs reduced the church to a shell.

5

Shortly before Allied forces landed at Anzio, General Patton paid a call on his old friend, General Lucas, commander of the U.S. VI Corps in Italy. Patton had been in limbo since the Sicilian campaign because of the furor over the slapping incidents. He had been living in exile in Palermo, busying himself by traveling through the Mediterranean, flying over the desert battlefields in Africa where Rommel and Montgomery had clashed, seeing the pyramids and King Tut's tomb in Egypt and touring the Holy Land.

Now he was being reassigned to England, where eventually he would command an army in the liberation of France. Before leaving the Mediterranean, he had a few words of advice for Lucas, who soon would be commanding the Anzio invasion. "John," said Patton, "there is no one in the Army I hate to see killed as much as you, but you can't get out of this alive. Of course, you might be badly wounded. No one *ever* blames a wounded general."

Patton's doubts only confirmed those Lucas already nurtured. "I felt like a lamb being led to the slaughter," Lucas wrote in his diary. He thought that his VI Corps and the naval forces involved had too little time to prepare for the operation and that the strength of the landing force, two divisions plus assorted battalions of Rangers, Commandos and paratroopers, was dangerously small. Harking back to the World War I landing in Turkey that had ended in disaster for the British and their allies, Lucas later said: "This whole affair had a strong odor of Gallipoli."

Winston Churchill, having spent decades living down his involvement in the planning of the Gallipoli campaign, would have been particularly incensed had he been aware of Lucas' words. Churchill shared none of this pessimism about his current pet project. He was sure that Operation *Shingle,* as the Anzio landing was called, would serve as a "cat-claw" to reach behind the Germans and get the Allies out of the interminable bloody fighting in the mountains of central Italy; ultimately it would lead to the quick capture of Rome.

General Alexander also thought the landing was a sound idea. "It will certainly frighten Kesselring," he said. The Allies were to establish a strong beachhead and then push inland about 25 miles to seize the Alban Hills and cut Highways 6 and 7, the Germans' main supply and escape routes. Alexander hoped the landing would cause the enemy to

THE OBSTACLE COURSE TO ROME

pull hastily out of the Winter Line and flee to the north.

But General Clark, the Fifth Army commander, was not sure the Germans would panic so easily. He suspected that as soon as they sized up the magnitude of the operation and realized that the Allies had shot their bolt and could not soon make other attacks elsewhere along the coast, the Germans would fight. They would concentrate all available forces against the beachhead, trying first to prevent the Allies from reaching the Alban Hills and then to deliver a heavy counterattack. "Don't stick your neck out, Johnny," Clark told Lucas. "I did at Salerno and got into trouble." He thought the best Lucas might do would be to seize and hold a beachhead without making a risky dash inland. He doubted that the establishment of the beachhead would cause the Germans to pull out troops from the Cassino front, but he realized that their reaction was unpredictable and he wanted to take no unnecessary chances at Anzio.

Clark was deliberately restrained in wording his orders to Lucas, who was "to seize and secure a beachhead in the vicinity of Anzio" and "advance on Colli Laziali" (the Alban Hills). If the phrase "advance on" seemed ambiguous, the limited nature of the assignment was underlined in a later passage in the orders, in which Lucas was instructed to "attack in the direction of Colli Laziali." Clark did not want to force Lucas into pushing inland at the risk of overextending the VI Corps and perhaps losing it. If conditions warranted a drive to the hills, Lucas was free to make one, but Lucas could decide for himself.

It was not in Lucas' nature to make Patton-style thrusts across the landscape. A modest man, he once remarked that "I am just a poor working girl trying to get ahead," and noted in his diary that "I am blessed in all my subordinates. They do all the work and most of the thinking." At 54, Lucas appeared considerably older—his men called him "Old Luke" or "Foxy Grandpa"—and his characteristics as a soldier were thoroughness and prudence. He may well have been miscast as leader of the Anzio operation, but his superiors knew his qualities when they selected him for the job, and they would have little reason later to blame him for not turning into a Churchillian wildcat.

The fortunes of the Anzio landing force and of the main body of the Fifth Army at Cassino were inextricably intermeshed. Strategically, the two forces would be engaged in the same battle. Success on one front could mean success on the other, and failure at either would imperil both. It was regrettable for the Allies that the respective roles of the two efforts were not more clearly defined at the outset. Lucas interpreted his orders to mean that Operation *Shingle* "was a 'diversion' to attract enemy troops from the front of the Fifth Army where the main effort was to be made." Churchill and Alexander, on the other hand, apparently regarded the landing as an envelopment substantial enough to cause the main line of German defense to crumble.

Because of the shortage of shipping and the fear of so weakening the Fifth Army on the Cassino front that the Germans might succeed wih a counterthrust there, Lucas' initial assault force was limited to only 40,000 men—the U.S. 3rd Division, accompanied by detachments of Rangers and paratroopers, and the British 1st Division plus a brigade of Commandos. Lucas particularly lacked the mechanized troops necessary for the kind of rapid advance that Churchill expected. (Clark would later send reinforcements, including the U.S. 1st Armored and 45th divisions.)

On the one-day voyage from Naples to Anzio, the Allied invasion fleet was not detected by the Germans, whose air force had been so whittled down that it could make few reconnaissance flights. On January 22, landing behind a dense barrage of naval rockets, the troops met only slight opposition on the beaches *(map, page 134)*. The port of Anzio was captured virtually intact, as was the nearby town of Nettuno. Lucas was elated: "We achieved what is certainly one of the most complete surprises in history." Inland they encountered only two depleted, exhausted German battalions, which had been pulled out of the Cassino area to rest and refit; they were soon overrun. By midday the British were two miles inland and the Americans had advanced to a depth of three miles. By the end of the day 36,000 troops and 3,200 vehicles were safely ashore.

Field Marshal Kesselring, being a skilled strategist, had plans to cope with a landing behind his lines, but his two reserve divisions from the area had been dispatched to cope with the British crossing of the Garigliano River four days earlier. There were so few German troops near Anzio that it seemed to Kesselring's intelligence officers that the landing might indeed bring the Cassino defenses "to a state of collapse." Hitler quickly agreed to move reinforcements from

Yugoslavia, Germany, France and northern Italy, and Kesselring immediately started drawing reinforcements down from the north. By nightfall of the first day, elements of three divisions were on their way from the Fourteenth Army, which was garrisoning northern Italy, and soon bits and pieces of four divisions were pulled out from the Cassino area and moved to the new front.

Thus, within 24 hours the Germans had set up a precarious defensive line around the beachhead. To Kesselring's great relief the Allies made no aggressive moves on the second day of the invasion beyond expanding their toehold slightly. Nor, except for small advances that deepened the beachhead to nearly 10 miles, was there much spirited action by the Allies on the third and fourth days. Lucas, aware of the "swiftness of the enemy build-up," was intent on getting in more men and supplies before taking aggressive action. "I must keep my feet on the ground and my forces in hand and do nothing foolish," he wrote. "This is the most important thing I have ever tried to do and I will not be stampeded."

By the fourth day Kesselring, out of what he called a "jumble of multifarious troops that streamed in from all directions," had put together a formidable defense, and he was sure the crisis had passed. The Germans now had elements of eight divisions deployed around the beachhead and parts of five more on the way. Kesselring brought down from northern Italy the Fourteenth Army commander, General Eberhard von Mackensen, put him in charge of the Anzio front and told him to prepare a counterattack as quickly as possible.

It was not until the ninth day of the invasion, January 30, that General Lucas launched a two-pronged drive toward the Alban Hills. On the left the British 1st Division managed to reach the town of Campoleone, 15 miles from Anzio and more than halfway to the hills, before it was stopped. But on the right the U.S. attack, spearheaded by two battalions of Rangers, met disaster.

At 1:30 in the bitterly cold winter morning the Rangers, carrying extra bandoleers of ammunition, started out in a column toward the town of Cisterna. They crept silently along the bottom of a large irrigation ditch, moving unobserved, they thought, past German sentries on the banks. In the darkness they could hear faint sounds all around them

Weighed down with gear, Allied troops disembark from LSTs docked at Anzio, 35 miles south of Rome. The first week after the January 22 landing, the Allies brought ashore 69,000 men, 508 guns, 237 tanks and 27,250 tons of supplies. So great was the surprise achieved by the predawn landing that of the 200 or more Germans captured, many were still in bed.

but there was no gunfire, no challenge. By dawn the column was strung out for a mile and a half and had penetrated far into the German lines. It seemed to the Rangers that they had surprised the enemy—but as they moved out of the ditch to deploy for an attack on Cisterna they were raked by fire from all sides. They had been ambushed. Rifles, machine guns, mortars and tank guns cut loose at them. They splintered into small groups. It was almost impossible to pull back; all they could do was fight until they dropped. They had run into the Hermann Göring Division and part of the 715th Infantry Division, newly arrived from France. Of the 767 Rangers who started toward Cisterna, six got back to the beachhead.

Nearby, soldiers of the U.S. 3rd Division also came to grief. One battalion, after being pinned down by enemy fire for 30 hours, rose up and fought its way into the outskirts of Cisterna and came within yards of cutting Highway 7. But the men were too far out in front of the troops on their flanks and were soon driven out of the long, narrow salient that they had gained. Approximately 650 of the 800 men in the battalion were lost.

After three days of fighting in which the Allies suffered 5,500 casualties and the Germans a similar number, Lucas' VI Corps was ordered by Generals Alexander and Clark to stop trying to break out of the beachhead and dig in behind a perimeter of barbed wire and mines. Intercepted and decoded messages indicated that the Germans were massing forces for a powerful counterattack; Lucas himself had thought all along that his men would soon be fighting for their lives. Yet if the concentration of enemy troops at Anzio was helping the main body of the Fifth Army to break through at Cassino, then the landing could be considered a success even though the beachhead itself was threatened. But the news from the Cassino front was not encouraging.

As soon as the surprise landing at Anzio had diverted the attention of the Germans in the south, General Clark ordered the main body of the Fifth Army to seize the moment and try once more to breach the Winter Line. With the disastrous failure of the January 20-22 Rapido River crossings fresh in their minds, the Allied commanders decided on a flank attack for their new effort. Instead of again trying to bull their way directly into the mouth of the Liri valley, the Allies would push up and over the spur of jumbled mountain peaks that juts southward from the central Apennines and culminates in the prominence of Monte Cassino itself (maps, page 144).

Known as the Cassino massif, the spur is a tormented volcanic wasteland strewn with jagged stones and boulders and gashed by V-shaped ravines. The sides of the spur are so

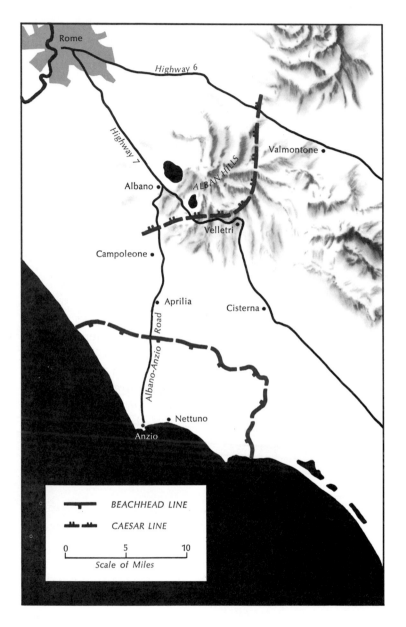

The surprise landing at Anzio was intended to relieve Allied forces stalled on the Cassino front. But the Allied commander, Major General John P. Lucas, failed to exploit the initial surprise. Instead of driving inland to cut Highways 6 and 7, the major supply and escape routes for the German forces to the south, he halted his forces in the beachhead and built them up against an anticipated enemy counterattack. When the counterattack was launched along the Albano-Anzio road on February 16, 1944, the Allies were driven back one and a half miles, but they had accumulated enough strength to beat off the attackers. The beachhead was saved, but the value of the Anzio operation would long be debated.

steep that from a distance they appear to rise vertically out of the ground.

Tucked under the southern end of the spur, next to the entrance to the Liri valley, lies the town of Cassino on the bank of the Rapido; perched atop Monte Cassino above the town, looking down on it from a height of 1,700 feet, is the Benedictine monastery. From the monastery and the ground around it there is a magnificent view of both the Liri and Rapido valleys. An observer can see for many miles, and if he happens to be an artillery spotter with a radio, he can call down a rain of shellfire on anything that moves below him. There has been no better military observation post since the invention of the cannon. Monte Cassino has been compared to the Rock of Gibraltar because of its dominance of the "strait" at the entrance to the Liri valley; in bygone years the Italian Military College had pointed it out to students as an example of a well-nigh impregnable natural defensive position.

If the Allies could reach the Liri valley by crossing the spur and going around behind Monte Cassino, they could pinch out that great bastion without having to assail it. On the far right of the Fifth Army front, General Alphonse Juin's French Expeditionary Corps—consisting of the 3rd Algerian and 2nd Moroccan divisions—was ordered to push across the spur in the vicinity of Monte Belvedere, a peak about five miles to the north of Cassino. On the inside of this French attempt to turn the German flank, the U.S. 34th Division would deliver the main blow. The 34th would cross the Rapido River north of the town of Cassino, where the river was shallow enough to be waded, fight its way up and over the Cassino massif, and then, having got beyond Monte Cassino and its monastery, wheel to the left and go down into the Liri valley. If all went well, this would open the highway to Rome.

An assault on the mountains was difficult enough in itself, but there were some preliminaries that made the assignment even harder. Before reaching the Rapido the soldiers of the 34th had to cross two miles of open, swampy ground that the Germans had flooded by diverting the river upstream. On the far side of the river they had to get through a wide belt of wire, mines, steel-reinforced concrete pillboxes and fortified stone houses. After that they had to seize two low hills and a large Italian barracks that was filled with German gun positions. Only then could they begin their climb up the steep slopes of the Cassino massif. And all of this had to be done under the eyes of comfortably entrenched enemy observers who could direct artillery and mortar fire on them.

The quickness and accuracy of the German artillerymen at Cassino were almost eerie. In daylight the movement of a single vehicle or the mere clustering of a handful of men often drew down precisely aimed shells. The Germans had dozens of excellent observation posts on the heights, but as shells burst near the men of the 34th Division, the GIs began to look in one direction: at the monastery on top of Monte Cassino. They were convinced that someone up there, certainly no peaceful monk, was directing fire at them. As it happened, the Germans had no troops in the monastery, nor did they need to have any; the high ground close by served just as well. But the Americans—and later the English, Indians, New Zealanders, Poles and French—did not believe this.

The monastery, founded by Saint Benedict in 529 A.D., was as famous and revered as any in Christendom. Destroyed by the Lombards in 581, by the Saracens in 883 and by an earthquake in 1349, it was rebuilt on a grander scale each time by architects who intended to make it proof against the assaults of man and nature. Within its walls the monks had copied and preserved a treasury of Latin literature that might otherwise have been lost—works of Ovid and Vergil, Cicero and Seneca, and many others.

Made of stone and with battlemented walls 10 feet thick, the monastery was about 150 feet high and 660 feet long. It had only one entrance, which was secured by a ponderous wooden gate, and its sides were pierced by long rows of narrow cell windows that from a distance looked like loopholes for guns. Dark with winter rain, silent, brooding, the colossal building seemed an almost living presence to soldiers below.

Under the eyes of the edifice the soldiers of the 34th Division began their attack on January 24, two days after the landing at Anzio, and it took them more than a week to gain a bridgehead across the Rapido and into the mountains beyond it. Then, while one regiment of the division remained on a shelf of relatively low ground and tried to drive south along it into the town of Cassino, the other two regiments went up into the mountains. The country was so rugged that advances could be made only by small groups of men picking their way through ravines, up flinty slopes and across steep ridges slippery with snow and ice. It was impossible to dig foxholes in the rocky ground. Men sheltered in crevices or behind boulders or little heaps of splintered stone. Many came down with pneumonia, dysentery, trench foot, but the men of the 34th kept clawing their way up the massif while a determined enemy, in bunkers and gun pits that had been prepared long in advance, cut them down.

Their casualties were frightful. The division lost 2,200 men; some rifle companies lost 75 per cent of their combat strength. Many of the wounded, caught on the bare slopes under clattering artillery barrages, were injured again by flying rock fragments.

For three weeks the men of the 34th fought as desperately and gallantly as any division in the War. They drove a salient two miles into the mountains, taking Monte Castellone and winning a foothold on a ridge that, because of its shape on military maps, came to be called Snakeshead. They took Hill 445, so named for its height in meters, and found themselves only 400 yards from the monastery.

On the right of the 34th Division, the French, who had begun their attack on January 25, conquered Monte Belvedere, but were soon stalled by heavy German counterattacks. A regiment of the U.S. 36th Division—the 142nd Infantry, which had been in reserve during the Rapido crossings and thus was still relatively intact—was inserted between the French and the 34th in an effort to sustain the momentum of the drive.

But General von Senger, commander of the German XIV Corps defending this part of the front, threw in everything that he had to stop the drive, committing his main reserve, the 90th Panzer Grenadier Division, and concentrating his artillery on the advancing Allies with devastating effect.

An Allied soldier blinded by a German shell at Anzio gets a hand from a buddy. On the small beachhead, where there was little cover from the constant barrage of German bombs and shells, 2,000 Allied troops were killed and 8,500 wounded in the first month of the operation.

One young American lieutenant, Harold L. Bond, described in an evocative memoir called *Return to Cassino* what it was like to be caught under the intense fire of the German guns. The bombardment began soon after his platoon had encamped for the night in their shallow holes covered with canvas from pup tents carried by the men. "The air was filled with sound as if every German gun in the valley had fired toward us at the same time. We pushed down as far as we could in terror, and the ground all around us shook with gigantic explosions. Huge showers of earth rained down on top of our canvas. The air was full of flying dirt and shrapnel. There was the frightening smell of gunpowder and crash after crash. I did not have time to wonder what was happening to my men. In such a shelling as this each man is isolated from everyone else. Death is immediately in front of him. He only knows that his legs and arms are still there and that he has not been hit yet; in the next instant he might be."

Bond was sharing his trench with a runner. "The young messenger started moaning softly to himself, but he did not say anything. I commented a couple of times how close the last one was, but I got no reply. Pity the poor man or beast caught out in this, I started to think, and then, 'Crash!' and I would grit my teeth and try to move my legs to see if they were still there." The bombardment lasted two hours. The next morning Bond found that his canteen cup, which had been left on the ground next to the trench, was riddled with large, jagged holes made by flying shell fragments. That day the frightened messenger slipped away from the platoon. Bond never saw him again.

Under such brutal punishment, many GIs sought excuses to get out of the front lines. Bond was surprised to find an American officer posted on a trail leading from the front, pistol drawn. "There was a regular stream of troops trying to get down from the ridge," Bond wrote. "He had orders to make everyone stay." A soldier was showing him a badly swollen hand. " 'But look, Lieutenant,' " he said, " 'I can't fire a rifle. I can't even pull the trigger.' "

" 'Go on back, goddamn you! Use your toes, then. My orders are that nobody goes out of here unless he's seriously wounded. Go on! Get back!' The soldier turned around and started the dreary trek to the top of the ridge. Two or three men, who had tags tied to their combat jackets to show that they were legitimate casualties, were allowed to go down. All the rest were turned back."

But most of the Americans did their duty without coercion. They came within a mile of making a breakthrough into the Liri valley. They could see Highway 6, and the Germans blocking their way were clinging to the tops of the precipitous slopes that led down to the vital road. But the heroic Allied efforts could not overcome the Germans' equally heroic stand. The Americans were worn out. They could go no farther.

On the shelf of ground beside the Rapido, where one regiment of the 34th tried to take the town of Cassino while the other units fought in the mountains above, the struggle was equally savage. The stone walls of the old Italian houses were so thick that it took as many as nine bazooka rockets to blow a hole three feet in diameter: among the houses, the Germans had built steel-reinforced concrete bunkers so strong that 105mm shells were ineffective against them. A maze of tunnels and trenches linked these strong points, enabling the defenders to dart back and forth at will. The Americans battered their way into a corner of the town but that small foothold was all they could obtain. The attempt to break the enemy defenses had failed.

On February 12 the 4th Indian Division, which along with the 2nd New Zealand Division had been brought over to Cassino from the Eighth Army's quiet front on the Adriatic, went into the line to relieve the exhausted Americans. The Indian troops, including battalions of Gurkhas long experienced in mountain warfare, were awestruck by what their allies had accomplished. "How the hell your chaps did it, I can't imagine," said a British officer with the Gurkhas as he surveyed the wedge the Americans had driven into the German line. As the relief was made it was found that 50 soldiers of the 34th Division were too numbed by fatigue and cold to move. They could still face the enemy and fire their guns, but they could not walk and had to be carried down from the massif on stretchers.

After this unsuccessful drive, the Allies battering at the Cassino defenses perhaps should have stopped, licked their wounds and renewed their energies for a big push later in the year, when reinforcements and better weather might have arrived. But they were not able to do so because now they were part of a two-front struggle. Operation *Shingle* had been launched to facilitate a breakthrough at Cassino. The breakthrough had failed, and now the situation was reversed. The troops at Cassino would have to keep pressing forward in order to take the pressure off the Anzio beachhead, which was now in dire trouble.

At Anzio, the Germans were getting ready for their all-out counterattack. Hitler was obsessed by the beachhead, which he called an "abscess" that must be removed at all costs, and personally ordered crack troops, more artillery and aircraft sent to the Anzio front.

General von Mackensen had transferred his headquarters to the Anzio front from Verona to take charge of the counterattack, and was planning to cut the beachhead in half by attacking down the Albano-Anzio road to the sea. Between February 3 and 10 he made several preliminary thrusts to gain what he considered a necessary starting line for his main attack. He knocked out a long, thin British salient on the road and took Aprilia, a modern brick town built by Mussolini as a model for Fascist farm settlements and called "The Factory" by Allied soldiers. By this time the German build-up had been so successful that Mackensen's troops outnumbered the Allies by about 95,000 to 76,000.

As Mackensen concluded his preliminary attacks, Churchill fumed in frustration over the failure of the Anzio operation to wreak havoc upon the Germans. "I had hoped that we were hurling a wildcat onto the shore," he complained, "but all we got was a stranded whale." He was exasperated by General Lucas' cautious, methodical management of the beachhead, with its mountainous accumulation of supplies, and demanded to know how many vehicles, exclusive of tanks, had been landed to serve 70,000 men. When told that there were 18,000 jeeps and trucks, he exploded. "How many of our men are driving or looking after 18,000 vehicles in this narrow space? We must have a great superiority of chauffeurs. I am shocked that the enemy have more infantry than we."

Lucas may not have needed all those wheels, but he did require great stocks of ammunition and other supplies to beat off the German counterattack, as events were soon to show. He had been using up his artillery ammunition faster than it could be replaced. "This is a national scandal," he

said. "We have been at war, or preparing for it, for four years and soldiers must die because guns have nothing to shoot. Where has it gone?"

On February 16, with the Germans outnumbering the Allies by about 125,000 to 100,000, Mackensen launched his major attack down the Albano-Anzio road. The brunt of it fell on the U.S. 45th Division, which was pushed back toward the sea but refused to break. Lucas called for air support and got more than 700 sorties against the oncoming Germans; he expended his dwindling stocks of ammunition to throw up barrages of fire from his artillery, tanks, tank destroyers and mortars, aided by a bombardment from two Navy cruisers lying offshore. One American artillery spotter in a small L-4 cub plane, seeing 2,500 German infantrymen and a column of tanks headed down the road, was able to concentrate the shells of more than 200 British and American pieces against them in a few minutes.

The German infantry attack was backed up by tanks, which set forth with high hopes but soon encountered the same problem that had plagued the Allies: mud. The tanks could operate only on the main roads, where they were most vulnerable to artillery fire—and when the tanks failed, German infantrymen, who had expected much help from them, were disheartened.

Disheartening too was the failure of an elite regiment, the Berlin-Spandau Infantry Lehr, sent to Anzio by Hitler to lead Mackensen's attack. The Infantry Lehr was a special demonstration unit that had been used in Germany to instruct troops in training. Its men were politically reliable and tough in appearance, but they had one major shortcoming: they had never been in a fight. Against his better judgment Mackensen obeyed Hitler's order and put them in the forefront. The veterans of the U.S. 45th Division, hard-bitten dogfaces who resembled cartoonist Bill Mauldin's weather-beaten GIs, Willie and Joe *(pages 114-115)*, cut them to bits. The Lehr regiment broke and ran, demoralizing other troops who were advancing behind them.

Still, the Germans were able to rally and press their counterattack for five days. They pushed the Americans back one and a half miles, but the beleaguered GIs, ordered by Lucas to hold a final beachhead line at all costs, dug in and refused to budge. Fighting at close range without sleep and in numbing cold, the shattered companies of the 45th

Division—some completely surrounded—seemed to deny a German breakthrough by sheer force of will. Their courage and determination prevented an Allied disaster at Anzio.

Finally acknowledging that they could not wipe out the beachhead, the Germans suspended their offensive on the 20th of February, although minor skirmishes continued for a few more days. Their losses since the day of the landing had totaled nearly 19,000 men, while Allied casualties had been about the same, reducing the combat units on both sides to impotence. At Hitler's insistence the Germans would make another, weaker attempt to crush the beach-

head defenders nine days later, but it too would collapse.

On February 22, after the first counterattack had died out, General Clark came to the beachhead and removed General Lucas from command, replacing him with the commander of the U.S. 3rd Division, General Truscott Clark liked Lucas and thought he had done a creditable job, but agreed with General Alexander, who wanted "a thruster like George Patton" at Anzio and felt that Lucas was worn out physically and mentally and "had no flash." Lucas was bitter. "I thought I was winning something of a victory," he said.

The blame for the failure to achieve a spectacular result at Anzio fell on him, but there was good reason to argue that he did not deserve the opprobrium. Lucas believed that if he had made an early dash for the Alban Hills, he would have seen his forces crushed. "Had I done so I would have lost my corps and nothing would have been accomplished except to raise the prestige and morale of the enemy," he wrote. "Besides, my orders didn't read that way."

The real failure at Anzio was perhaps most accurately pinpointed by the German commander of both the Anzio and Cassino fronts, Albert Kesselring. "The landing force was initially weak, only a division or so of infantry, and without infantry armor," he said to an American newsman after the War. "It was a half-way measure as an offensive that was your basic error."

Churchill was pleased with the replacement of Lucas by Truscott, although the change of command had no immediate effect on the grim stalemate in which both fronts were now locked. Tacitly admitting that the gamble at Anzio—which was primarily his gamble—had failed, Churchill said no more about stranded whales and tried to look at the bright side. "A large secondary front in Italy is not unwelcome to the Allies," he said. "We must fight the Germans somewhere."

The Germans made no further major efforts to eradicate the beachhead, but continually pounded the Allied troops with air raids and shellfire. The beachhead was so small that every square inch was within the range of German artillery, including tunnel-hidden 280mm railroad guns, "Anzio Annie" and "The Anzio Express," that threw shells for 20 miles. "Our heavy artillery and Luftwaffe bombers saw to it that even when 'resting' their soldiers had no rest," Field Mar-

Monks in the abbey at Monte Cassino fill a crate with precious books, after being advised by the Germans to evacuate the monastery. As the Allies neared the Cassino area, monks and German troops packed and removed thousands of parchments, manuscripts and printed books, including Cicero's De Republica, Saint Augustine's sermons, the Dialogues of Seneca, and the 11th Century De Lingua Latina, the oldest grammar book in existence. The priceless works—many of them richly illuminated by Cassino monks in the 11th Century—were safely stored in the Vatican.

shal Kesselring said of his penned-in enemy. "It must have been damned unpleasant."

The Allies sought protection below ground. Command posts were located in wine cellars, and troops dug in and built thousands of small underground homes from sandbags, scrap lumber, empty ammunition boxes or old wine barrels. Hospital tents were sunk halfway into the ground and buttressed with sandbags, but even so they were dangerous places to be in. The Germans did not purposely fire on them, but in the crowded beachhead the tents were necessarily surrounded by supply dumps and other legitimate targets, and shells often missed their mark. When a bombardment or air raid began, doctors and nurses could not leave their patients on operating tables and take cover. Casualties among medical personnel were high: 92 were killed, 387 wounded and 60 reported missing in action.

Allied troops learned to accept the constant deadly fire as routine, and got on with life in spite of it. They watched movies in two large underground theaters and played baseball and volleyball games, which were frequently interrupted by air raids or incoming shells. And they whiled away many hours listening to the German broadcaster, "Axis Sally," who played popular American records, dispensed propaganda and told the Allied soldiers that Anzio was "the largest self-supporting prisoner-of-war camp in the world."

While the Germans were massing their forces for the counterattack at Anzio in February, the Fifth Army in the Cassino area, alerted by intercepted enemy messages, had hurriedly organized another major effort to break through the de-

Major General John P. Lucas, commander of the U.S. VI Corps, was relieved on February 22, 1944, for not showing more aggressiveness at Anzio. Before the landing, Lucas had accurately predicted his own fate. "They will end up by putting me ashore with inadequate forces and get me in a serious jam," he wrote in his diary. "Then, who will take the blame?"

fenses on that front into the Liri valley. The U.S. 34th and 36th divisions had been badly mauled, and now General Alexander gave the task to the newly arrived 2nd New Zealand and 4th Indian divisions. Later they were joined by the British 78th Division. The New Zealand Corps, as this temporary formation was called, was commanded by New Zealand's Lieut. General Sir Bernard Freyberg.

Freyberg, a huge, rugged man who had won the Victoria Cross in World War I, studied maps of the area and decided that this time the Allies should try to capture Monte Cassino instead of bypassing it. He would send the 4th Indian Division into the mountains to take "Monastery Hill"—the name Allied troops had given to the abbey-crowned peak— and press on beyond it into the valley while the 2nd New Zealand, down below, fought its way into the town. He

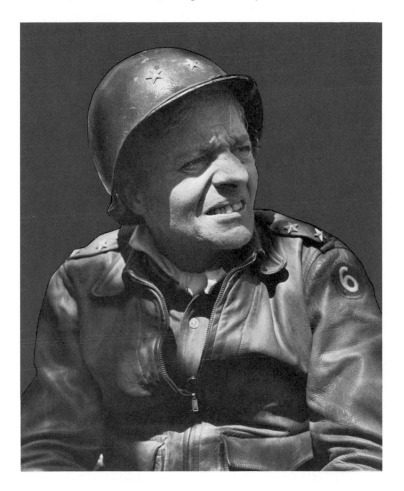

would use more troops than the Americans had employed and, just before his attack went in, he would have the monastery bombed.

The decision to destroy the monastery was reached after Major General F. I. S. Tuker of the 4th Indian Division did some research about the building. When his division was assigned the wretched task of assaulting Monastery Hill, Tuker naturally asked the Fifth Army's intelligence branch to give him some information about the structure. Intelligence was no help.

For months, ever since Salerno, it had been evident that the Allies somehow would have to deal with Monte Cassino in order to get past it to Rome, and for weeks the Fifth Army had been just beneath the mountain and the huge abbey on its summit. Yet Army intelligence was unable to provide detailed information of the building's construction. Frustrated, General Tuker drove to Naples and prowled through bookshops until he found an 1879 volume that contained what he needed: a description of the abbey's construction, its dimensions, the thickness of its walls.

Tuker now knew what he was up against. He told Freyberg he found it unreasonable to ask his men to move against a position that was crowned by an enormous, intact fortress. It did not matter, Tuker told Freyberg, whether the monastery was garrisoned by Germans at the outset or not; Tuker was sure they would move into it during the battle. The building was so strong, he added, that it would take blockbuster bombs to deal with it. He wanted it removed.

Freyberg agreed and relayed the request to Alexander. Alexander asked the commander of the Twelfth Air Force, U.S. Major General John Cannon, whether bombs could in fact reduce the monastery. Cannon replied: "If you let me use the whole of our bomber force against Cassino we will whip it out like a dead tooth."

American and British airmen were convinced that battles could be won from the sky. It was only necessary to obliterate the target, and then the infantry could move in. The airmen were particularly enthusiastic about the Cassino operation because it would give them a chance to demonstrate the power of the heavy bomber, which had never before been used in concentrated numbers in direct support of infantry trying to take a specific objective.

General Clark and other senior American ground com-

The man who succeeded Lucas was Major General Lucian K. Truscott Jr., the tough-minded commander of the U.S. 3rd Division. A sensitive man, Truscott was keenly aware of his friend's feelings about being relieved of his command. "While Lucas was deeply hurt," Truscott would recall later, "he had no ill feeling toward me, and our friendship was unbroken. . . . It was one of my saddest experiences of the war."

manders were strongly opposed to the bombing. They had several reasons. First they felt it would be shameful for religious and cultural reasons to destroy the monastery and its treasures. (Neither the Americans nor the British knew it, but the Germans had already removed the most valuable of the monastery's books, manuscripts and paintings to Rome and deposited them for safekeeping at Castel Sant'Angelo.) Also, as had already been demonstrated in Sicily and Italy, a ruined town or a ruined building with all its rubble can provide better protection for defenders than one that is intact. Finally, there were civilian refugees in the monastery and there was no clear evidence that the Germans were actually inside the building, although they had observation posts and gun positions within 200 yards of it.

But the Allied foot soldiers and junior officers who were doing the fighting believed there were enemy troops in the monastery. So did two American generals, Ira C. Eaker, commander of the Mediterranean Allied Air Forces, and Jacob Devers, Deputy to the Supreme Allied Commander, Mediterranean. Eaker and Devers flew over the building in a Piper Cub at 200 feet and stated flatly afterward that they had seen a military radio antenna on the monastery and had observed German soldiers there.

General von Senger, the German commander at Cassino, fervently maintained later that he never used the abbey for military purposes. Senger was in a painfully ironic position. He admired and was sincerely concerned with preserving the legacy of Italian culture. He was a devout Catholic and a lay brother of the Benedictine order, fighting in a Catholic country, with the venerable Benedictine abbey in the center of his line. His conduct was scrupulous. He stationed German military police at the gates of the monastery to prevent his soldiers from entering. When he visited the abbey to dine with the abbot and attend mass on Christmas Eve, 1943, he even refrained from looking out the windows.

But General Alexander, who knew the psychological hold the monastery had on Allied soldiers, decided in favor of the bombing. It seemed not only sensible but obligatory to give the attacking troops all the support that could be mustered. "Was the destruction of the monastery a military necessity? Was it morally wrong to destroy it?" Alexander later wrote. "The answer to the first question is 'yes.' It was necessary more for the effect it would have on the morale of the attackers than for purely material reasons. The answer to the second question is this: when soldiers are fighting for a just cause and are prepared to suffer death and mutilation in the process, bricks and mortar, no matter how venerable, cannot be allowed to weigh against human lives."

Because it was known that the Germans were about to launch their big counterattack at Anzio, it was important to get the Cassino attack moving as soon as possible. In the haste, some details were overlooked. It was assumed, but not decisively worked out, that before the air raid the refugees in the monastery would be given a reasonable time to leave and that the 4th Indian Division was to be in position, fully supplied and ready to follow up the raid with a strong assault on the ruins of the building.

The timing of the raid was left up to the airmen, who needed a forecast of 24 hours' clear weather. At first it was thought that the bombers would strike on February 16. When the sky suddenly cleared, the timing was advanced by a day, but some Allied units on the ground were not informed. On the afternoon of February 14, leaflets were dropped on Monte Cassino warning the civilians—the abbot, about 10 monks and lay brothers, and more than 800 refugees—to get out of the building at once. But before they could leave, the harried monks had to parley with the equally harried Germans in the midst of battle and prepare the refugees, many of whom were ill or elderly (the abbot himself was 80 years old). It was decided that all should go out on foot via a mule path through the German lines at 5 a.m. on February 16. When the raid began at 9:45 a.m. on the 15th the monks and refugees were still in the building.

The 4th Indian Division, having entered the front line only three days before, was not ready to follow up the bombing with its own attack. In that tortured terrain where the fighting was at close range, the weapons that mattered most were hand grenades and mortars. But the Indians had lost most of their grenades and mortar shells in vehicle accidents, and these critical items had to be transported in small quantities at night by mule over a long, devious route. The 4th Indian Division was not only unprepared but outraged when the raid began a day earlier than expected.

Attacking in waves for several hours, medium and heavy bombers dropped nearly 600 tons of high explosive on the monastery. Between waves, Allied artillery pounded the building with volley after volley. At intervals the smoke and dust cleared, revealing the great walls in various stages of demolition. American foot soldiers, watching, wept with joy. If the men of the 34th Division had any regret, it was only that the monastery had not been bombed earlier. Inside the building the monks and the refugees prayed and died. Perhaps 300 of them—the exact number was never known—were crushed and buried in the rubble, or killed by artillery fire as they attempted to escape. The abbot and 40 others survived in the depths of the abbey's crypt.

When the raid was over it could be seen that although the monastery had been terribly battered the lower part of it was still standing. The base of the walls, 10 feet thick, had not been breached; no holes had been made through which infantrymen could easily enter; and the ruins, as General Clark and others had predicted, now provided ideal lodgments for German mortar and machine-gun crews. Soon after nightfall the men of the 4th Indian Division, unready and still lacking supplies, made a brave attempt to reach the monastery but were repulsed by Germans on the nearby slopes. The Indians tried again the next night and again on February 17, and both times were turned back. Meanwhile, at the foot of the mountain, two companies of New Zealand Maoris attacked and seized the railway station at the southern edge of the town of Cassino, but they, too, were driven back by counterattacks.

Two days after the bombing, having made arrangements with the Germans, the aged abbot came out of the ruins of the monastery holding aloft a large wooden crucifix. Behind him stumbled a forlorn column of monks and refugees. After they had made their way to safety, tough German

paratroops quickly moved into the ruins. "Now," General von Senger said later, "we would occupy the Abbey without scruple. The Germans had a mighty commanding strong point, which paid for itself in all the subsequent fighting."

After the failure to take Monastery Hill, the Allies might well have decided to halt the attack at Cassino for the remainder of the winter. The Germans at Anzio, having failed with their counterattack, no longer threatened to wipe out the beachhead but were content to contain it, and there was now no urgent need to unite the divided Fifth Army. Perhaps this was the time for the Allies to rest and refit, to wait until spring weather dried the sodden ground and allowed them to use their great superiority in armor, guns, transport and air. But General Freyberg and his New Zealand Corps were determined to make one more attempt to crack the defenses. Possibly the Germans, in order to strengthen their forces at Anzio, had so weakened their Cassino front that it might now be broken in a last effort.

Again Freyberg would try to fight his way into the Liri valley by sending the 2nd New Zealand Division through the town of Cassino and onto Highway 6 at the base of the mountain massif, while the 4th Indian Division attacked Monastery Hill from below. The attack was to be preceded by a tremendous aerial bombardment of the town, heavier than the raid on the monastery, that would wipe out most of the German defenders and leave the survivors too dazed to offer much resistance. Before the bombardment, however, there had to be three days of clear weather during which the ground would become dry enough to support tanks.

All the preparations for the attack were completed by February 24, but the weather remained foul for three weeks.

The Girl You Left Behind

'Poor little Joan! She is still thinking of Bob.......'

THE WAY OF ALL FLESH

When pretty Joan Hopkins was still standing behind the ribbon counter of a 5 & 10 cts. store on 3rd Avenue in New York City, she never dreamed of ever seeing the interior of a duplex Park Avenue apartment. Neither did young Bob Harrison, the man she loves. Bob was drafted and sent to the battlefields in Europe thousands of miles away from her. Through Lazare's Employment Agency Joan got a job as private secretary with wily Sam Levy. Sam is piling up big money on war contracts. Should the slaughter end very soon, he would suffer an apoplectic stroke.

Now Joan knows what Bob and his pals are fighting for.

Joan always used to look up to Bob as the guiding star of her life, and she was still a good girl when she started working for Sam Levy. But she often got the blues thinking of Bob, whom she hadn't seen for over two years. Her boss had an understanding heart and was always very kind to her, so kind indeed, that he often invited her up to his place. He had always wanted to show her his "etchings". Besides, Sam wasn't stingy and each time Joan came to see him, he gave her the nicest presents. Now, all women like beautiful and expensive things. But Sam wasn't the man you could play for a sucker. He wanted something, wanted it very definitely.....

Poor little Joan! She is still thinking of Bob, yet she is almost hoping that he'll never return.

Look for the other pictures of this series.

German propaganda leaflets like this one were scattered by artillery shells over Anzio. Here the drawing and clumsy anti-Semitic message were calculated to play on the GI's fear of losing his wife or girl friend to men back home.

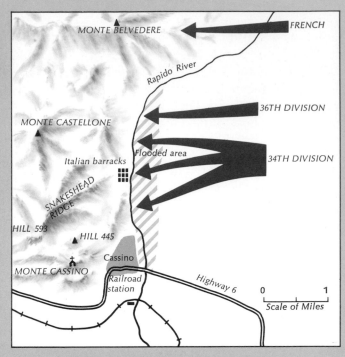

In the first phase of the battle of Cassino after the Rapido disaster (map, page 105), the U.S. 34th Division attacked through lowlands that had been flooded by the Germans. Aided by the French Expeditionary Corps and a regiment of the U.S. 36th Division, the 34th captured a heavily defended army barracks, drove toward the town of Cassino and fought to within 400 yards of the monastery.

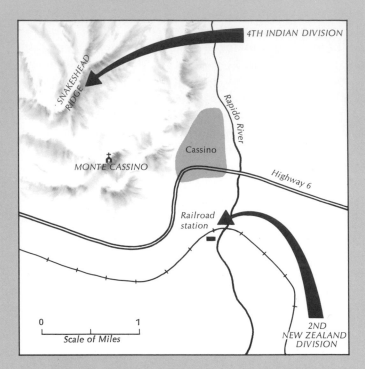

The troops of the initial assault were relieved by the 2nd New Zealand and 4th Indian divisions on February 12. Three days later, after the monastery had been bombed, the Indians opened the second phase by trying to take the abbey from the rear; they failed. Meanwhile, the New Zealanders, attacking Cassino from the south, seized the town's railway station but were then driven back.

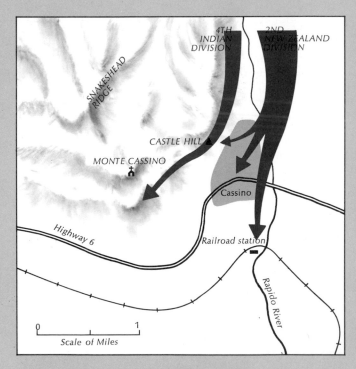

The third phase began on March 15 with an aerial bombardment of the town. The 2nd New Zealand Division then attacked Cassino from the north. One element reached the railroad station, another was stalled in town and a third veered off to take Castle Hill. The 4th Indian Division used the hill as a jump-off point for its attack on the monastery, only to be stopped 250 yards away.

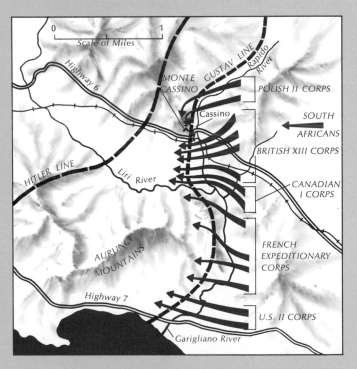

In the final stage the Allies massed 14 divisions against the Germans, with the 6th South African Armored Division in reserve. The U.S. II Corps crossed the Garigliano River near its mouth. The French Expeditionary Corps, attacking a lightly held area, made the decisive breakthrough. The Canadian I Corps and the British XIII Corps broke into the Liri valley, and the Polish II Corps took the monastery.

144

Each day the infantry awaited a code signal, "Bradman batting tomorrow," in reference to the redoubtable Australian cricketer of the 1930s, Don Bradman, and each day they heard only "Bradman not batting." It was not until March 15 that conditions were right.

When Bradman finally did bat, 435 aircraft, including heavy bombers based as far away as England, dropped 1,000 tons of explosive in the Cassino area. British war correspondent Christopher Buckley described the scene: "Sprout after sprout of black smoke leapt from the earth and curled slowly upward like some dark forest. One wave had no sooner started on its return journey than its successor appeared over the eastern skyline. I remember no spectacle so gigantically one-sided. Above, the beautiful, arrogant, silver-grey monsters performing their mission with what looked like a spirit of utter detachment; below, a silent town, suffering all this in complete passivity." Meanwhile, nearly 750 Allied guns and howitzers threw another 4,000 tons of shells into the target area.

A German lieutenant, who lived through the bombardment while walls and ceilings fell around him and huge chunks of masonry and uprooted tree stumps flew through the air, later recalled that "we could no longer see each other; all we could do was touch and feel the next man. The blackness of night enveloped us and on our tongues was the taste of burnt earth. I had to grope my way forward through a dense fog, and then down came the bombs again. Direct hits here, here, and here. The same unspoken thoughts were in all our minds—when would it be our turn?"

But when the New Zealand infantry moved into what remained of the town of Cassino, they found that heavy bombardment alone cannot wipe out determined troops in fortified positions. Most of the Germans of the 1st Parachute Division had survived in their deep tunnels and bunkers and two-man steel shelters that could hold six men in an emergency. Moreover, the survivors were still undaunted and full of fight. As General von Senger proudly noted, "Iron tenacity and unswerving resolution of true soldiers had overcome a concentration of materials on a narrow front which probably had no precedent in this war."

The Germans came out of their bunkers and met the New Zealanders with rifles, grenades and machine guns in the rubble. When Allied tanks were sent in, they had great difficulty maneuvering among the mountains of debris and the bomb craters, some of which were 50 feet across. A pouring rain began and the craters quickly filled with water. After a week of close-quarter combat the Germans still held much of the town. And on the mountain above, where soldiers of the 4th Indian Division managed to fight their way to within 250 yards of the monastery, the German paratroopers still held the battered building. The attack, despite what the airmen called "the greatest concentration of air power in the world," had failed.

By this time Churchill's questions for Alexander were becoming increasingly tart. "I wish you would explain to me," said the Prime Minister to the ground commander, "why this passage by Cassino, Monastery Hill, etc., all on a front of two or three miles, is the only place which you must keep butting at. About five or six divisions have been worn out going into those jaws."

Alexander did not intend to keep butting at one place. He was planning a coordinated assault by all his troops along the main battle line that stretched for 25 miles from the Cassino vicinity to the sea. He decided now to abandon the profitless Adriatic front, except for a screening force, and transfer the Eighth Army to the Cassino area. Then, after he had regrouped and rested his veteran divisions and reinforced them with new ones brought in from the U.S., Africa and the Middle East, he would make four main thrusts.

On the left two U.S. divisions, the newly arrived 85th and 88th, would fight their way up the coast along Highway 7. Beside them the French Expeditionary Corps under General Juin, now numbering four divisions, two Moroccan, one Algerian and one French, would attack through the Aurunci Mountains that formed the left shoulder of the Liri valley. In the center one Indian division, two Canadian divisions, a Canadian armored brigade and three British divisions would cross the Rapido and break into the valley at the point where the U.S. 36th Division had been turned back. The 6th South African Armored Division was in reserve in this sector. On the right the Polish II Corps, consisting of two infantry divisions and an armored brigade, would attack Monte Cassino across the mountaintops. If all went as planned, the Germans would crack, and as they retreated north toward Rome, the Allied divisions penned in at Anzio

ANGELS OF MERCY IN HELL'S HALF ACRE

A U.S. nurse puddle-jumps in the Anzio hospital area.

The unsung heroes of Anzio were the men and women of the Army medical corps who staffed the beachhead hospitals. Because the Allied toe hold was so small, the four evacuation hospitals—no more than tents—were frequently hit by shells. The area was nicknamed "Hell's Half Acre," and conditions were so harrowing that one wounded man asked General Lucian Truscott to send him back to the front because "we are better off there than here."

The U.S. hospitals were equipped with X-ray labs, the latest drugs and supplies, full stores of blood plasma and 3,500 beds. From January to May 1944, they accommodated a total of 33,128 patients.

The battlefront work of the almost 200 nurses inspired the troops with an "if-the-nurses-can-take-it-so-can-we" attitude. In pursuit of their duties at Anzio, six of the nurses were killed and four became the first women ever to win the Silver Star.

Soldiers remove debris from the wreckage of a hospital hit by German shells.

A severely wounded man receives a transfusion in a tent at Anzio. In four months Allied medics at Anzio used a total of 14,309 pints of whole blood.

would burst out of the beachhead, cut the escape routes of the enemy forces and trap them.

The Germans, whose reconnaissance planes had been effectively driven from the sky, had scant means of detecting the regrouping and reinforcement, which Alexander carried out at night in radio silence and with masterful use of camouflage by day. Field Marshal Kesselring, who thought he was facing six Allied divisions on the main front, was in fact now facing more than 15. He was not sure of the size and location of the French Expeditionary Corps and did not even know that the Poles had been brought into the line. Kesselring was also deceived by amphibious maneuvers that Alexander staged ostentatiously near Naples and that were reported to the German commander by intelligence agents. To Kesselring it appeared that the Allies were preparing to make another major landing on the west coast of Italy, probably at Civitavecchia north of Rome, and to counter it he kept his mobile reserves in that area.

Though he was thoroughly fooled, Kesselring did not remain inactive while Alexander prepared to strike. At a distance of five to 10 miles beyond the Cassino defenses, he was building another defensive position, the Hitler Line, and in the Alban Hills north of the Anzio beachhead he was preparing still another, the Caesar Line. Both contained mines, barbed wire and pillboxes. They were as yet unfinished, and not as strong as the Winter Line, but Kesselring was sure his men could hold them for as long as need be.

It took more than six weeks for Alexander to make all his preparations, but at last on May 11 he was ready. At 11 p.m. the Allies opened the most devastating cannonade the Italian war had yet seen. More than 1,600 guns along the 25-mile front began to fire at every known German position, covering the mountains with bright splashes of fire and filling the valleys with incessant reverberations and smoke. Before the echoes died away the infantry moved forward.

The Germans were stunned—but not for long. As they had done so often before, they recovered from the pounding and skillfully fought back. The Americans along the seacoast were halted after making small gains; the British Eighth Army, trying to break into the mouth of the Liri valley, could establish only a shallow bridgehead across the Rapido; and the Poles on Monastery Hill were turned back

with heavy losses. Only in one sector, where the French attacked through the Aurunci Mountains, was there much progress—but that, as it soon turned out, was enough.

The German defenses in the Auruncis were thinner than anywhere else on the front. Kesselring was relying on the exceptionally difficult terrain to stop any enemy advance there. He had not taken account of the mountain-bred French North Africans, who were completely at home in such rough country. General Juin, one of the most able—and least publicized—of Allied ground commanders in Italy, sent his troops knifing through the mountains with startling speed. Using mules for transport along the rugged trails, Juin's soldiers took only a few days to brush aside the Germans and reach a point several miles west of Cassino where they could turn to their right, break into the Liri valley and threaten to cut off the enemy. Sparked by the French advance, the Americans soon began to push forward along the coast while the Eighth Army steadily enlarged its bridgehead across the Rapido.

On the scarred slopes around the abbey the Poles, under Lieut. General Wladyslaw Anders, continued to probe the German defenses and to take severe casualties. Many of the Poles had been captured by the Russians in the fall of 1939, when the western half of their homeland had been seized by Hitler and the eastern half by Stalin, and had been held in jails and labor camps in Russia. General Anders had been confined for many months in Lubianka Prison in Moscow. Finally released under an amnesty, the Poles had been allowed to organize an army in Russia. Later, the army was dispatched to Italy and equipped by the British to face the Germans again. All the men had lost their country, many had lost their families, few had much hope for the future. They fought, as they said, for revenge and honor, and they were a grim sight to the Germans who saw them coming.

By May 17, after six days of fighting, the British had advanced far enough from their Rapido bridgehead into the Liri valley to outflank the ruins of the town of Cassino and the monastery above. That night the Germans withdrew from both places. The 1st Parachute Division did not want to yield; Kesselring personally had to order it to retire. On the 18th of May, the Poles occupied the monastery and raised their flag above it. In the Cassino operation they lost nearly 4,000 men, many of whom are buried in a cemetery on nearby Snakeshead Ridge, beneath this inscription:

> We Polish soldiers
> For our freedom and yours
> Have given our souls to God
> Our bodies to the soil of Italy
> And our hearts to Poland.

By the 23rd of May, the German Tenth Army was in retreat all along the main battlefront, and it was time for the troops at Anzio—now numbering some seven divisions—to break out of the beachhead. According to General Alexander's plan, the Anzio force was to thrust north to the town of Valmontone and cut Highway 6, thus blocking the Germans' escape route.

Clark did not think that blocking the highway would trap the Germans. He believed that they would be able to es-

Poring over a map, Polish Lieut. General Wladyslaw Anders (second from right), commander of the Polish II Corps, confers with British officers at Cassino. Said British General Sir Harold Alexander of Anders and his men, who succeeded in capturing the monastery at Cassino where others had failed: "He had a great fighting corps of gallant Polish soldiers, whose performance was unexcelled by that of any other corps under my command, and he led them with considerable distinction."

149

cape by several secondary routes farther inland. He felt, too, that if he marched north to Valmontone, he would expose his left flank to a possible enemy counterattack in the Alban Hills. And anyway, he thought Alexander's main reason for the plan was to make it easy to pull the British Eighth Army up to the Rome area, "like throwing them a rope." Clark felt strongly that his own American troops had earned the grand prize. Possibly, while Americans were occupied at Valmontone, the British might slip past and enter Rome,

and Clark wanted it for the American Army and himself.

At 5:30 on the morning of the 23rd, 500 Allied guns opened fire from the beachhead. At the same time, 60 light bombers struck at Cisterna. Then four divisions launched an all-out attack toward the town.

Meanwhile, the U.S. II Corps pushed northward from the shattered Cassino front. Shortly after daylight on the 25th, engineers from the beachhead linked up with troops coming up from the south. Cisterna fell that day, and men of the

On the day of the Allied breakout from Anzio, May 23, 1944, GIs of the U.S. 3rd Division take cover behind a jeep as an ammunition truck explodes on the road to Cisterna. Germans in the town put up fierce resistance but were overwhelmed on May 25. Ten days later, Allied troops entered Rome, causing Winston Churchill to note with satisfaction, "At long last, we began to reap the harvest from our winter sowing at Anzio."

U.S. VI Corps, now commanded by the aggressive General Truscott, lunged toward Valmontone, hoping to trap large numbers of Germans retreating from the south. At that point Clark interceded. With an eye on Rome, he ordered Truscott to divert the attack. Clark could not entirely ignore Alexander's wishes, so he directed that less than one third of the American forces were to go on striking toward Valmontone while the others were to wheel northwest toward Rome. To Churchill, watching with fascination from a distance, this seemed outrageous. It also seemed outrageous to Truscott and other U.S. commanders. And most British generals shared the view of their colleague General W. G. F. Jackson that Clark "overnight threw away the chance of destroying the right wing of von Vietinghoff's Tenth Army for the honour of entering Rome first." If Clark had closed the trap, possibly the Germans might not have escaped. No one can say. The only certainties are that this was not a high watermark in Anglo-American military relations and that the bulk of the German forces from the Cassino area deftly side-stepped the Allies and got away.

When Clark wheeled west toward Rome he still had to cut through the Germans' unfinished Caesar Line on the southern slopes of the Alban Hills. This line had not yet been fully occupied, and by chance a reconnaissance patrol of the U.S. 36th Division discovered a large hole in it. Behind the town of Velletri there was a vital piece of high ground, Monte Artemisio, that lay on the boundary between two German units. Neither unit had bothered to put strong forces on the mountain; there were only some scattered sentries.

On the night of May 30, 1944, two regiments of Americans, some 8,000 men, set out to make a silent march through the German lines. "We marched all night," recalled one soldier. "We had all been cautioned to maintain absolute silence, and when the troops learned what we were doing, this became the quietest bunch of guys I have ever seen. All night long I never heard so much as a small clink from a piece of equipment."

When lone Germans were encountered they were killed quietly with wire garrotes or knives. It was not a pleasant undertaking, but these GIs were not in a pleasant mood. They belonged to the 36th Division, which had suffered cruelly at Salerno and San Pietro and had somehow survived the disaster at the Rapido. Now they were going to even the score. "Sentries were crawled upon and jumped from the rear," one soldier remembered. "The thumb and the index finger held the German's nose and the other three fingers of the left hand were placed over the mouth, jerking the head full back, exposing the jugular. Holding the knife in the right hand, the blade was swiftly inserted between the vein and the neck bone. As it was pushed through the skin and behind the jugular and air pipes, the knife came out under the chin. The guard bled to death without a sound except bubbles of blood."

By dawn the two regiments had gained the high ground behind the Caesar Line, and though fighting continued for a few more days the line was broken. The Germans, declaring Rome an open city, withdrew to the north. Some of the enemy stayed behind outside Rome to delay the Allies. The 1st Special Service Force was dealing with some troublesome German self-propelled guns on the outskirts of the city on the afternoon of June 4. According to war correspondent Eric Sevareid, Major General Geoffrey Keyes, II Corps commander, arrived in a jeep and challenged Brigadier General Robert Frederick, 1st Special Service Force commander: "General Frederick, what's holding you up here?"

"The Germans, sir," Frederick replied.

"How long will it take you to get across the city limits?" Keyes asked.

"The rest of the day. There are a couple of SP guns up there."

"That will not do. General Clark must be across the city limits by four o'clock."

"Why?"

"Because he has to have a photograph taken," Keyes said. Frederick mulled that over briefly and replied, "Tell the general to give me an hour." Frederick's men silenced the guns and the way was cleared for the general to have his picture taken in Rome.

General Alexander's massive offensive had succeeded, but at a fearful price. Allied casualties in the drive on Rome totaled 40,000 dead, wounded and missing, while the Germans had lost 38,000. Allied troops could now enter the Italian capital for a fleeting moment of triumph before the attention of the world was diverted by another event to the north—the Allied landing in Normandy.

THE CAMPAIGN'S BIGGEST BATTLE

Clouds of smoke erupt from the summit of Monte Cassino during the bombing of the Benedictine monastery there by the Allies on February 15, 1944.

THE ALL-SEEING EYES OF MONTE CASSINO

After the Allied forces had fought their way through the mountains north of Naples and entered the Rapido River valley at the beginning of 1944, they found themselves confronting one of the most formidable defensive positions in the world. Before them lay the flooded Rapido, its banks heavily mined, the minefields bristling with trip wires that could set off deadly explosions at a touch. Beyond the river lay a range of heavily defended hills and the town of Cassino, a fortified obstacle course whose buildings concealed tanks, gun emplacements and machine-gun nests.

Looming over the valley was 1,700-foot Monte Cassino, birthplace of the Benedictine order in the Sixth Century and a natural observation post from which to spot almost anything that moved. The slopes of this humpbacked mountain and the surrounding heights were strewn with mines and laced with barbed-wire entanglements; amid this jungle were cannon carefully presighted on the valley.

From January to late March, as the Allies battered themselves against one barrier after another, troops on both sides suffered almost every conceivable hardship. Fighting at the height of Italy's worst winter in decades, they endured driving rains, knee-deep mud, bone-chilling winds, snowdrifts and freezing temperatures. Soldiers who were unable to keep their feet dry were hobbled by trench foot; others fell victim to frostbite. Many became infested with fleas and lice, or developed flu or pneumonia. Shells ricocheting off the iron-hard slopes of the mountain cast splinters of rock into men's heads and eyes. There was hardly any escape from the murderous fire; even the wounded on stretchers were killed as they awaited evacuation—a process that could take as long as eight hours because of the tortuous terrain. Dead soldiers lay where they fell for weeks, some with their throats eaten out by packs of scavenger dogs.

So enormous was the strain that Kesselring's Austrian mountain troops, fresh from the rigors of the Russian front, "would rather return to Russia on all fours," according to their commanding officer, than have to put up with the ordeal of another Cassino.

Before its destruction, the Cassino abbey included a cathedral, a seminary, an observatory, a boys' college and a library some 200 yards long.

U.S. artillery fire lands behind Castle Hill (center), a 300-foot stronghold above the town of Cassino that blocked the most direct Allied approach to the monastery.

COSTLY EFFORTS TO GRAB A FOOTHOLD

Before the first phase of the battle of Cassino began, Allied leaders were full of optimism. They expected that a linkup between the Cassino and Anzio forces would occur in a matter of days, followed by a quick march to Rome. A Fifth Army intelligence summary offered the view that German forces were so exhausted "it would appear doubtful if the enemy can hold the organized defensive line through Cassino against a coordinated army attack."

One man who disagreed with this optimistic view was Major General Fred L. Walker, commander of the U.S. 36th Division, charged with the task of crossing the Rapido River. "We might succeed, but I do not see how we can," Walker confided to his diary.

His pessimism was justified. The 36th Division was thrown back across the river, losing 1,681 men in 48 hours. Though the British X Corps carved a small bridgehead beyond the Garigliano River, it did so at a cost of 4,000 men; the U.S. 34th Division lost 2,200 troops in gaining a toehold in the heights near Monte Cassino. The message of the first phase was painfully clear: there would be no easy road to Rome.

From a mountain perch, a U.S. 34th Infantry Division officer scans German movements on Cassino.

A U.S. Fifth Army Sherman tank lies abandoned after bogging down in mud created when the Germans diverted the Rapido to flood the plain above Cassino.

U.S. engineers use smoke pots to screen the 36th Division's advance to the edge of the Rapido River.

British engineers load their equipment into a boat to recross the Garigliano River after clearing a mined area in the new bridgehead on the river's north bank.

The Monte Cassino abbey stands gutted after the bombing. Among the sections left intact were the tomb and cell of the monastery's founder, Saint Benedict

Waiting to attack, New Zealand infantrymen crouch along the Rapido during the Allied bombardment.

U.S. soldiers from a chemical-mortar battalion strain to pull their weapon up a rocky slope near Cassino.

A NEEDLESS BOMBING THAT BOOMERANGED

The second phase of the battle began with Allied planes dropping 600 tons of bombs on the monastery. A British correspondent who viewed the attack observed that "a bright flame . . . spurted swiftly upwards at half-a-dozen points. Then a pillar of smoke five hundred feet high broke upwards into the blue." When the smoke cleared, "the west wall had totally collapsed."

Meanwhile, inside the monastery, the 80-year-old abbot and six monks were saying prayers in a chapel underground. As the bombs struck, the abbot gave the monks absolution, and they calmly awaited death.

Deep in the shelter, the monks all survived. There were no German casualties either. After the abbey had been destroyed, the Allies learned that the Germans had never used it for military purposes.

The final irony occurred when the Allies launched their ground assault against the monastery. The attackers were repulsed by Germans taking advantage of the protection now offered by the rubble.

From a butchery in Cassino, German troops watch an Allied shelling. One man (left) holds a letter from home; his comrade (foreground) clutches a magazine

MAKING THE MOST OF AN UNEASY CALM

In the lull between the second and third phases of the attack, troops of the crack 1st German Parachute Division moved into Cassino. They had been there some three weeks when Allied planes and artillery resumed the attack and hit the town so hard that one German reported "the ground is shaking as if there was an earthquake."

The seven-hour assault left many paratroopers buried under mountains of debris. They had lost all of their antitank weapons and most of their ammunition, and had nothing to drink and little to eat. But when the Allies attacked again, the Germans fought back so hard that the Allied commander, General Sir Harold Alexander, later called the paratroopers "the best fighting unit in the German Army."

Armed with a machine gun and grenades, a German paratrooper watches out for enemy movement.

A German officer (facing front) and his men wait beside a self-propelled gun for the next attack.

Smoke billows from the town of Cassino as it is pulverized by tons of Allied bombs in March 1944.

After the bombing, turbaned Indian troops trudge into the smashed town to take up assault positions.

A New Zealand soldier waits to advance behind a Sherman tank firing on German snipers holed up in the debris between Castle Hill and the outskirts of Cassino.

Shielded by boulders and thickets, two Polish infantrymen hurl grenades into German positions at Monte Cassino in May of 1944.

Visiting the monastery at Monte Cassino months after the battle, clergymen wend their way through the rubble. Before the War's end, reconstruction of the abbey was begun with the aid of Italian soldiers and German POWs.

SWEET REVENGE FOR THE POLES

In the final phase of the battle, the honor of taking the monastery itself went to the 46,000 men of the Polish II Corps under Lieut. General Wladyslaw Anders. Discussing their role in the victory, General Mark Clark later commented: "The Polish Corps fought with utter bravery and disregard for casualties." They were highly motivated. Earlier in the War, they had seen the Germans gobble up half of their country; they were burning for revenge.

The Poles attacked in waves, suffering heavy casualties with each assault. When they ran out of ammunition, they threw stones at the Germans. No matter what happened, the Poles' spirit remained unbroken. Said one dying soldier to his comrades: "My dear friends, you don't know how dreadful death can be. Now I shall have to miss the rest of the battle." It took the Poles eight days of bloody fighting, but on May 18 they planted their flag on the ruins of the monastery, and the battle of Cassino was over.

FRANCE'S AWESOME FIGHTERS

A French soldier probes amid the rubble moments after German shells struck jeeps and other vehicles advancing past the village of Esperia in May of 1944.

BOLD ATTACK AGAINST AN ENEMY STRONGHOLD

Of all the Allied units in Italy, few lashed out more boldly at the Germans than the French Expeditionary Corps, or FEC. Composed of regular French Army troops, Tunisians, Algerians and Moroccans from France's North African colonies, and led by General Alphonse Juin, one of the Italian campaign's outstanding ground commanders, the FEC's 90,000 men were determined to redeem the honor of France after its crushing defeat at the hands of the Germans in 1940.

The FEC went into action in January 1944, in the rugged mountains north of Monte Cassino. After three weeks' fighting, the troops managed to rip through German defenses and advance more than six miles, overrunning one enemy position, penetrating another and capturing 1,200 prisoners before the fighting became stalemated.

Four months later, in the final phase of the epic struggle on the Cassino front, the 2nd Moroccan Infantry Division clambered up a roadless, barren stretch of the Aurunci range. The terrain was so forbidding that the Germans thought it impassable, but the sure-footed, knife-wielding Moroccans stormed the craggy 3,100-foot peak of Monte Majo to make the decisive breakthrough in the defenses south of Cassino, disrupting the Germans' communications and forcing them to pull back all along the line. After this crucial stroke, the FEC fanned out across the mountains in pursuit of the Germans. Pack animals—4,000 in one sector alone—had to be used on the tortuous slopes to carry supplies and rations. And the men had to thread their way along treacherous trails that were mere goat paths.

It fell to the 3rd Algerian Infantry Division to take the town of Esperia *(right),* an all-important link between two German corps, and a critical stronghold in the forward area of the defensive position known as the Hitler Line. Led by General Aimé de Goislard de Monsabert—an aristocratic officer who was given to constantly twirling the ends of his white moustache—the Algerians swept through the villages of Castelforte and Ausonia toward Esperia. As they closed in, LIFE photographer George Silk was on hand to record their painful progress in a series of rare color photographs.

Generals de Gaulle (right), who had flown over from his headquarters in England, Juin (wearing goggles) and de Monsabert map out tactics.

The key mountain town of Esperla lies shattered in the wake of Allied bombing and shelling before the overland attack by the French Expeditionary Corps.

On the road to Esperia, North African troops drive a line of pack animals past bombed-out buildings.

STUMBLING BLOCKS TO VICTORY

As they attacked toward Esperia, the Algerians were aided by Moroccan Goums and by tanks of the U.S. 1st Armored Division. Making use of their mountaineering skills, the Goums silently scaled the 3,800-foot cliffs of Monte Fammera south of Esperia in a predawn attack. They killed a group of German sentries with knives, gagged others with scarves and captured more than 100 surprised defenders on the summit.

With their southern flank secured by the Goums, the Algerians pushed along the road to Esperia, only to be given some alarming news. An Allied artillery observer, flying in a Piper Cub, reported that a German mechanized column was advancing toward their objectives from the far side of town. FEC artillerymen swung into action and raked the road with devastating effect, wiping out the column before it was able to reach the village.

Supported by U.S. medium tanks, the Algerians pressed on and encountered elements of the 90th Panzer Grenadier Division. Fortunately, the Germans, who were merely a rear guard, did not put up a serious fight. But so quickly had the Algerians advanced on the town that the Germans still in Esperia did not have a chance to escape. Holed up in the ruins of stone houses, they fought to their last bullet. The survivors were in such a state of exhaustion that some collapsed upon surrendering.

In a meadow of poppies south of Esperia, American tank crewmen pause for a breather beside their partially camouflaged M4 Sherman used in support of the FEC.

Under heavy German mortar fire, Algerian infantrymen scramble behind a disabled scout car north of Esperia. The partially blocked road, running along a

A CAREFULLY LAID GERMAN TRAP

After the Algerians captured Esperia, they made a critical mistake. In their haste to push on, they did not take the time to clear the summit of Monte d'Oro, a 2,700-foot peak northwest of town. Their failure to do so was to lead them into a deadly trap.

Heading out of Esperia in tanks, in jeeps and on foot, they discovered that the road on the other side of the town was partial-ly blocked with wrecked German vehicles from the previous day's artillery bombard-ment. As the lead French vehicle—a light tank—started to crawl through the wreck-age, Germans on top of Monte d'Oro, who had carefully zeroed in on the bottleneck in the road, unloosed a savage 15-minute mortar barrage.

Correspondent Will Lang, who covered

FEC soldiers wearing U.S. uniforms, one using a battery commander's telescope, adjust artillery fire.

cliff, provided no room to maneuver vehicles.

An abandoned self-propelled gun (right) lies beside the blazing vehicle also shown on page 167, right.

the action with George Silk, described the bedlam that followed. "Screams pierced through clouds of smoke as the Germans poured their fire into the exposed men and machines. The tank exploded with a roar and belched a mass of flame and smoke as the ammunition inside caught fire. Other vehicles were catching fire as their frantic, crazed occupants scrambled out, running up the road toward the shelter of thick-walled old buildings in the village."

Casualties were heavy, and a poignant scene was enacted on the road as Padre Baudouin, a French chaplain, wearing a brass cross on his helmet and a large silver crucifix on a chain around his neck, bent down to pull his bleeding comrades out of their jeeps, bind up their wounds and drag them under the vehicles for safety.

While the survivors scrambled back to Esperia and regrouped, French foot soldiers inched up Monte d'Oro and knocked out the German mortars to seal the hard-earned victory.

"Now at last," said General Monsabert as the FEC resumed its advance, "we are beginning to pay them back for 1940."

His face masked in pain, a North African soldier, wounded during the German shelling, is lifted up a rocky slope by stretcher-bearers for evacuation to an aid station near Esperia.

Killed by a mortar round, an Algerian and his mule—yellow grain spilled around its head—sprawl on the road along which the retreating Germans had presighted their weapons.

Exhausted German prisoners—among the hundreds taken by the North Africans during the fighting around Esperia—stare dejectedly through the barbed wire of a POW compound.

Beside the road to Esperia, triumphant FEC soldiers gather around a table, brought from the stone house at left, to enjoy their rations and a bottle of wine after the grueling battle.

6

At 9 p.m. on June 4, 1944, a young woman in Rome named Vera Signorelli Cacciatore saw the last of the Germans leaving town. A military truck dashed through the darkened and quiet Piazza di Spagna; as it passed her house, a soldier riding in it fired a burst from a machine pistol, for no reason apparent to Mrs. Cacciatore, shattering windows in the house next door.

"There was a brilliant full moon," she later recalled, "and the light in the Piazza reminded me of a painting by di Chirico. When the truck was gone I looked out again and saw two civilians, one dead, the other wounded.

"For half an hour there was quiet and then far off down the Via Due Macelli someone yelled that the Americans were coming. Soon a few tanks went through the Piazza and then the soldiers came marching in the moonlight. They were silent, very tired, marching almost like robots. The people came out of the houses to cheer them but they only smiled, waved and kept on going. One company of them disappeared, then another, but finally an order was given and hundreds of soldiers came to a halt. The civilians crowded around them, patting them on the back, kissing them. The soldiers asked for something to drink, water or wine, and when they had drunk they slumped down on the stones and fell asleep.

"They slept on the street, on the sidewalks, on the Spanish Steps. Some of them climbed into Bernini's dried-up fountain, The Old Boat, which had been empty since the aqueducts were bombed, and slept there. The stones were still warm from the sun and the Piazza seemed like an enormous bed. Next morning the air, the smell of Rome had changed. Before, Rome had always smelled of cooking, wine, dried fish, garlic. Now suddenly it was Chesterfields."

Later that day, two American soldiers approached Mrs. Cacciatore and told her that they had been assigned to guard her house. It had been singled out for protection because of its literary associations. The poet Keats had died there in 1821; the small stone dwelling had long been a memorial to him and to his contemporaries in Italy—Shelley and Leigh Hunt and Lord Byron. The house contained manuscripts and relics that belonged to them and a 10,000-volume library devoted to their work. Mrs. Cacciatore was the curator. During the German occupation of Rome she had closed the house, although she continued to live in it,

PURSUIT TO THE ALPS

and faced down the few Germans who tried to enter. Now that the Americans had liberated the city, she opened the house once again.

One of the soldiers assigned to guard duty at the Keats-Shelley house was an Italian-American, Mrs. Cacciatore recalled. "I doubt that he had heard of Keats or Shelley. But the other was a college student, or had been. His name was Leonard Rosenberg. He asked me if he could go in the house and stand for a minute in the room where Keats died. I told him there was no electricity but that I would take him there with a candle. Rosenberg handed his gun to the other soldier and we went up into the room. He stood there for quite a while and in the dim light I saw that tears were coming out from under Rosenberg's thick eyeglasses.

"We went outside again. Rosenberg took back his gun and the two soldiers took places near the door. In a few hours two other soldiers came and replaced them. Rosenberg went away and I never saw him or heard from him again. I hope he lived through the war."

For Mrs. Cacciatore that was the fall of Rome. For the footsore and exhausted Allied soldiers, the capture of the Eternal City provided only the briefest of respites. They accepted the Romans' offerings of wine and fruit and flowers, caught a few winks and marched on to the north, following the German retreat.

As the Germans withdrew, they left a trail of demolitions behind them to slow the pursuing Allies. They fought short, sharp rear-guard actions, gaining time to sort out their battered formations.

Field Marshal Kesselring's strategy called for checking the Allied pursuit at another series of temporary defensive lines. Although he knew that none of these lines would stop the Allies for long, he had to buy time. In the icy peaks of the northern Apennines, 155 miles north of Rome, engineers were working feverishly to prepare the principal German bastion, the Gothic Line (map, page 21). Kesselring wanted to stall the Allies until the permanent fortifications of the Gothic were ready, then withdraw into the mountain refuge where he might stop the Allies for the winter.

After two weeks of retreat from Rome, the mauled German troops managed to regroup, and Kesselring established the Trasimeno line across the peninsula, centered on Lake Trasimeno about 85 miles north of Rome. It was not a mighty bulwark by any means, but Kesselring held the American Fifth and British Eighth armies at bay for 10 days. Then in an orderly, disciplined retreat, the Germans slowly pulled back about 30 miles to still another line, the Arezzo line. There they held for another 10 days before resuming their gradual withdrawal.

In falling back the Germans were obliged to give up the valuable ports of Ancona on the Adriatic coast and Leghorn on the Ligurian Sea; as the troops withdrew they wrecked the ports as they had Naples. They also introduced a variety of deadly little booby traps. When soldiers of the U.S. 34th Division arrived in Leghorn, they found the expected clutter of sunken ships, wrecked cranes and mines in the harbor, and they encountered a variety of devious gadgets. "We had had a great deal of experience with all kinds of hidden and concealed explosives in the past, but Leghorn turned out to be filled with many new ones, all of them tricky," wrote General Clark. "Here they used articles such as chocolate bars, soap, a package of gauze, a wallet or a pencil which, when touched or molested, exploded and killed or injured anyone in the vicinity. Others were attached to windows, doors, toilets, articles of furniture and even the bodies of dead German soldiers. We found over 25,000 of these hideous devices and many of our lads were killed or injured as a result."

It was the 4th of August, two months after the fall of Rome, before Kesselring grudgingly drew back into a new bulwark, the Arno Line, which ran along the Arno River from Pisa through Florence and then over the Apennines to the Adriatic. As he retreated, he issued orders that his troops were to avoid fighting in Florence, although, as an expedient, German engineers blew up all the city's bridges except the historic Ponte Vecchio to prevent the Allies from using them. The old bridge could not have supported much military traffic, but the Germans did not take any chances and blocked access to it by demolishing the houses at both ends and mining the rubble.

Kesselring had little hope of holding the Arno Line, but this was not a cause for despair. Just 20 miles to the north was his mountain bastion, the Gothic Line, and there he planned to make his stand. Running diagonally across Italy, winding through the northern Apennines, the Gothic Line was a wide belt of fortifications consisting of antitank minefields, barbed-wire entanglements, and elaborate artillery and machine-gun emplacements carved into rock or fashioned from concrete. But the longer Kesselring could put off retreating into the Gothic Line, the better off he would be. He was skillfully consuming time, eating up the good summer weather that was so valuable to the highly mechanized Allies. Even the smallest delay at the Arno would be to his advantage. September rain and November snow would soon come to his aid, and then the Allies might be hung up in the mountains for the winter, just as they had been hung up at Cassino a year earlier.

Although he had no inkling of it, Kesselring was getting help—from the Allies. The fall of Rome had revived an old strategic debate between the British and the Americans. Churchill had never given up hope of striking into the Balkans and now, as the Russian armies advanced steadily into middle Europe, he was anxious to meet—or confront—them as far east as possible. The phrase "Iron Curtain" had perhaps not yet occurred to him but he foresaw the shape of the postwar world. In his view the Allied armies in Italy should smash the Germans and then drive with all speed through the Ljubljana gap, across Yugoslavia and on to Vienna, possibly even to Budapest and Prague, denying the Russians as much territory as possible.

General Alexander held the same opinion, as did General Clark, who cited a quotation from the French writer André Garteiser, saying that a military commander must strive "above all to terminate the war in such a manner that the military situation at the end of the conflict should be the one which his country should desire to see realized for political reasons."

Roosevelt and the U.S. Army Chief of Staff, General Marshall, were still solidly opposed to any venture into the Balkans. Their steady object was to defeat Germany without delay and then turn the full power of the U.S. against Japan. The year before, it had been agreed among the Allied leaders that Allied forces in the Mediterranean, after knocking Italy out of the War, should wheel west and launch an invasion of southern France, preferably synchronized with the landings in Normandy. Now, insisted Roosevelt and Marshall, the time had come to carry out that plan. What was more, General Eisenhower's armies were in sore need of supply ports, and the capture of Marseilles would be a tremendous help.

After months of sporadic debate, Roosevelt said in June 1944 that if Churchill was not ready to agree to an invasion of southern France, the matter should be referred to Stalin for adjudication. Well aware that Stalin would side with Roosevelt, Churchill conceded the point, and the Supreme Allied Commander in the Mediterranean, General Wilson, began preparing for the invasion of southern France.

For the invasion, which was to take place on the Riviera on August 15 (Churchill would be on hand in a British warship to watch), seven first-rate Allied divisions were withdrawn from Italy: the U.S. 3rd, 36th and 45th, plus all four divisions of the French Expeditionary Corps. Their removal was a sad disappointment for General Alexander, who was convinced that if his armies had only been left intact, he could have broken through the Gothic Line before the Germans had an opportunity to man it and that shortly thereafter he might have thrust into Yugoslavia on the way to Vienna.

Still, the withdrawal of the seven Allied divisions did not throw the odds completely in the Germans' favor in Italy, though it appeared that way. The Allies were left with 20 divisions facing 22 German divisions, and the Germans continued to have the advantage of being on the defense; according to standard military opinion, troops on the attack require a 3-to-1 numerical superiority, at least at the point of breakthrough, to crack a well-defended line.

But the Allies had overwhelming air superiority, and fortunately for them, several of the German units were undermanned and others were not up to snuff. Some were made up of overage or convalescent troops, suitable only for garrison duty or coastal defense. Two were Luftwaffe divisions, composed of antiaircraft and other air-base troops, and one was a curious outfit called the 162nd Turkoman. It had German officers and noncoms, but the troops were former Russian prisoners from Soviet Turkestan. They were avowedly anti-Communist, but there remained some doubt as to how doggedly these Turkic tribesmen might fight in the cause of Adolf Hitler. In sum, although the seven-division withdrawal seriously weakened the Allies, it left the two sides about evenly matched.

At the beginning of August, the Germans and the Allies

faced each other across the Arno Line. The Allies anticipated that the Germans would merely attempt a delaying action at the Arno before withdrawing some 20 miles northward into the Gothic Line, in the northern Apennines. Beyond the frigid heights of these mountains lay the broad valley of the Po River, the plain of Lombardy, the best tank country in Italy. There the Allies would be able to maneuver and take full advantage of their superiority in motorized equipment. For the men of the British and American armored divisions, who had been wandering for such a long time in the wilderness, the Po Valley was a promised land. They were certain that if they could break out onto the wide plain with their tanks, they could end the campaign.

Before this could happen, however, the Allies would have to crack the Arno Line and come to grips with the Gothic Line. They spent the first three weeks of August shifting their troops for the attack. Originally, General Alexander had planned to pierce the Gothic Line in the high, mountainous central sector north of Florence, where it appeared to be thinly defended, and to spearhead his attack with the Moroccan and Algerian divisions that had been so successful in breaking the Cassino line. But these had been withdrawn for the landing in southern France, and now, lacking skilled mountain troops, Alexander had to revise his idea. The new plan involved shifting the mass of the Eighth Army from the middle of the peninsula over to the Adriatic coast, where the hills were lower and less forbidding. After the Eighth Army, commanded by Lieut. General Sir Oliver Leese since Montgomery's departure for France back in January 1944, had launched a drive in the direction of the seacoast town of Rimini and drawn German reserves to its front, the

Fifth Army would attempt to fight its way through the Apennines and head for Bologna.

On August 25, with only a few good weeks of fighting weather remaining, the Eighth Army began its assault toward Rimini. As the Allies had anticipated, the Germans reacted by shifting troops from the center of the line to meet the attack. At first the British army, spearheaded by two crack Polish divisions, made swift progress, crossing the Arno Line, punching through the Gothic's defenses and capturing some 4,000 prisoners. But soon the autumn rains began and the Eighth was bogged down several miles short of its objective, Rimini. However, the German transfer of troops left the center of the line weak and allowed the Fifth Army to make an almost unopposed crossing of the Arno River. On September 2 the Fifth moved into Pisa, and soon afterward passed through the undefended city of Pistoia, 15 miles beyond the river.

On the 13th of September the Fifth Army arrived at the well-prepared defenses of the Gothic Line 15 miles north of Florence and ran into heavy opposition. There were only two mountain passes through which Clark's troops could continue moving toward Bologna, Futa Pass on the principal road north and Il Giogo Pass on a secondary road. Reasoning that Futa Pass was likely to be the more strongly held, Clark made a feint in that direction and threw his main effort toward Il Giogo.

The route through that pass was no larger than a two-lane rural road and had many sharp curves that were under the direct observation of German gunners on the heights on both sides. On the left was the 3,000-foot massif of Monticelli and on the right was Monte Altuzzo, equally high. Both mountains were cut by numerous ravines and laced with belts of barbed wire, and the logical climbing routes were mined and covered by machine guns in concrete pillboxes. The terrain and the defenses made it impossible for the attacking Americans to deploy large numbers of troops. The cutting edge of the Fifth Army, which then numbered over 262,000 men, was limited to small groups of infantrymen—often only a platoon and in some cases only a single man. It was with the smallest of spearheads that the Americans attacked the heights protecting Il Giogo Pass.

The assault on the Monticelli massif on the left side of the pass was led by 200 men of Company B of the 363rd Regi-

Allied officials visit Grotto Via Ardeatina, a cave near Rome where more than 330 Italian civilians were machine-gunned to death by the Gestapo on March 24, 1944. The massacre was in reprisal for the deaths of 32 German soldiers, victims of a partisan attack. The Germans dynamited the entrance to the cave (here partially reopened) in an attempt to hide the atrocity. Field Marshal Albert Kesselring, top German commander in Italy, later was tried and condemned to death for his responsibility in the act, but the sentence subsequently was commuted to life imprisonment.

181

ment, 91st U.S. Infantry Division. For two days these men crawled and clawed their way toward the crest. When they reached it in a bayonet charge, only 70 of them remained. The Germans made repeated counterattacks, reducing their number to 50, but the Americans hung on. Their position became so desperate that their left flank was being held by a solitary man, Private First Class Oscar G. Johnson, who was cut off from his comrades.

Attacked by dozens of the enemy who came at him in waves, Johnson steadfastly drove them back. During lulls in the fighting he collected weapons and ammunition from the dead and wounded, arranging the guns around him so that he could keep up a steady stream of fire. He fought alone from late afternoon all through the night and into the next morning before help finally reached him. In front of his position lay the bodies of at least 40 Germans, and Johnson was grimly waiting for the next onset. For his action he got the Medal of Honor.

The tenacious grip of Private Johnson and Company B on the slope of Monticelli allowed reinforcements to break through the German defenses and finally take the summit. At the same time, in fierce, isolated hand-to-hand engagements, infantrymen inched their way to the crest of Monte Altuzzo on the right side of the pass. At a cost of 2,731 American casualties, the two hills that protected Il Giogo were in American hands, and soon Fifth Army troops were moving through the pass, headed toward Bologna. The Germans, recognizing that the capture of Il Giogo had outflanked their position in Futa Pass, promptly withdrew from the pass and fell back to try to build another defense line in the mountains to the north.

The Gothic Line had been broken in the center, and it appeared that the Allies might have victory in their grasp before winter. By early October the Fifth Army had advanced so far that Clark noted that he "could see for the first time the Po Valley and the snow-covered Alps beyond. It seemed to me that our goal was very close."

It was close indeed, but it remained out of reach. Although the Germans at last were running out of mountains, they were prepared to fight bitterly for the toe hold that remained to them. Hitler, unwilling to give up another inch of Italian territory, had ordered Kesselring to make a back-to-the-wall defense in the northern Apennines. Clark's troops were on the edge of exhaustion and there were few replacements to bring their ranks up to strength. Now torrential rains began to fall almost daily, while fog and low-hanging clouds interfered with air and artillery support. On October 22, only about 10 miles short of the Po Valley, the Fifth Army made a last attempt to break through the improvised but stoutly defended German line—and failed. Soon afterward, Clark's men went into defensive positions and found themselves, exactly as Kesselring had hoped, stalled for another winter in the freezing mountains of sunny Italy.

Although the Fifth Army was halted, the Eighth Army had renewed its stalled offensive, capturing the port of Rimini and continuing to struggle forward along the Adriatic coast. Churchill had not forgotten Vienna and hoped to forestall the Russians with a thrust up the Adriatic coast and through the Ljubljana gap. Beyond Rimini, the Eighth Army emerged on the Romagna Plain, an area of low, flat marshy ground. Thought to be good tank country, it turned out to be a nightmare for armored-division troops.

Pinched between the Adriatic on the right and the Apennines on the left, the Eighth Army was obliged to drive straight ahead across the Romagna Plain, which is crossed by no fewer than 13 rivers that rise in the mountains and flow northeast across the flatland toward the sea. The rivers, swollen by fall rains, ran in dredged channels with lofty flood embankments, some of which rose 40 feet above the soft, watery meadows that surrounded them—and between the rivers there was an intricate network of deep drainage ditches. For more than three months the Eighth Army slogged and wallowed along in the "Battle of the Rivers," crossing seven of them.

At last in late December the British were forced to call a halt. The Allies would undertake no more offensive operations until April. Churchill, watching sadly as the Allied armies went into winter quarters, lost hope of being first into Vienna and did not press the matter again.

As another dread winter in Italy approached, the morale of the Allied armies began to ebb. Many of the troops, it seemed, lacked a strong sense of purpose. No longer could they look forward to a specific goal—such as Rome—but only to more mountains, more rivers, more snow, mud and German defenses. And although the average foot soldier knew little of strategy, he sensed that the War was not going to be settled in Italy. The decisive blows were being struck by Eisenhower's armies in northwest Europe and by the Russians in the east. Why should a man take risks now when, by being cautious, he might last out the War?

The number of desertions from Allied divisions began to rise. In the British Army the death penalty for desertion had been replaced by a jail term, and many soldiers believed there would be an amnesty that would free them after the War. Although the U.S. Army retained the death penalty it was not, for all practical purposes, invoked. In all of World War II only one Allied soldier, in France, was executed for desertion. Meanwhile, the number of men who were merely AWOL, a less serious but still troublesome breach of military law, continued to go up.

Some U.S. troops, as in the valiant 34th Division, simply became battle-weary. They came down with various complaints including combat fatigue, an affliction similar to the First World War's shell shock. The 34th had fought in North Africa, at Cassino and in the drive on Rome, and the old-timers in the ranks were making it very plain that they wanted to go home. General Clark, in a reference to the 34th in his war diary, referred to the division as "diseased." General Keyes, commander of the II Corps, made an extensive study of the 34th Division and concluded that the unit was so worn out after two and a half years overseas that selected personnel should be sent home. The proposal was vetoed by the War Department on the grounds that it was impractical and would set an impossible precedent for the rotation of troops.

As far as motivation went, the Germans appeared to have the edge. Although they had been retreating in the Mediter-

ranean theater for nearly two years—since the Battle of El Alamein—they were being driven closer to their homeland, and there was little need to explain to them why they were fighting. Their backs were to the wall.

With the campaign stalled in northern Italy, two U.S. divisions were coming into the line. One fared well, while the other did not. The inadequacy of the latter—which can be understood in the context of the time—was revealed by the last Axis counteroffensive in Italy, a short, sharp jab directed at a single U.S. division, the 92nd Infantry. The 92nd was made up of black enlisted men, commanded mostly by white officers. (The long-standing Army practice of keeping black enlisted men in segregated units, begun during the Civil War, persisted throughout World War II.)

During the summer and fall of 1944, the 92nd Division had been sent in installments to Italy and by Christmas was holding a position on the extreme left flank of the Fifth Army, from the Ligurian Sea inland approximately six miles to the valley of the Serchio River. This was a quiet section of the front but a potentially dangerous one—if the German troops could strike swiftly down the Serchio valley, they might reach the port of Leghorn and disrupt the Fifth Army's supply line.

Signs of a German attack in the Serchio area were detected in mid-December, and accordingly the Fifth Army brought in the veteran 8th Indian Division to backstop the 92nd, which had seen almost no action. When the Germans struck on December 26, the troops of the 92nd were driven back in confusion for five miles, fleeing through the ranks of the Indians to safety behind them. The Indians stopped the Germans and soon recovered the lost ground.

Leonardo da Vinci's Last Supper—shielded by a makeshift roof and scaffolding (center of photograph), and protected by a sandbag barrier—remains unharmed in the ruins of the refectory of Santa Maria delle Grazie in Milan. On the 14th of August, 1943, bombs demolished most of the 15th Century building, missing the famous fresco by only yards.

A month later, when the 92nd had undergone some retraining, the division was ordered to make a limited attack to improve its position. This too ended in failure. The troops became disorganized, panicked and hid in ditches, barns or wherever they could find shelter. "We have no reserve except our command post," signaled a distraught regimental commander. "Search all houses and places for stragglers . . . report every hour on progress and number of men rounded up."

The performance of the 92nd Division was deeply rooted in the racial discord that had plagued the outfit ever since its training-camp days back in the States. Many of its white officers resented being assigned to the division. The enlisted men felt that their commanders considered them inferior soldiers, and the distrust became mutual. Under the stress of combat, this current of racial animosity flowed through the ranks. Treated as second-class citizens, the men had little incentive to fight. Why should they put their lives on the line? Indeed, some of the black GIs in the Serchio valley were prepared to believe the worst—that they were deliberately being led into suicidal situations.

"The Negro soldier needed greater incentive," Clark later said, "and a feeling that he was fighting for his home and country and that he was fighting as an equal." The failure of the 92nd did not reflect on the courage of black soldiers, he pointed out, but on the society that had denied them equality. Even in the division's most dismal hour there were instances of heroism, perhaps exemplified best by the artillery forward observer who, after his supporting infantry retreated, called in fire on his own position as the Germans overran it. "I have decorated for bravery Negro officers and

men of the 92nd Division," Clark said, "and have known of others who were killed in extremely valorous actions on the field of battle."

The record compiled by another new division—the 10th Mountain—illustrated what green but properly motivated troops can do. More than half of its soldiers were college students or graduates. Many had been signed up by the National Ski Patrol, a civilian organization that had been asked by the War Department to recruit volunteers. The core of the division was described by one journalist as "a mammoth ski club" of downhill and cross-country racers, jumpers and winter-sports instructors. There were also a good many amateur and professional mountain climbers, lumbermen, ranchers and farmers from the Cascades, the Rockies and the High Sierras. A captured German intelligence report spoke of them as young men from wealthy or politically important families. That was only partially true, but the 10th Mountain had an aristocratic flavor that was not always appreciated by the men of other U.S. divisions. In the rest-and-recreation bars of Florence, it was common for tough survivors of Cassino and Anzio to say to the newcomers, "Let's see how blue your blood really is," and then the brawls would begin.

It turned out that the 10th Mountain could fight exceptionally well. In mid-February, to see what the college boys could do, the Fifth Army assigned the division to take several high peaks southwest of Bologna needed for the general offensive that would begin in April. In a night operation that involved moving an 800-man battalion by ropes and pitons up the ice-glazed, clifflike face of 3,000-

Wearing white parkas to blend with the snow, a reconnaissance platoon of the elite 10th Mountain Division, the U.S. Army's only mountaineering outfit, trudges upward over the drifts on a slope in the northern Apennines. Rigorously trained in the American Rockies, the crack 10th Mountain troops awed the Germans with their ability to climb, ski—and fight.

foot Riva Ridge, the 10th fell upon the astonished German defenders on the summit and overran them. Then the mountain troops moved on to take the heights of Monte della Torraccia and Monte Belvedere overlooking the Po Valley. General Clark noted that the 10th had performed miraculously, while a rueful German officer later observed, "We didn't realize that you had really big mountains in the United States, and we didn't believe your troops could climb anything quite that awkward."

After the 10th Mountain seized its objectives, an eight-week lull settled on the Italian front, with both sides preparing for a climactic battle in the spring. The War was going so badly for the Germans now that in February, General Karl Wolff, commander of the German SS forces in Italy, got in touch with Allen Dulles, the American intelligence chief in Switzerland, and began secret negotiations for the surrender of Kesselring's armies. But these negotiations were hamstrung by protests from the Russians, who feared that the Americans and British would make a separate peace with their mutual foe. The spring offensive in Italy, then, would commence as planned.

The Germans did what they could to strengthen their positions. On the Romagna Plain, where the Eighth Army still had to cross a few more rivers, they set up three successive lines with female names—the Irmgard, the Laura and the Paula—and to cover Bologna on the Fifth Army front they patched together a line called the Genghis Khan. If these were broken, the Germans could fall back to the Po River, but the Po was too long to be held for more than a few days. The final defense line in Italy, and the one that concerned the Allies the most at this point, was the Venetian, which ran from the Alps near Lake Garda along the Adige River to the Gulf of Venice. The Venetian Line was short and well fortified, and if the Germans could reach it in good order, they might hold there for a considerable time.

As spring came on, American and British planes bombed and strafed without opposition in the Po Valley and the Alpine passes. To keep even a modest flow of supplies moving, the Germans built bridges a few inches underwater, where they could not be seen by Allied airmen, and made pontoon structures that were swung into place at night, then withdrawn and camouflaged by day. By this time the Allies had refined the techniques of coordinating air and ground forces. Their fighters and bombers could now be called on to strike with dependable accuracy targets that were pointed out by the infantry—and there were so many planes that, as the Germans later lamented, even lone motorcycle riders were attacked on the roads.

In the meantime, Italian partisans worked with increasing boldness behind the German lines. Some 50,000 strong, they were armed with weapons captured from the Germans or dropped by Allied aircraft, and were often trained and organized by Allied officers who penetrated enemy lines or parachuted behind them. Sensing that the time was ripe for action, partisan bands stepped up their activity, cutting telephone wires, ambushing troops and dynamiting culverts, bridges, roads and railroad tracks.

Kesselring himself acknowledged the effectiveness of the partisans, although he deplored their methods, which, he said, "contradicted every principle of clean soldierly fighting. . . . In small groups or singly they ran amok without restraint, doing their nefarious work everywhere, in the mountains, in the Po Valley, in woods and on roads, under cover of darkness or of fog—but never openly. . . . The German soldier in the infested areas could not help seeing in every civilian of either sex a fanatical assassin or expecting to be fired at from every house."

For every German soldier killed or wounded by partisans, the Germans routinely executed 10 civilians of military age, but even this grim retaliation did not suppress the Italian guerrilla uprising. In northern Italy many partisan groups, well armed and organized, were controlled by the Communist Party. In addition to attacking the German soldiers and officers, they waylaid and killed Fascist Blackshirts (Mussolini's hard-core supporters) and their own political opponents, whether of the right, left or center, pinning labels marked *Spia Tedesca* (German spy) on the clothing of the dead. A good many other murders were committed simply for reasons of revenge or hatred, but *Spia Tedesca* served to cover them all. It was the Germans who were most frequently shot, however, and the partisan uprising in the north was a significant contribution to their defeat.

In their preparations for their last, crushing attack in July, the Allies stockpiled artillery ammunition and vast supplies of gasoline and brought in weapons new to the Italian

SWIFT TRIUMPHS FOR THE URBAN PARTISANS

Italian workers in Milan make use of a variety of weapons to protect a factory from the Germans.

Escorted by a wary partisan armed to the teeth, two high-ranking German officers hide their faces from the camera as they lead their forlorn subordinates down a Milan street to a place of confinement.

When the Allies ripped through German defenses in northern Italy in April 1945 and surged into the Po Valley, bands of urban partisans in the major industrial cities rose up on signal to join in this victory. In a few days they staged insurrections in Genoa, Milan (shown here) and Turin.

Following carefully laid plans, the partisans quickly seized power stations and factories to prevent their sabotage by the Germans. They captured office buildings, German command posts and radio stations. Bolstered by bands of rural comrades who swept out of the hills, they sealed roads to prevent a German retreat from the cities and then surrounded enemy garrisons. When the Allied troops arrived, anticipating German resistance, they found instead thousands of prisoners of war and proud, jubilant partisan throngs to greet them.

Sporting a variation of the feathered an[...]

peaked Alpine hats worn by Italian mountain troops, partisans from northern Italy's hill country parade in triumph through Milan after the city's liberation.

campaign. Some of these were flamethrowing Churchill tanks called Crocodiles, amphibious troop carriers known as Fantails, Sherman tanks with heavy guns and armored bridging equipment. By early April, as the ground dried out and clear weather returned, the Allies were ready to strike.

The battle plan devised by Alexander was in the familiar pattern used by the Allies throughout the Italian campaign: a one-two punch, with one army attacking first to rivet the Germans' attention while the second army, a few days later, delivered its blow on another front. In this case the British Eighth Army struck first on April 9 in the area of Lake Comacchio and the American Fifth several days later near Bologna. As the British launched their main assault, Allied heavy bombers dropped 175,000 twenty-pound fragmentation bombs on German positions, and then hundreds of medium bombers and fighter-bombers roared in to attack specific targets. When the airmen were through, more than 1,000 artillery pieces with an allotment of two million shells opened up on the enemy. In spite of this tremendous pounding the Germans still put up a brave fight before, inevitably, giving way.

On April 14 the Fifth Army threw the second punch. Led by the 10th Mountain Division, it sliced through the last of the Gothic Line defenses in front of Bologna. General von Vietinghoff, who had taken over command of the German armies when Kesselring was transferred to northwest Europe in March, in desperation asked Hitler for permission to fall back. But he was told, "The Führer expects now as before the utmost steadfastness in the fulfillment of your present mission, to defend every inch of the north Italian areas entrusted to your command." On April 20, when it was already far too late, Vietinghoff ordered a withdrawal on his own initiative. By that time the Americans were breaking out onto the Po Valley plain and their armored columns were beginning to dash across it.

On the extreme left of the Allied front the 442nd Regimental Combat Team, the vanguard of a reshuffled 92nd Division, was also moving forward through the ridges that descended to the Ligurian Sea, toward Genoa and Turin. The 442nd, composed of 8,400 Japanese-Americans, was perhaps the most decorated of all U.S. infantry regiments in World War II. Many of its soldiers had parents or other relatives who were interned in U.S. relocation camps. In-

spired by their regimental motto, "Go for Broke," they were determined to make the ultimate demonstration of their loyalty to their country.

The Japanese-Americans in the 442nd were proud soldiers and crack troops by any standards. They had fought first in Italy with the 34th Division in the advance to the Arno Line in July 1944, then in France in the fall of 1944 in the Vosges Mountains and now had been brought back to Italy for this final drive.

On April 20 the 442nd's objective was a critical road juncture at the inland village of Aulla, whose capture would cut off retreat for German troops stationed at the La Spezia naval base. Aulla was being well defended by German troops on ridges ringing the village. It fell to Company E, 2nd Battalion, to assault Colle Musatello, one of the heavily defended ridges. Leading the attack on April 21 was Second Lieutenant Daniel K. Inouye, whose bravery typified the grit of the 442nd.

Inouye's 3rd Platoon made good progress up the slope of the ridge, until it came under fire from three separate machine-gun emplacements. Grenade in hand, Inouye sprinted toward one of the German gun nests. "Somebody punched me in the side, although there wasn't a soul near me, and I sort of fell backward," Inouye later wrote. "Then I counted off three seconds as I ran toward that angry splutter of flame at the mouth of the nearest machine-gun. I threw the grenade and it cleared the log bunker and exploded . . . and when the gun crew staggered erect, I cut them down with my tommy gun."

Bleeding from the wound in his side, Inouye lurched up the hill to the second machine-gun nest, realizing that his

With the war-wrecked buildings of Leghorn in the background, U.S. Secretary of the Navy James V. Forrestal and General Mark Clark review an honor guard from the 100th Battalion of the highly decorated 442nd Regimental Combat Team. The Japanese-American soldiers who made up the regiment earned no fewer than 3,600 Purple Hearts for action in France and Italy, in addition to one Medal of Honor, 47 Distinguished Service Crosses, one Distinguished Service Medal and 354 Silver Stars.

men would be hopelessly pinned down in the coverless terrain if it were not destroyed. "I lobbed two grenades into the second emplacement before the riflemen guarding it ever saw me. But I had fallen to my knees. Somehow they wouldn't lock and I couldn't stand and I had to pull myself forward with one hand. . . .

"At last I was close enough to pull the pin on my last grenade. And as I drew my arm back, all in a flash of light and dark I saw him, that faceless German, like a strip of motion picture film running through a projector that's gone berserk. One instant he was standing waist-high in the bunker, and the next he was aiming a rifle grenade at my face from a range of 10 yards.

"And even as I cocked my arm to throw, he fired and his rifle grenade smashed into my right elbow and exploded and all but tore my arm off. I looked at it, stunned and unbelieving. It dangled there by a few bloody shreds of tissue, my grenade still clenched in a fist that suddenly didn't belong to me anymore. . . . The grenade mechanism was ticking off the seconds. In two, three, or four, it would go off, finishing me and the good men who were rushing up to help me.

"Get back! I screamed, and swung around to pry the grenade out of that dead fist with my left hand. Then I had it free and I turned to throw and the German was reloading his rifle. But this time I beat him. My grenade blew up in his face and I stumbled to my feet, closing in on the bunker, firing my tommy gun left-handed, the useless right arm slapping red and wet against my side."

Inouye's men were overrunning the emplacement, and it was almost over. But a final burst from the machine gun caught Inouye in the right leg, and he fell and rolled, over and over, down the hill. Later, he stopped the bleeding from his nearly severed arm and refused to be evacuated, directing the final assault that carried the ridge. Inouye survived, despite his terrible wounds, and was awarded the Distinguished Service Cross for his valor. (He was also rewarded, later in life, by the people of Hawaii; in 1962 they elected him United States Senator.)

The village of Aulla fell on April 25, and the 442nd began a mad dash up the Ligurian coastline. By then, German resistance in the coastal sector had all but collapsed, and when the Japanese-Americans entered Genoa, and later Turin, they found both cities under partisan control.

On April 21 the Fifth and Eighth armies had linked up beyond Bologna, and the Germans were fleeing in disorder across the Po Valley while armored spearheads, moving in great arcs, encircled them. In two days the U.S. 88th Infantry Division alone took 11,000 prisoners, moving so fast that it captured a German field bakery with bread still warm in its ovens and a confused German paymaster with bundles of *Deutschmarks* in his hands. Allied planes constantly swooped down on the enemy, leaving the roads clogged with burning wreckage. When German troops reached the Po they found all the bridges bombed out. Many got across the river in small boats or by swimming but were obliged to leave their heavy weapons behind. Meanwhile, the Allies, with their own bridging equipment, swiftly crossed the Po and hurried on to the Venetian Line, getting there before the retreating Germans could put up a defense.

And all across northern Italy the partisans rose up. On signal, railway workers sabotaged tracks in a number of provinces to prevent the movement of German troops and supplies. In Genoa partisan groups cut off water and electric service to German barracks and established roadblocks to prevent enemy troops from escaping, or from being reinforced. In a pitched battle they thwarted German demolition squads bent on destroying the city's port installations. Their ranks swelled with overnight volunteers, the Genoa partisans—and guerrilla brigades in dozens of other Italian cities, including Milan and Turin—forced the surrender of German garrisons and were firmly in control by the time the Allied troops arrived.

By now, the German armies were disintegrating, their exhausted and discouraged troops surrendering by the tens of thousands. Allied armored units, exhilarated by victory, raced wildly toward the Austrian and French borders to seal the Alpine passes and bar exit to German units trying to escape from Italy. The American and British armies had fulfilled their mission. For 20 months, the longest sustained Allied drive of the War, they had kept some 20 German divisions tied up—enemy forces that might have been dispatched with devastating effect to other, more critical fronts. The campaign for Italy, a grinding, bloody, inch-by-inch slog through mountains that seemed to go on forever, was finally coming to an end.

DICTATOR ON THE RUN

A photographer's hurried snapshot shows the ailing Mussolini being escorted to a rescue plane by Germans who have just freed him from imprisonment.

THE DECLINE AND FALL OF THE DUCE

Few men in the 20th Century have risen to such heights as Benito Mussolini—or have had a greater fall. As Italy's dictator for 21 years, he ruled with an iron fist. When he spoke from his balcony in Rome, oceans of worshipful admirers roared their approval. At his signal, armies were launched into Ethiopia, Greece and Yugoslavia. Throughout his career scarcely a word of criticism was tolerated.

Then in midsummer of 1943, while Sicily was being over-run by Allied armies and Italy's economy was crumbling, his erstwhile supporters turned on him. It all came to a head on July 24, when the Duce met with the Grand Council of the Fascist Party, a rubber-stamp assembly that he had not deigned to convene for three and a half years. With unexpected fury, Dino Grandi, a respected council member, shouted: "In this war, we already have a hundred thousand dead, and we have a hundred thousand mothers who cry: 'Mussolini has assassinated my son!' . . . You have imposed a dictatorship on Italy that is historically immoral." After six hours of heated debate, the party leaders in the early hours of July 25 voted 19 to 7 for a motion of no confidence in the aging dictator. That same day, King Victor Emmanuel III divested Mussolini of his powers and had him arrested.

Mussolini's political decline was accompanied by a diminution of his physical and mental powers. Agonizing abdominal pains, stemming from an ulcer or gastritis, forced him to rest frequently and drove him to morphine addiction. When he became too weak to work long hours, he kept a light on at night in his empty office for show. His moods alternated between outbursts of anger and periods of deep despair. He compared himself to Jesus and Napoleon, and blamed his failure on others—especially the Italian people. He said his countrymen were a "mediocre race of good-for-nothings—only capable of singing and eating ice cream," and he expressed a ghoulish delight when Naples was bombed by the Allies.

He lived for almost two years after his arrest, enduring a series of bizarre and humiliating experiences before finally coming to a grisly and inglorious end.

In the days before the Allied invasion, the Italian King greets Mussolini. Later he had him arrested, saying, "You are the most hated man in Italy."

A bullet-ridden portrait of Mussolini hangs from a tree in Sicily following the Duce's downfall. All over Italy, Fascist emblems were defaced and destroyed

1. The Hotel del Gran Sasso, where Mussolini was held as a prisoner for two weeks, was a ski resort on a 6,500-foot mountain plateau.

3. Bundled against the cold, Mussolini prepares to board the rescue plane. A pilot himself,

HAIR-RAISING RESCUE FROM A SECLUDED PRISON

After his arrest, Mussolini was taken to a ski lodge on Gran Sasso d'Italia in the Apennine mountains about 75 miles northwest of Rome. The lodge was accessible only by a funicular railroad and had been built so recently that it was not marked on military maps or on mountain climbers' charts. But German intelligence agents under the direction of SS Captain Otto Skorzeny had learned of Mussolini's whereabouts, and at Hitler's direction a rescue mission was organized.

To determine the feasibility of a landing on the peak, Skorzeny flew over the Gran Sasso at 15,000 feet in a Heinkel-111. Leaning out the window in a numbing 200-mile-an-hour wind, he took pictures while a companion held on to his legs. The pictures showed a little rock-strewn meadow beside the lodge where it might just be possible to land a few gliders.

When Skorzeny and his company of 90 men swept silently down on the lodge in 12 gliders, they discovered to their great dismay that the meadow had a precipitous drop-off at its end. "It was much like the platform for a ski jump," Skorzeny later said. He ordered his pilot to make a "vertical landing," which tore open his flimsy glider but brought it to a halt in less than 30 yards.

Leaping out of the gliders, Skorzeny and his men swept past a handful of astonished, unresisting guards, and without firing a shot, made their way to Mussolini. "I knew that my friend Adolf Hitler would not desert me," the old dictator said.

Soon a small Storch observation plane alighted on the meadow. When Skorzeny and Mussolini climbed into it, the pilot was appalled: with both men aboard, the plane would surely crash. But Skorzeny insisted on going along.

The Storch bounced along the meadow, glanced off a rock and careened over the edge of the plateau. It dropped dizzily through the thin air, then nosed up and headed toward Rome.

2. Following a dangerous landing, German commandos dash from their glider toward the ski lodge to rescue the Italian dictator.

4. As the tiny rescue plane gets ready for takeoff, Mussolini sits hunched in the back seat, with Skorzeny doubled over the dictator.

5. Skimming along at an altitude of only 320 feet to keep out of sight of Allied fighters, the plane wings its passengers toward Rome.

Hitler extends a warm greeting as Mussolini disembarks from the Ju-52 that transported him to the Führer's headquarters near the Russian front. Hitler was

appalled by Mussolini's physical appearance.

At Rastenburg, Mussolini appears with Hermann Göring, who once envied the dictator's strength.

THE WOLF INVITES
THE LAMB TO HIS LAIR

From Rome, Mussolini was flown to Vienna, then to the Wolf's Lair, Hitler's headquarters at Rastenburg in East Prussia. The Führer greeted the Duce with tears in his eyes. He was bent on restoring Mussolini to power, but the Duce spoke of retiring from public life so as to avoid plunging Italy into civil war.

Hitler was aghast. He argued that only a strong Fascist government in northern Italy could save the Italian people, and that only Mussolini could lead such a regime. Hitler was particularly chagrined because Mussolini displayed no eagerness to wreak vengeance on the members of the Grand Council who had betrayed him—presumably because one of the traitors was his son-in-law, Count Galeazzo Ciano.

After the meeting, Hitler told his Minister of Propaganda, Joseph Goebbels, of his disenchantment with Mussolini, saying that the Duce—whom he had once greatly admired—seemed a far smaller man than before. "I have never before seen the Führer so disappointed as he was at this time," Goebbels later noted in his diary.

Hitler and Mussolini conferred for three days, and the Führer finally had his way. On the 15th of September, Mussolini approached him and said bitterly, "I have come for my instructions." The instructions were brutal: A new Fascist republic would be estabilshed in northern Italy under Mussolini, but the Germans would assume control of its foreign policy and many of its economic resources and would govern part of the country. In addition, all of the members of the Grand Council who had voted against Mussolini would be tried and executed.

The Duce listened humbly to the man he had once considered his protégé. On the 27th of September, he flew to the village of Gargnano, north of Salò, to establish the headquarters of his new republic in German-occupied northern Italy.

197

A NAZIONALE
CISTA REPUBBLICANO

issued a manifesto that censured the monarchy and supported the workers.

Mussolini inspects troops defending his new republic on the Adriatic front.

The Duce chats with his doctor, Georg Zachariae, who was sent by Hitler.

UNHAPPY REIGN FOR THE PUPPET DICTATOR

As Hitler's puppet, Mussolini came to be called "the prisoner of Gargnano." German guards tapped his phone and watched his every move. "They are always there, like the spots of the leopard," he complained. His key appointments had to be approved by the Germans, and each Italian official was assigned a German adviser.

Mussolini tried to revitalize the Army and to swell the ranks of his new socialist-fascist party by promising better working and living conditions. But his time was running out: the people had deserted him, the Allies were penetrating deeper into Italy, and he was growing physically and mentally weaker.

Count Pierluigi Bellini Delle Stelle, known by the pseudonym "Pedro," commanded the partisan brigade that captured Mussolini.

A partisan's photograph shows the truck carrying Mussolini as it neared the guerrillas' roadblock outside the town of Dongo.

The partisans' blockade—a felled tree and a heap of stones—awaits the arrival of Mussolini's convoy on the far side of the tunnel.

A DESPERATE FLIGHT AND A PAIR OF TELLTALE BOOTS

As the Allies moved into northern Italy in April 1945, Mussolini fled toward Austria. Near the town of Dongo his truck convoy was ambushed by partisans. The Duce was dressed in a German soldier's greatcoat and steel helmet, but his expensive leather boots gave him away. The partisans took him to a farmhouse, where he was joined by his mistress, Claretta Petacci, who had begged to be reunited with him.

The following day, a Communist partisan drove Mussolini and Claretta to a nearby villa. The partisan ordered them out of the car and leveled a machine gun at them. The gun jammed. He grabbed another and fired a deadly burst at Claretta. Then Mussolini, holding back the lapels of his jacket, said, "Shoot me in the chest." The partisan fired twice, and the Duce was dead.

In a picture taken shortly before his capture
by the partisans, Mussolini—now 61 years old—
is a haggard version of his once-robust self.

Mussolini's mistress, Claretta Petacci—seen
here in earlier days—abandoned her husband
for the Duce and was his lover for 13 years.

A white cross by the entrance to the Villa
Belmonte marks the spot where Mussolini and
his mistress were gunned down by a partisan.

A locket with the dates on which Claretta met
Mussolini and received this keepsake from him
reads, "Clara, I am you and you are me. Ben."

ike butchered animals, the Duce, Claretta and a cohort hang in Milan.

THE BLOODTHIRSTY MOB OF THE PIAZZALE LORETO

On the morning after Mussolini and his mistress were slain, the partisans dumped their bodies in front of a garage in Milan's Piazzale Loreto. A crowd gathered around; some people shouted obscenities, others laughed. One woman fired a pistol at Mussolini five times to "avenge her five dead sons." Eventually, the two mutilated bodies were strung upside down for everyone to see. For hours the crowd jeered and spat at Mussolini's body. On the following day he was buried in the family tomb in the village of Predappio.

Upon his arrest two years earlier, he had prophetically spoken his own epitaph as well as that of the bloody era he represented. "That's my fate," he said: "from dust to power and from power back to dust."

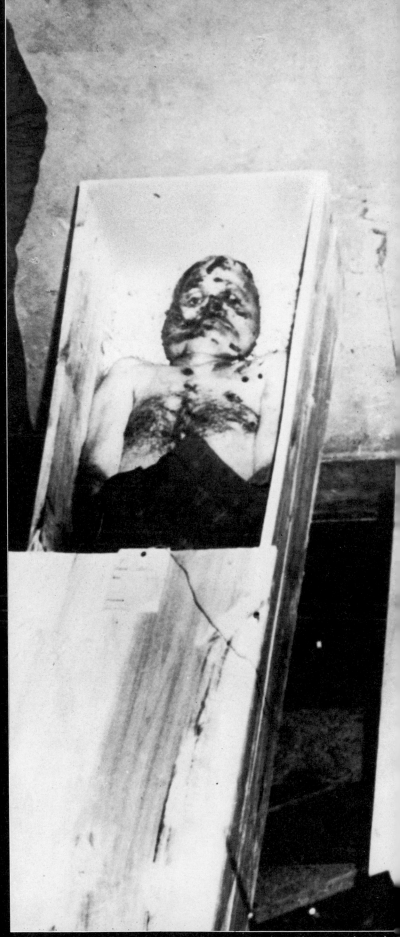

A partisan inspects the battered corpses of Mussolini, Claretta and anothe

ACKNOWLEDGMENTS

The index was prepared by Mel Ingber. For help given in the preparation of this book the editors thank the Association of the United States Army, Washington, D.C.; Ulysses Auger, Washington, D.C.; Ernst-Otto Baade, Eschwege, Germany; Hans Becker, Adn-Zentralbild, Berlin; Professor Herbert Bloch, Belmont, Massachusetts; Carole Boutte, Senior Researcher, U.S. Army Audio-Visual Activity, The Pentagon, Washington, D.C.; Colonel Oreste Bovio, Archivio Storico, Ministero Della Difesa, Rome; William R. Brady, Dickinson, Texas; Joseph J. Cain, Tallahassee, Florida; Phyllis Cassler, Carlisle Barracks, U.S. Army Office of Military History, Carlisle, Pennsylvania; Cecile Coutin, Curator, Musée des Deux Guerres Mondiales, Paris; Department of Photographs, The Imperial War Museum, London; V. M. Destefano, Chief of Reference Library, U.S. Army Audio-Visual Activity, The Pentagon, Washington, D.C.; Joe Dine, Washington, D.C.; Ulrich Frodien, Süddeutscher Verlag Bilderdienst, Munich; Bianca Gabbrielli, Rome; Herman Graml, Institut für Zeitgeschichte, Munich; Colonel Maurice Guilhamat, Paris; Général Augustin Guillaume, Paris; Randy Hackenburg, Carlisle Barracks, U.S. Army Office of Military History, Carlisle, Pennsylvania; Frederick Hartt, University of Virginia, Charlottesville, Virginia; Dr. Matthias Haupt, Bundesarchiv, Koblenz, Germany; Werner Haupt, Bibliothek für Zeitgeschichte, Stuttgart, Germany; Heinrich Hoffmann, Hamburg, Germany; Colonel William S. Hutchinson Jr., Jacksonville, Florida; Billy Kirby, Clifton, Texas; Dr. Roland Klemig, Bildarchiv Preussischer Kulturbesitz, Berlin;

A. F. Kohutek, Membership Secretary, 36th Division Association, Abilene, Texas; Franz Kurowski, Dortmund, Germany; William H. Leary, National Archives and Records Service, Audio-Visual Division, Washington, D.C.; Carolyn Lee, Chief Librarian, Theological Library, Catholic University, Washington, D.C.; Beverly Lindsey, Command History, John F. Kennedy Center for Military Assistance, Fort Bragg, North Carolina; Professor Otto Mazzucato, Rome; Brün Meyer, Militärarchiv, Freiburg, Germany; Robert Olesen, Racine, Wisconsin; Professor Carlo Pietrangeli, Rome; Pietro Pullini, Rome; Charles R. Rummel, Clifton, Texas; Axel Schulz, Ullstein, Berlin; Dr. George Siefert, Head, Classics Department, Catholic University, Washington, D.C.; George Silk, Westport, Connecticut; Rodolfo Siviero, Delegazione per le Restituzioni, Ministero degli Affari Esteri, Rome; John Slonaker, Carlisle Barracks, U.S. Army Office of Military History, Carlisle, Pennsylvania; Dr. Richard Sommers, Carlisle Barracks, U.S. Army Office of Military History, Carlisle, Pennsylvania; Hank Strano, Motion Picture Depository Division, Tobyhanna Installation, Tobyhanna, Pennsylvania; Alex Szima, Cape Coral, Florida; John Taylor, National Archives, Modern Military Branch, Washington, D.C.; Reverend Al Tovey, Panama City Beach, Florida; Général Maurice Tricon-Dunois, Paris; Joachim von Metzsch, Stuttgart, Germany; Paul White, National Archives and Records Service, Audio-Visual Division, Washington, D.C.; Marie Yates, U.S. Army Audio-Visual Activity, The Pentagon, Washington, D.C.

PICTURE CREDITS

Credits from left to right are separated by semicolons, from top to bottom by dashes.

COVER and page 1: Robert Capa from Magnum.

SICILY: DOORSTEP TO ITALY—6 through 9: The Imperial War Museum, London. 10, 11: U.S. Army. 12, 13: Keystone Press, London. 14 through 17: The Imperial War Museum, London.

THE FIRST BITE OF EUROPE—21: Map by Elie Sabban. 23: U.S. Air Force. 25: Map by Elie Sabban. 28: Robert Capa from Magnum for LIFE. 29: King Features Syndicate, Inc. 30: U.S. Army. 32: Bundesarchiv, Koblenz.

ROME UNDER THE GERMAN HEEL—34 through 37: Copied by Aldo Durazzi, courtesy Museo di Roma. 38: Copied by Aldo Durazzi, courtesy Museo Storico Liberazione di Roma. 39: Copied by David Lees; copied by Aldo Durazzi, courtesy Museo Storico Liberazione di Roma. 40 through 43: Copied by Aldo Durazzi, courtesy Museo di Roma. 44: Copied by David Lees. 45: Copied by David Lees; copied by Aldo Durazzi, courtesy Museo di Roma. 46, 47: Copied by Aldo Durazzi, courtesy Museo di Roma.

CLOSE CALL AT SALERNO—50: Publifoto Notizie, Milan—Rizzoli, Milan. 52: Farabola, Milan. 55: Wide World. 57: The Imperial War Museum, London. 58, 59: Map by Elie Sabban. 60: The Imperial War Museum, London. 62: Wide World.

HEADING 'EM OFF AT THE PASS—64, 65: Robert Capa from Magnum. 66: National Archives. 67: U.S. Army. 68, 69: Robert Capa from Magnum. 70, 71: The Imperial War Museum, London. 72: Robert Capa from Magnum. 73: Robert Capa from Magnum—The Imperial War Museum, London. 74, 75: Robert Capa from Magnum.

"SEE NAPLES AND DIE"—78: Sandro Aurisuchio de Val. 80: United Press International. 82, 83: U.S. Army. 84: Margaret Bourke-White for LIFE.

FRIENDS AMONG THE FOE—86, 87: King Features Syndicate, Inc. 88: Robert Capa from Magnum. 89: National Archives. 90, 91: National Archives—Robert Capa from Magnum for LIFE; Photo Trends. 92, 93: National Archives (2); E.C.P. Armées, Paris. 94: John Phillips for LIFE—National Archives. 95: Robert Capa from Magnum for LIFE—National Archives. 96, 97: National Archives. 98, 99: Patellani, Milan; National Archives.

THE DEFIANT MOUNTAINS—102: Margaret Bourke-White for LIFE. 105: Map by Elie Sabban. 107: The Public Archives of Canada. 108, 111: U.S. Army. 112:

Keystone, Munich. 114: John Phillips/Photo Researchers, 1975; Drawing copyrighted 1944, renewed 1972, Bill Mauldin; reproduced by courtesy of Bill Mauldin. 115: Drawings copyrighted 1944, renewed 1972, Bill Mauldin; reproduced by courtesy of Bill Mauldin.

THE MENACE TO ITALY'S ART—118, 119: Ministero degli Affari Esteri/Delegazione per le Restituzioni, Rome. 120: George Silk for LIFE. 121: Fotolocchi, Florence. 122: Capitoline Museum, Rome—Publifoto Notizie, Milan. 123: Farabola, Milan. 124, 125: German Archeological Institute, Rome; Hanns Hubmann. 126: Delegazione per le Restituzioni, Rome; Alinari, Florence (2). 127: Alinari, Florence. 128, 129: Alinari, Florence; George Silk for LIFE.

THE OBSTACLE COURSE TO ROME—132, 133: E.C.P. Armées, Paris. 134: Map by Elie Sabban. 136: Robert Capa from Magnum. 139: Bundesarchiv, Koblenz. 140: U.S. Army. 141: George Silk for LIFE. 143: U.S. Army. 144: Maps by Elie Sabban. 146: Margaret Bourke-White for LIFE—U.S. Army. 147: Margaret Bourke-White for LIFE. 149: The Imperial War Museum, London. 150: United Press International.

THE CAMPAIGN'S BIGGEST BATTLE—152, 153: George Rodger for LIFE. 154: United Press International. 155, 156: U.S. Army. 157: U.S. Army—The Imperial War Museum, London. 158, 159: Photo Trends; U.S. Army (2). 160, 161: Bundesarchiv, Koblenz. 162, 163: The Imperial War Museum, London, except top left, U.S. Army. 164, 165: The Imperial War Museum, London; Heinrich Hoffmann.

FRANCE'S AWESOME FIGHTERS—166 through 177: George Silk for LIFE.

PURSUIT TO THE ALPS—181: Carl Mydans for LIFE. 183: Gabinetto Fotografico Nazionale, Rome. 184: U.S. Army, courtesy Walter L. Galson. 186, 187: Farabola, Milan, except top left, Publifoto Notizie, Milan. 188: Photo Trends.

DICTATOR ON THE RUN—190, 191: Fototeca Storica Nazionale, Milan. 192: Rizzoli, Milan. 193: National Archives. 194, 195: United Press International; Rizzoli, Milan—Mondadori, Milan; Rizzoli, Milan; Fototeca Storica Nazionale, Milan. 196, 197: Office of Strategic Services; Heinrich Hoffmann. 198, 199: Rizzoli, Milan; Wide World—Madeleine Mollier, Rome. 200, 201: Publifoto Notizie, Milan—Rizzoli, Milan; Fototeca Storica Nazionale, Milan; Roma's Press, Rome; Rizzoli, Milan—Rizzoli, Milan; Roma's Press, Rome. 202, 203: United Press International.

BIBLIOGRAPHY

Adelman, Robert H., and Colonel George Walton:
  The Devil's Brigade. Chilton Books, 1966.
  Rome Fell Today. Little, Brown and Company, 1968.
Alexander, Field-Marshal The Earl of Tunis, *The Alexander Memoirs: 1940-1945.* Cassell & Company Ltd., 1962.
Altieri, James:
  Darby's Rangers. Seeman Printery Inc., 1945.
  The Spearheaders. The Bobbs-Merrill Company, Inc., 1960.
Anders, Lieut. General W., *An Army in Exile: The Story of the Second Polish Corps.* Macmilan & Company, Ltd., 1949.
Anzio Beachhead (22 January—25 May 1944). Washington Historical Division, Department of the Army, 1947.

Battaglia, Roberto, *The Story of the Italian Resistance.* Odhams Press Ltd., 1957.
Bloch, Herbert, *The Bombardment of Monte Cassino (February, 14-16, 1944): A New Appraisal.* No publisher, 1976.
Blumenson, Martin:
  Anzio: The Gamble That Failed. J. B. Lippincott Company, 1963.
  Sicily: Whose Victory? Ballantine Books Inc., 1968.
Bohmler, Rudolf, *Monte Cassino.* Cassell & Company Ltd., 1964.
Bojano, Filippo, *In the Wake of the Goose-Step.* Cassell & Company Ltd., 1944.
Bond, Harold L., *Return to Cassino: A Memoir of the Fight for Rome.* Doubleday & Company, Inc., 1964.
Bourke-White, Margaret, *Purple Heart Valley: A Combat Chronicle of the*

War in Italy. Simon and Schuster, 1944.

Bradley, Omar N., A Soldier's Story. Henry Holt and Company, 1951.

Burton, Hal, The Ski Troops. Simon and Schuster, 1971.

Chambe, René, La Bataille du Garigliano. Ernest Flammarion, 1952.

Churchill, Winston S.:
The Second World War. Bantam Books.
Volume V, Closing the Ring, 1962.
Volume VI, Triumph and Tragedy, 1953.

Clark, General Mark W., Calculated Risk. Harper & Brothers, 1950.

"Clark-Rittgers Interview" (Interview of General Mark Clark by Colonel Rittgers). Carlisle Barracks, U.S. Army Office of Military History.

Clough, Shepard B., The Economic History of Modern Italy. Columbia University Press, 1964.

Coates, John Boyd, Jr., ed., Preventive Medicine in World War II, Vol. V, Communicable Diseases Transmitted through Contact or by Unknown Means. Office of the Surgeon General, Department of the Army, 1960.

Craven, Wesley Frank, and James Lea Cate, eds., The Army Air Forces in World War II, Vol. III, Europe: Argument to V-E Day, January 1944 to May 1945. The University of Chicago Press, 1951.

De Gaulle, Charles, The Complete War Memoirs of Charles de Gaulle. Simon and Schuster, 1964.

Eisenhower, Dwight D., Crusade in Europe. Doubleday & Company, Inc., 1948.

Esposito, Vincent J., chief editor, The West Point Atlas of American Wars, Vol. II. The Department of Military Art and Engineering, The United States Military Academy, 1959.

Farago, Ladislas, Patton: Ordeal and Triumph. Ivan Obolensky, Inc., 1964.

Fermi, Laura, Mussolini. The University of Chicago Press, 1961.

Gallo, Max, Mussolini's Italy, translated by Charles Lam Markmann. Macmillan, 1973.

Hartt, Frederick, Florentine Art under Fire. Princeton University Press, 1949.

Haupt, Werner, Kriegschauplatz Italien 1943-1945. Mortorbuch Verlag, 1977.

Hibbert, Christopher:
Anzio: The Bid for Rome. Ballantine Books, Inc., 1970.
Il Duce: The Life of Benito Mussolini. Little, Brown and Company, 1962.

History of the Second World War, United Kingdom Military Series. Her Majesty's Stationery Office:
Ehrman, John, Grand Strategy, Vols. V and VI, 1956.
Howard, Michael, Grand Strategy, Vol. IV, 1972.

Hughes, Serge, The Rise and Fall of Modern Italy. The Macmillan Company, 1967.

Inouye, Daniel K., with Lawrence Elliott, Journey to Washington. Prentice-Hall, Inc., 1967.

Jackson, W. G. F.:
The Battle for Italy. Harper & Row, 1967.
The Battle for Rome. Bonanza Books, 1969.

Juin, Alphonse, La Campagne d'Italie. Guy Victor, no date.

Kesselring, Albert, Kesselring: A Soldier's Record. William Morrow & Company, 1954.

Kurzman, Dan, The Race for Rome. Doubleday & Company, Inc., 1975.

La Farge, Henry, ed., Lost Treasures of Europe. Pantheon Books, 1946.

Lee, Ulysses, United States Army in World War II, Special Studies: The Employment of Negro Troops. Office of the Chief of Military History, United States Army, 1966.

Libraries Guests of the Vaticana during the Second World War with the Catalogue of the Exhibition. Apostolic Vatican Library, 1945.

Linklater, Eric:
The Art of Adventure. Macmillan & Company Ltd., 1948.
The Second World War, 1939-1945: The Campaign in Italy. His Majesty's Stationery Office, 1951.

Lucas, Major General John P., From Algiers to Anzio. Department of the Army, 1948.

Majdalany, Fred:
The Battle of Cassino. Mayflower Books Ltd., 1975.
The Monastery. Houghton-Mifflin Company, 1946.

Molony, Brigadier C. J. C., History of the Second World War, United Kingdom Military Series, The Mediterranean and the Middle East, Vol. V, The Campaign in Sicily 1943 and the Campaign in Italy: 3rd September 1943 to 31st March 1944. Her Majesty's Stationery Office, 1973.

Morison, Samuel Eliot, History of United States Naval Operations in World War II, Vol. IX, Sicily-Salerno-Anzio. Little, Brown and Company, 1954.

Nicholson, Lieut. Colonel G. W. L., Official History of the Canadian Army in the Second World War, Vol. II, The Canadians in Italy 1943-1945. Edmond Cloutier, 1957.

Phillips, N. C., Official History of New Zealand in the Second World War, 1939-1945, Italy, Vol. I, The Sangro to Cassino. War History Branch, Department of Internal Affairs, 1957.

Pond, Hugh, Salerno. William Kinger and Company, Ltd., 1961.

Pyle, Ernie, Brave Men. Henry Holt and Company, 1943.

Roxan, David, and Ken Wanstall, The Jackdaw of Linz. Cassell & Company Ltd., 1964.

Scrivener, Jane, Inside Rome With the Germans. The Macmillan Company, 1945.

Sevareid, Eric, Not So Wild a Dream. Alfred A. Knopf, 1946.

Shirer, William L., The Rise and Fall of the Third Reich. Simon and Schuster, 1960.

Shirey, Orville C., Americans: The Story of the 442nd Combat Team. Infantry Journal Press, 1946.

Skorzeny, Otto, Skorzeny's Secret Missions. E. P. Dutton & Company, Inc., 1950.

Smith, Denis Mack, Italy: A Modern History. The University of Michigan Press, 1969.

Smith, E. D., The Battles for Cassino. Ian Allan Ltd., 1975.

Starr, Lieut. Colonel Chester G., ed., From Salerno to the Alps: A History of the Fifth Army, 1943-1945. Infantry Journal Press, 1948.

Tannenbaum, Edward R., and Emiliara P. Noether, eds., Modern Italy: A Topical History since 1861. New York University Press, 1974.

Tompkins, Peter, A Spy in Rome. Simon and Schuster, 1962.

Truscott, L. K., Jr., Command Missions. E. P. Dutton & Company, Inc., 1954.

Tutaev, David, The Man Who Saved Florence. Coward-McCann, Inc., 1966.

United States Army in World War II, The Mediterranean Theater of Operations. Office of the Chief of Military History, United States Army:
Blumenson, Martin, Salerno to Cassino, 1969.
Fisher, Ernest F., Jr., Cassino to the Alps, 1977.
Garland, Albert N., and Howard McGaw Smyth, Sicily and the Surrender of Italy, 1965.

United States Army in World War II, The Technical Services. Office of the Chief of Military History, United States Army:
Coll, Blanche D., Jean E. Keith, and Herbert H. Rosenthal, The Corps of Engineers: Troops and Equipment, 1958.
Ross, William F., and Charles E. Romanus, The Quartermaster Corps: Operations in the War against Germany, 1965.

Vita di Mussolini. Edizioni di Novissima, 1965.

Von Senger und Etterlin, Frido, Neither Fear Nor Hope. E. P. Dutton & Company, Inc., 1964.

Waagenaar, Sam, The Pope's Jews. A Library Press Book, no date.

Wagner, Robert L., The Texas Army: A History of the 36th Division in the Italian Campaign. Austin, Texas, 1972.

Walker, Fred L., From Texas to Rome. Taylor Publishing Company, 1969.

Wiltse, Charles M., United States Army in World War II, The Medical Department: The Medical Service in the Mediterranean and Minor Theaters. Office of the Chief of Military History, Department of the Army, 1965.

Works of Art in Italy: Losses and Survivals in the War, Part II. His Majesty's Stationery Office, 1946.

INDEX

Numerals in italics indicate an illustration of the subject mentioned.